The Dissenting Tradition in American Education

"James C. Carper and Thomas C. Hunt have long been the preeminent students of dissenting religious traditions in American education. This book is the culmination of decades of scholarship, and it is a monumental contribution to the field of educational history. Anyone interested in the relationship of religion and education will find here an illuminating, provocative, and carefully crafted work. It should be required reading for both historians and policy-makers."

B. Edward McClellan, Indiana University

"As informed people have known for some time, systematic public schooling was established in the mid-1800s, primarily because the Protestant majority, deeply concerned about rearing its young as committed Christians, thought that publicly run schools, supplemented by the efforts of churches, would serve that purpose well by remaining mainstream-Protestant (and therefore, in a predominantly Protestant nation, presumably neutral). Equally important, most Protestants assumed that public schools would foster good citizenship in virtually all the nation's young, partly by counteracting a frightening influx of Catholics and crime-prone immigrants.

In this compelling, utterly timely book, Carper and Hunt demonstrate that several leading Protestant thinkers recognized, surprisingly early, that the dream of the 'neutral,' basically Protestant public school was not only unfair to Catholics (since it deprived them of the equal right to educate their children, via tax support, in keeping with Catholic principles) but was doomed to backfire as the nation became increasingly diverse, even to the point of much militant secularism. Since every element of a school reflects overarching beliefs and values, agreeing to the public school contract guaranteed, ultimately, the religious mis-education of the descendants of every person of deep faith, with exceptions, often unofficial, where religious parents are very influential.

Carper and Hunt demonstrate, with overwhelming evidence, that in every era since Protestants signed the public school contract, some major group has dissented openly and justly from the public school model. That dissent continues and intensifies. Its current forms include open refusal to include theistic interpretation of evidence on evolution in science classes, sex education that violates the deep convictions of many parents, and disciplinary policies that permit behavior many parents regard as morally corrupting, and a great deal more. If all citizens, and especially all people of religious conviction, would read this book, we'd get drastic educational re-arrangements mighty soon."

Donald Erickson, Professor Emeritus, University of California, Los Angeles

The Dissenting Tradition
in American Education

PETER LANG
New York • Washington, D.C./Baltimore • Bern
Frankfurt am Main • Berlin • Brussels • Vienna • Oxford

James C. Carper and Thomas C. Hunt

The Dissenting Tradition
in American Education

PETER LANG
New York • Washington, D.C./Baltimore • Bern
Frankfurt am Main • Berlin • Brussels • Vienna • Oxford

Library of Congress Cataloging-in-Publication Data

Carper, James C.
The dissenting tradition in American education /
James C. Carper, Thomas C. Hunt.
p. cm.
Includes bibliographical references and index.
1. Church and education—United States—History. 2. Religion in the public
schools—United States—History. 3. Dissenters, Religious—
United States—History. I. Hunt, Thomas C. II. Title.
LC111.C28   379.2'80973—dc22   2007001951
ISBN 978-0-8204-7920-0

Bibliographic information published by **Die Deutsche Bibliothek**.
Die Deutsche Bibliothek lists this publication in the "Deutsche
Nationalbibliografie"; detailed bibliographic data is available
on the Internet at http://dnb.ddb.de/.

Cover design by Lisa Barfield

The paper in this book meets the guidelines for permanence and durability
of the Committee on Production Guidelines for Book Longevity
of the Council of Library Resources.

© 2007 Peter Lang Publishing, Inc., New York
29 Broadway, 18th floor, New York, NY 10006
www.peterlang.com

Printed in the United States of America

James C. Carper and Thomas C. Hunt
dedicate this book

■   ■   ■

to our wives of thirty-eight years, Kathy and Karen,
for their unswerving love and tireless support.

"To compel a man to furnish contributions of money for the propagation of opinions which he disbelieves and abhors, is sinful and tyrannical. . . ."

THOMAS JEFFERSON, *BILL FOR ESTABLISHING RELIGIOUS FREEDOM*, 1779

■ ■ ■

"A general State education is a mere contrivance for molding people to be exactly like one another; as the mold in which it casts them is that which pleases the predominant power in the government—whether this be a monarch, a priesthood, an aristocracy, or the majority of the existing generation—in proportion as it is efficient and successful, it establishes a despotism over the mind. . . ."

JOHN STUART MILL, *ON LIBERTY*, 1859

■ ■ ■

"And in matters of conscience, the law of the majority has no place."

MOHANDAS GANDHI, *YOUNG INDIAN*, 1920

■ ■ ■

"If there is any fixed star in our constitutional constellation, it is that no official, high or petty, can prescribe what shall be orthodox in matters of politics, nationalism, religion, or other matters of opinion."

JUSTICE ROBERT JACKSON,
WEST VIRGINIA STATE BOARD OF EDUCATION V. BARNETTE, 1943

■ ■ ■

"Injustice anywhere is a threat to justice everywhere."

MARTIN LUTHER KING, JR., *LETTER FROM THE BIRMINGHAM JAIL*, 1963

■ ■ ■

"Under the doctrine of *Meyer v. Nebraska*, we think it entirely plain that the Act of 1922 unreasonably interferes with the liberty of parents and guardians to direct the education and upbringing of children under their control. . . . The fundamental theory of liberty upon which all governments in this union repose excludes any general power of the State to standardize its children by forcing them to accept instruction from public teachers only. The child is not the mere creature of the State. . . ."

JUSTICE JAMES MCREYNOLDS, *PIERCE V. THE SOCIETY OF SISTERS*, 1925

■ ■ ■

"The history and culture of western civilization reflect a strong tradition of parental concern for the nurture and upbringing of their children. This primary role of the parents in the upbringing of their children is now established beyond debate as an enduring American tradition."

CHIEF JUSTICE WARREN BURGER, *WISCONSIN V. YODER*, 1972

■ ■ ■

"The school has become the established church of secular times."

IVAN ILLICH, *NEW YORK REVIEW OF BOOKS*, 1969

TABLE OF CONTENTS

ACKNOWLEDGMENTS

James Carper acknowledges Rick Jones, reference librarian at Louisville Presbyterian Theological Seminary, and the library staff at Columbia International University for their assistance with locating materials on Charles Hodge and Robert Dabney. He would also like to thank Marci Carper and Kathy Carper for proofreading most of the final draft of this work, Val Morton and Janet Hawkins, Administrative Assistants in the Department of Educational Studies at The University of South Carolina, for their assistance in preparing the manuscript for submission, and Zan Peters Tyler for her contribution to Chapter 9. Finally, The University of South Carolina graciously granted James Carper sabbatical leave to work on this project. Thomas Hunt acknowledges with gratitude the Dean of the School of Education and Allied Professions at The University of Dayton, Thomas J. Lasley II, his Associate Dean, C. Daniel Raisch, and the Chair of the Department of Teacher Education, Kathryn Kinnucan-Welsch, for their support of his professional endeavors. He would also like to thank Dianne Hoops and her colleagues in the Roesch Library at The University of Dayton for their assistance.

Some of the material in the following chapters originally appeared in articles published in various journals and is used with permission: Chapter 3, Thomas C. Hunt, "The Impact of Vatican Teaching on Catholic Education

Policy in the United States During the Late Nineteenth Century," *Paedagogica Historica* 24 (1984): 437–60; Chapter 4, Thomas C. Hunt, "The Bennett Law of 1890: Focus of Conflict between Church and State," *Journal of Church and State* 23 (Winter 1981): 69–93; Chapter 5, Thomas C. Hunt, "The Edgerton Bible Decision—The End of an Era," *The Catholic Historical Review* 67 (October 1981): 589–619; Chapter 6, James C. Carper, "William Morgan Beckner: The Horace Mann of Kentucky," *The Register* 96 (Winter 1998): 29–60; Chapter 7, James C. Carper and Jack Layman, "Independent Christian Day Schools: The Maturing of a Movement," *Catholic Education: A Journal of Inquiry and Practice* 5 (June 2002): 502–14; Chapter 8, James C. Carper, "The *Whisner* Decision: A Case Study in State Regulation of Christian Day Schools," *Journal of Church and State* 24 (Spring 1982): 281–302; and Chapter 9, James C. Carper, "Pluralism to Establishment to Dissent: The Religious and Educational Context of Home Schooling," *Peabody Journal of Education* 75 (2000): 8–19 and Zan P. Tyler and James C. Carper, "From Confrontation to Accommodation: Home Schooling in South Carolina," *Peabody Journal of Education* 75 (2000): 32–48.

· 1 ·

INTRODUCTION

Most Americans interested in religion, education, and politics remember the year 1963. In June of that year, Pope John XXIII, known for his commitment to ecumenism and "modernization" of the Catholic Church, died in Rome. Two months later, Martin Luther King, Jr.'s public sermon on racial equality, in which he proclaimed, "I have a dream," echoed across the Washington Mall. C. S. Lewis, the noted medieval and Renaissance literary scholar and creator of the ever popular *Chronicles of Narnia*, and the youthful President John F. Kennedy, the first Catholic Chief Executive and "Cold War Warrior" fresh from his famous Berlin Wall address, passed into eternity the same day in November. Lewis bequeathed a body of apologetic literature that still influences the worldview thinking of millions of conservative Christians. Kennedy's vision of a broader role for the national government in education was fulfilled by his successor Lyndon Baines Johnson, the "Education President," whose unmatched political skills contributed mightily to the passage of the landmark Elementary and Secondary Education Act (ESEA) of 1965. Praised by many as a long overdue response to educational inequality and criticized by some as an unconstitutional intrusion by the federal government into a state and local matter, the ESEA certainly marked a major step in the federal government's efforts to shape public school policy and practice. Likewise, the three Bible-reading and prayer decisions by the Supreme Court of the United States, the last two of which were rendered in 1963, garnered both praise as rightful readings of the Establishment Clause of the First Amendment and condemnation as an example of an overly activist federal court misreading the intent of the clause that led to "godless" public schools. Moreover, these controversial decisions removing devotional Bible-reading and state-sanctioned prayer from the public schools played an important role in the growth of Christian day schools in the 1970s and Christian homeschooling in the 1980s.

In the midst of these significant culture-shaping events in 1963, two scholars published insightful volumes regarding religion and education. Indeed, Sidney E. Mead's classic study of religious freedom, *The Lively Experiment: The Shaping of Christianity in America*, and Rousas J. Rushdoony's provocative examination of leading educators' beliefs regarding the religious nature of public education, *The Messianic Character of American Education*, inform the present work. Mead, one of the outstanding historians of American religion in the latter half of the twentieth century, was among the first modern scholars to assert that public schooling functions as our established church. He argued that one of the prominent reasons for the development of compulsory public education in the United States was to "guarantee the dissemination and inculcation among the embryo citizens of the beliefs essential to the existence and well-being of the democratic society." Such beliefs, he claimed, "are certainly religious." Thus the state, he continued, "in its public-education system is and always has been teaching religion" because the stability of the nation-state requires a foundation of shared beliefs, the "religion of the nation" in his terms. "In other words," he concluded, "the public schools in the United States took over one of the basic responsibilities that traditionally was always assumed by an established church. In this sense, the public school system of the United States *is* its established church."[1]

Rushdoony, the late Presbyterian theologian, educator, and leader of the often-maligned Christian Reconstruction movement whose goal is to reconstruct society according to Old Testament law, also argued that since its inception in the middle decades of the nineteenth century, public education has functioned as the established church of the United States. Furthermore, in his survey of the educational thought of well-known American educators, such as Horace Mann, James G. Carter, William T. Harris, John Swett, Francis Parker, G. Stanley Hall, John Dewey, William H. Kilpatrick, and George Counts, Rushdoony documents the messianic language and expectations they associated with public schooling. Mann, for example, believed that common schooling could alleviate crime, poverty, vice, and social discord by teaching "true religion," which closely resembled his Unitarian faith, while Parker spoke of the "gospel of common education" and the "regeneration of the world from the teaching of the common schools of America." Others proclaimed that public education must be "intensely religious" in its teaching of the "democratic faith," and George Counts claimed that the "school is looked upon as a worker of miracles."[2] Many of these educational theorists took a dim view of those who dissented from the prevailing orthodoxy of public education, which Rushdoony described as a "man-centered" faith in the perfectibility of society by means of state education. At the 1891 meeting of the National Education Association, for example, Parker claimed, "The republic says to its citizens, 'You cannot be educated outside of the common school, for the common school is the infant republic.'" To oppose the expansion of public education and maintain private schools, he continued, "is bigotry." In a similar vein, William H. Kilpatrick feared that nonpublic schools might breed antidemocratic attitudes and compromise the welfare of the society as a whole.[3]

Though Mead and Rushdoony were among the first to point out that public education has functioned as our established church, that messianic language and expectations have been part of its history, and that the state school system always has conveyed a particular worldview or orthodoxy, they have not been the only scholars to do so. Since the early 1960s, a number of students of religion have discussed these themes. Elwyn A. Smith, for example, averred that public education has since its origins been viewed as an

> instrument for the moral elevation of the people; and George Washington warned in 1796 that it was perilous to separate morals from religion. The vehemence of the disputes that swirl around public education are largely to be explained by widespread agreement with Washington's judgment, which perhaps justifies the suggestion that the American public school system is the nation's equivalent to the European established church.[4]

In a similar vein, Robert Michaelsen, a longtime student of American religion, suggested that public education always has been expected to transmit beliefs supposedly common to most Americans or what some scholars have called our "civil religion."[5] Warren Nord also has devoted considerable time to analyzing the role of religion in public education. In his influential work, *Religion & American Education: Rethinking a National Dilemma*, he expresses general agreement with the contemporary religious conservative contention that state schools inculcate "the religion of secular humanism." According to Nord:

the underlying worldview of modern education divorces humankind from dependence on God; it replaces religious answers to many of the ultimate questions of human existence with secular answers; and, most striking, public education conveys its secular understanding of reality essentially as a matter of faith. Indeed, I will argue that at least in its textbooks and formal curriculum students are *indoctrinated* into the modern (secular) worldview and against religion.[6]

As Michaelsen, Nord, and others have pointed out, however, citizens often have objected to the propositions of knowledge and dispositions of belief and value transmitted by our "established church." As a result, the public school frequently has been at the center of heated debate about the content of our public theology. The current brouhaha regarding the "under God" clause in the Pledge of Allegiance and intelligent design as an alternative to naturalistic explanations of human origins and biological diversity are current cases in point.

In sum, then, we contend that the public school is the functional equivalent of an established church, buttressed with religious language, expected to embrace all people, legitimating and transmitting an orthodoxy or worldview, and underwritten by compulsory taxation.[7] As was the case with the traditional established churches in Old Europe and early America, however, individuals and groups have expressed objections to our established church. Since its inception in the mid-1800s, they have dissented on religious, cultural, philosophical, and/or pedagogical grounds. The present volume focuses on episodes of religiously and/or culturally motivated dissent from the prevailing orthodoxy of public education, universal taxation for public schools, government responsibility for schooling, and state attempts to control nonconforming schools. It is not a comprehensive history of dissent in American education. We mention contemporary pedagogical dissenters, such as John Holt, Paul Goodman, and Ivan Illich, and nineteenth-century dissenting religious bodies, such as Missouri-Synod Lutherans and Seventh-day Adventists, only in passing.[8] Though we discuss three noteworthy Protestant dissenters in the nineteenth century, our focus in the 1800s is the Roman Catholic experience with what some scholars have called the "pan-Protestant" public school establishment. In the twentieth century, we concentrate on evangelical Protestant dissent from an institution they generally supported until the latter part of the 1900s. We focus on these examples, in part, because they are the most tangible manifestations of dissent from the public school paradigm. Moreover, the authors have spent most of their professional careers as students of the educational experience of Roman Catholics (Hunt) and conservative Protestants (Carper) with America's established church and have been longtime members of those faith communities. Despite our differing theological traditions and educational experiences, we believe that, regardless of some recent steps in the direction of enhancing the liberty of parents to direct the education and upbringing of their children, for example, tax credits and deductions for educational expenses, the current structure of public education is incompatible with America's confessional pluralism (citizens embrace different answers to "first order" questions, such as "What is the nature of the cosmos?") and our sacred commitment to universal liberty of conscience in matters of education and religion.[9]

In the following chapters, we recount the experience of individuals and groups, who as a matter of conscience, dissented in various ways from our established church, the state school. Four chapters deal with nineteenth-century dissenters. Chapter 2 features the dissenting role of the aggressive nineteenth-century Catholic Bishop of New York City, John Hughes, called "Dagger John" by one of his biographers.[10] Hughes, arguing that it was a violation of conscience to tax Catholics for schools that their faith would not permit their children to attend, was unsuccessful in his fight to secure public funds for Catholic schools in New York. The conflict, described by historian Diane Ravitch as "The First School War," resulted in the eventual demise of the New York Public School Society, an allegedly nonsectarian, but in reality, a general Protestant association.[11] This Society had held a monopoly of public funds for the schooling of poor children, many of whom were Irish Catholic, in New York City. Hughes won what some have called a "Pyrrhic victory," because it led to the gradual secularization of public schools, something Hughes could not have desired.[12] Neil McCluskey, commenting on Hughes' influence on the American Catholic position in education, wrote in 1959 that it had not changed since the days of Bishop Hughes in New York City, more than 100 years before.[13] Historians have traced the separate, dissenting "system" of Catholic schools to his efforts.

Chapter 3 discusses the nineteenth-century Catholic parish school and the controversies surrounding this dissenting institution. The Catholic bishops, individually and in Council, called on the faithful to avoid attendance at what they viewed originally as bastions of Protestantism and later secular, sometimes called "Godless," schools. They were aided in this cause by pronouncements from Vatican offices and the teaching of popes. The major thrust of the hierarchy's teaching was the danger of loss of faith of Catholic children who failed to attend Catholic schools and the necessity of Catholic schools for the survival of Catholicism in the nation. German-American Catholics were especially supportive of parish schools as enclaves of maintaining nationalistic culture as well as religiosity. The nation's bishops, gathered at the Third Plenary Council of Baltimore in 1884, strongly endorsed the necessity of Catholic school attendance and placed all decisions regarding those schools in the hands of the local bishop. Nonetheless, the motto of "Every Catholic child in a Catholic school" was never close to fulfillment in the century. The period closed with an internal struggle between the "Americanizer" faction of bishops, led by Archbishop John Ireland of St. Paul who called for compromise with the public schools, and the "conservative" bishops, who held firmly to the necessity of attendance at Catholic schools, a fracas that many called "The school controversy." Pope Leo XIII ultimately settled the strife by direct intervention in 1893.

Chapter 4 describes the struggle to maintain the independence of dissenting schools from state control in Wisconsin. The Bennett Law of 1889, whose objectionable features defined a school as a place where certain subjects were taught in the English language and students were required to attend school in the public school district in which they resided, sparked the controversy. Catholics and Lutherans objected, and united in their opposition to the legislation they believed constituted state interference with their schools and was motivated by the desire to control, if not eliminate, their schools. Governor William Dempster Hoard and his partisans stoutly defended the Bennett Law as necessary to build citizenship, in the process holding that Catholic and Lutheran schools did not foster patriotism and placed the church ahead of civil society. The controversial law became the major contention in the election of 1890. Governor Hoard was soundly defeated in his bid for reelection, and the replacement of the Bennett Law was the first act of the Wisconsin legislature in 1891. Catholics and Lutherans achieved a measure of independence for their nonconforming schools.

Wisconsin was once again the battleground for events recounted in Chapter 5, which traces the legal struggle of a group of Catholics to unseat the visible symbol of Protestant ascendancy in the supposedly nonsectarian common schools, namely, the devotional reading of the King James Version of the Bible. Wisconsin, a state whose demographics changed drastically due to immigration in the second half of the nineteenth century, was an apt place for this struggle to occur. The result of the battle was the decision by the Supreme Court of Wisconsin in 1890, the first of its kind in the nation, that Bible-reading constituted sectarian instruction and thus was an unconstitutional activity in the schools. Most of the state and nation's mainstream Protestants—Baptists, Congregationalists, Methodists, and Presbyterians—greeted the decision with alarm and chagrin, while many Catholics, Unitarians, and liberals rejoiced. The

Edgerton decision, as it is usually termed, presaged the *Schempp* decision of the Supreme Court of the United States some seventy-three years later. The efforts of these dissenters led to a policy that contributed significantly to the secularization of public education.

Though most Protestants strongly supported public education in the nineteenth century, a minority dissented in varying degrees from the state school paradigm. Chapter 6 discusses the thought and work of three Presbyterian dissenters. Charles Hodge, one of the most widely recognized theologians of his day who taught for more than fifty years at Princeton Seminary, conditioned his support of the common school on its provision of religious instruction in the basic doctrines of Protestantism, for example, sin and salvation by faith alone. Mere devotional Bible-reading and moralizing would not suffice. Absent adequate religious education, Hodge strongly advocated the establishment of Presbyterian parochial schools. Robert L. Dabney, a product of the Old South, a critic of Reconstruction and efforts to establish a public school system in Virginia, and a well-known Union (Virginia) Seminary theologian, argued that education was a family, not a government, responsibility. Like Hodge, he was sharply critical of Roman Catholic theology and polity. Nevertheless, both he and his Princeton counterpart believed Catholics had a legitimate claim to a share of tax dollars for education. Often thought to be out of touch with his times, in the late 1870s Dabney predicted the complete removal of the Bible, prayer, and other vestiges of religion from the public school. Less well-known than Hodge and Dabney, William M. Beckner, a Presbyterian layman and reformer from Kentucky, supported the fledgling public school system in the 1870s and 1880s. At the Constitutional Convention of 1890, however, he expressed concern about the possibility that if the state ever passed a compulsory school attendance law, it might lead to an attempt to force all children to attend public schools. Professing a strong commitment to freedom of conscience and aware of anti-Catholic sentiment in Kentucky and elsewhere, Beckner authored an addition to the Kentucky Bill of Rights that forbade the state from forcing parents to send their children to a school to which they were conscientiously opposed. His concern for and protection of nonconformists anticipated by thirty-two years Oregon's shameful effort to coerce universal state school attendance, which the Supreme Court of the United States declared unconstitutional in 1925 in the *Pierce* decision.

Chapter 7 describes one of the most visible dissenting movements of the late twentieth century. Energized by the Supreme Court's prayer and Bible-reading decisions of 1962 and 1963, conservative Protestants began to scrutinize public education. Convinced that the government school system was becoming increasingly hostile to their beliefs, some of them attempted to reintroduce Christian symbols and views into the public schools. Others simply exited the public school system that they had once considered "theirs" and founded and/or patronized Christian day schools. Though varying in teaching philosophy, internal climate, governance, and curriculum, these schools universally profess the centrality of Jesus Christ in all aspects of education and attempt to transmit a Christian worldview. By the 1970s, these dissenting schools were part of the educational landscape throughout the country and were often involved in clashes with state authorities regarding regulatory issues.

Chapter 8 examines one of these disputes that culminated in an important decision by the Ohio Supreme Court. Disturbed by the increasingly secular character of public education and convinced that the church should reclaim its responsibility for the provision of education, Pastor Levi Whisner and his congregation in rural Darke County, Ohio founded Tabernacle Christian School in 1973. That action sparked nearly three years of controversy and litigation regarding the extent to which the state could regulate a Christian school without conflicting with constitutional protections of free exercise of religion and parental rights in education. In 1976, Ohio's highest tribunal handed down its decision in the *Whisner* case. It ruled that Ohio's detailed accreditation standards violated those protections and that religious schools in the state were not subject to regulations that in effect compromised the ability of the schools to carry out their mission. Though not binding on other states, the *Whisner* decision served as an important reference point for similar cases in other jurisdictions.

Homeschooling, the most radical form of dissent in recent decades, is the subject of Chapter 9. Though numbering only around 15,000 in the mid-1970s, most scholars estimate that as of 2006, parents teach approximately two million children at home. While homeschooling parents are an increasingly diverse lot, the vast majority are conservative Christians whose primary, though seldom sole, motivation is religious. Regardless of motivation, homeschoolers are committed to the integrity of the family and the belief that parents are children's best teachers. Like the nonconforming Christian schools in the 1970s and early 1980s, homeschooling families have often clashed with school and state officials about reporting, approval and supervision, teacher certification, and testing. In South Carolina, a state in which both sides were frequently in court in the late 1980s and early 1990s, a group of homeschool advocates mounted a successful effort to pass legislation that recognized the supervisory authority of an association run by and for homeschoolers as an alternative to government approval. This unique law ended the litigious environment in South Carolina and freed radical dissenters from control by state school officials.

In Chapter 10, we discuss several themes that emerge from these episodes. We reiterate that traditional religious establishments always bred dissent, which, in turn, frequently led to persecution of nonconformists. Likewise, public education, our established church, has since its genesis bred dissent. Nonconformists often have objected to the prevailing orthodoxy of the public schools, unjust taxation, and the government's attempts to regulate or eliminate their schools. We also note that in the mid-1800s, a few Catholics and Protestants agreed that as a matter of freedom of conscience and simple justice, education tax dollars should be distributed to groups with differing concepts of an appropriate education. Though longstanding Protestant/Catholic animosity precluded the creation of an educational arrangement that recognized the confessional pluralism of the times, we suggest that current conditions may present an opportunity at least to consider the "disestablishment" of public education.

Notes

1. Sidney E. Meade, *The Lively Experiment: The Shaping of Christianity in America*, New York: Harper & Row, 1963, 67–68.
2. Rousas J. Rushdoony, *The Messianic Character of American Education*, Nutley, NJ: The Craig Press, 1963, 29–32, 103–4, 246.
3. Ibid., 105, 207–8.
4. Elwyn A. Smith, ed., *The Religion of the Republic*, Philadelphia: Fortress Press, 1971, vii–viii.
5. Robert Michaelsen, *Piety in the Public School*, New York: The Macmillan Company, 1970, 9–11.
6. Warren A. Nord, *Religion & American Education: Rethinking a National Dilemma*, Chapel Hill, NC: University of North Carolina Press, 1995, 159.
7. For a discussion of a functional definition of religion, see Richard A. Baer, Jr., "Why a Functional Definition of Religion Is Necessary If Justice Is to Be Achieved in Public Education," in *Curriculum, Religion, and Public Education: Conversations for an Enlarging Public Square*, eds. James T. Sears and James C. Carper, New York: Teachers College Press, Columbia University, 1998, 105–15.
8. For a discussion of several prominent pedagogical dissenters of the 1960s and 1970s, see David Skinner, "Libertarian Liberals," *Education Next* 5 (Fall 2005): 74–80. Adventist, Lutheran, and other dissenting religious groups are covered in Thomas C. Hunt and James C. Carper, eds., *Religious Schools in the United States: A Source Book, K–12*, New York: Garland Publishing, 1993.

9. Justice Robert Jackson's opinion in *West Virginia State Board of Education v. Barnette* (1943), which declared unconstitutional the mandatory participation in the Pledge of Allegiance, suggests, unintentionally, the incompatibility of a government school system that compels attendance and universal taxation for its support and confessional pluralism. He wrote: "If there is any fixed star in our constitutional constellation, it is that no official, high or petty, can prescribe what shall be orthodox in politics, religion, or other matters of opinion or force citizens to confess by word or act their faith therein."

10. Richard Shaw, *Dagger John: The Unquiet Life and Times of Archbishop John Hughes of New York*, New York: Paulist Press, 1977.

11. Diane Ravitch, *The Great School Wars in New York City, 1805–1973*, New York: Basic Books, 1974.

12. Michaelsen, *Piety in the Public Schools*, 87.

13. Neil G. McCluskey, *Catholic Viewpoint on Education*, Garden City, NY: Hanover House, 1959, 167.

· 2 ·

JOHN HUGHES

Catholic Dissent in Nineteenth-Century New York City

Writing in 1959, Neil G. McCluskey observed that the Catholic position on schooling had not changed since the days of Archbishop Hughes in New York City.[1] Historian Harold Buetow added that Hughes was "the figure that stands out in bold relief" during the mid-nineteenth century in Catholic education, as the "champion of Catholic educational rights."[2] James Cardinal Gibbons supported that assessment when he said in 1916 that if Catholic schools "are so thoroughly established and developed throughout the land, the result is due in no small measure to the bold and timely initiation of the Archbishop of New York."[3] Who is this Catholic cleric and how did he come to earn the plaudits of American Catholic leaders? And how does he qualify as a "Dissenter"?

Early Life

John Hughes was born in Ireland in 1797.[4] One of seven children, Hughes was studying for the priesthood when he was called home to help on the farm. He was angered at the time of his sister Mary's death when British authorities did not allow the priest to enter the cemetery to preside at graveside services.[5] Henry Brann contends the "place, the time, the influences that surrounded his youth, helped to make him a strong character. . . ."[6] Shortly after the cemetery incident Hughes emigrated to the United States, and obtained work as a gardener. He entered the seminary at Mt. St. Mary's in Emmitsburg, Maryland and was ordained a priest in 1826.[7]

Assigned to a post in Philadelphia, Hughes encountered and challenged the Trustee System of Catholic Church governance in that city, a system that gave authority over Church matters, including hiring (and dismissing) the pastor to lay trustees. By his writings and speaking, Hughes developed a reputation as a forceful and articulate defender of the faith within the Church.[8] In 1837, he was appointed coadjutor Archbishop of New York City and as administrator of that Diocese in 1839.[9] He was soon to be involved in the school controversy.

The New York Free (Public) School Society

In 1805 Thomas Eddy, a wealthy Quaker, concerned about the growing number of illiterate poor boys in New York City, apparently became convinced that education would be a remedy for their condition. Accordingly, he headed up a group, heavily Quaker, in establishing a school for those boys, As William Bourne comments, "about one hundred of the most respectable men in the city" viewed with "painful anxiety the multiplied evils which have accrued, and are daily accruing, to this city, from the neglected education of the children of the poor."[10] The deplorable condition of these children, said to be brought about by parental neglect, had produced "ignorance and vice, and all those manifold evils resulting from every species of immorality." All this was due to a lack of a *virtuous education.* This situation the Society would address via free schools, i.e., charity schools, at no cost for the urban poor children.[11]

Subsequent to incorporation by the state of New York, the President of the Society, DeWitt Clinton, addressed the public on the dire straits of these children, who being brought up in "ignorance, and amidst the contagion of bad example are in imminent danger of ruin," and were likely to become the "burden and pests of society." "Early instruction," combined with "fixed habits of industry, decency, and order," which are the "surest safeguards of virtuous conduct," was the answer to this growing social cancer. The Society would address this problem, Clinton told his fellow New Yorkers, by means of schools in which in addition to the "elements of learning usually taught in schools, strict attention will be bestowed on the morals of the children."[12] The Society claimed to be nonsectarian, an antipoverty institution that would directly counter the evil influences of the poor home, and simultaneously safeguard the community's welfare.[13]

The Society adopted the Lancaster monitorial system of education, which had proven to be "successful" in the teaching of urban poor children in England. The system relied on monitors, and was both inexpensive and effective, in terms of moral education.[14] Kaestle describes the priority that moral education occupied in this system:

> The central intent of the curriculum, seen both explicitly in the teaching materials and implicitly in the procedures of the schools, was to inculcate the values of obedience, subordination, promptness, regularity, cleanliness, thrift, and temperance. . . . The school, with its neat uniformed rows and its regimented activity, would teach poor children the discipline so sorely lacking in the chaotic world of poverty outside its doors. School officials constantly testified that manners were improved and crime reduced by the stable of Lancasterian schools.[15]

Society President Clinton lavished praise on the Lancaster method. Speaking at the opening of a new school building in New York City in 1809 he averred that ignorance was both the cause and effect of bad government in England and that the Lancaster method would propagate knowledge and diffuse virtue in New York City.[16] He acclaimed the moral achievements of the method in its instillation of both a "spirit of emulation" and a "purity of morals." The system, he claimed, had created a "new era in education, as a blessing sent down from heaven to redeem the poor and distressed of this world from the power and dominion of ignorance."[17]

Ten years later, in 1819, Clinton spoke to the parents and guardians of the students in the Society's schools, emphasizing that the schools had been established for the happiness of them and their children, "both here and hereafter." He reminded them that their children's minds should be "early cultivated and moral instruction inculcated, and that, by example as well as precept."[18] Clinton admonished the parents that it was their responsibility to lay the foundation of "usefulness and respectability, both in civil and religious society," including becoming bound by every "moral obligation to avail themselves of the advantages" presented them, especially that the children be "improved in morals and manners."[19] He pointed out the benefits of the "gratuitous education" their children enjoyed, something that they had not had the privilege of, and said that the Society's labors and generosity would be in vain without their cooperation.[20] He told the parents that their children must be "clean and decent" when they went to school; that they should observe the Sabbath, because "public worship is a duty" we owe our Creator; and should see that their children attend Sunday school. It was the parents' obligation, Clinton intoned, to instruct their children "early in the principles of the Christian religion," so that they would understand the "unspeakable love and infinite wisdom of their Almighty Creator."[21] The most basic purpose of education was to "form habits of virtue and industry, and to inculcate the general principles of Christianity," grounding their children in the "nurture and admonition of the Lord."[22]

As he neared the conclusion of his remarks, Clinton turned to the debt the parents and guardians owed those in the forefront of the Free School movement. The Society, he said, had been established with "much labor and personal exertions" on the part of its patrons. The school buildings erected and the teachers hired have resulted in "great expense." All of this, he maintained, had been done to "promote the good of your children, and to improve their condition." Parents and guardians, he contended, had to feel a "weight of obligation to the friends and patrons of such an institution."[23]

Diane Ravitch writes that the society's trustees believed that their program was completely nonsectarian and thus should be acceptable to all religious groups in New York.[24] Nonetheless, the Society's monopoly of nondenominational free education was challenged by church schools as early as the 1820s. In 1820, for example, the Bethel Baptist Church opened a school for poor children of all faiths and obtained a portion of the common-school fund, which ultimately included erecting buildings, as was the practice with the Society. The New York legislature directed the City's Common Council to take charge of the fund; the Council sided with the Society's position that it alone provided nonsectarian religious education for poor children and in 1825 outlawed using any common-school funds to a religious society, thus giving the Society official sanction.[25]

In 1826 the state legislature acted again, this time giving the Society a new charter and changing its name to the Public School Society. The Society was allowed to accept all children, regardless of economic level or religion, and was permitted to charge a nominal tuition if circumstances permitted. The new charter required that the Society's property be transferred to the City, which then granted the Society a perpetual lease as long as the facilities were used for education. The Society was now a quasi-public agency.[26]

The Society became enmeshed in more controversy when the Catholic Orphan Asylum, along with the Methodist Episcopal Church, applied for a share of the public funds. The council denied the latter's request but approved the Catholic petition, which had pointed out that the New York Orphan Asylum, which was commonly called the "Protestant Orphan Asylum," received funding, and the Catholic Asylum served as both home and school to its inhabitants.[27]

Irish Immigration

The arrival in New York City of thousands of Irish immigrants in the 1820s and 1830s exacerbated the situation. Poor, Catholic, and with the memories of English repression in their homeland fresh in their memories, the Irish were not ready to docilely accept the yoke of Protestantism in schools. The magnitude of the problem is revealed in the fact that New York City's population grew from 120,000 in 1820 to more than 300,000 in 1840. The percentage of aliens increased from eleven percent in 1825 to thirty-five percent by 1845, and by 1855 more than one-half of the city's residents were foreign-born and over half of that number was Irish.[28] Ravitch asserts that the Society's trustees failed to understand Catholic opposition to participation in the Society's schools— only several hundred of the approximately 12,000 Catholic children in New York City in the late 1830s were enrolled in the public schools, which were among the best in the nation at that time, and enrolled nearly 20,000 pupils by 1838. Catholics rejected the allegedly nonsectarian schools of the Public School Society on "*principle*."[29]

The Conflict Begins

William Seward, a Whig, and Protestant, was Governor of New York in 1839. A trip to Ireland in 1833 apparently had informed him of that country's plight under English control and led him to believe that the Irish immigrants deserved equal treatment in New York City, including schooling.[30] Seward believed that the Irish Catholic children should have the opportunity to go to school "in which they may be instructed by teachers speaking the same language with them and professing the same faith."[31] These schools would be supported by public funds.[32]

Nationally, the Catholic Church was growing in the rapidly expanding nation. The Vatican had created four dioceses in 1808; New York was one of these, and the bishops of those dioceses had met with the top-ranked Catholic cleric in the nation, the Archbishop of Baltimore, several times, beginning in 1829. One of their most compelling concerns in the pastoral letters (a pastoral letter was a communication from a Catholic bishop to his flock that dealt with religious matters) that resulted from these gatherings was the education of Catholic children, which they felt should be in schools that nourished and protected their faith.[33] The allegedly nonsectarian schools of the New York Public School Society (PSS) did not meet those criteria.

Bishop Hughes was in Europe in the late 1830s, seeking money for Catholic institutions in his diocese when the controversy started. Catholics sought public money from the New York City Common Council for eight parish schools, which enrolled about 3,000 students; they were joined by Scotch Presbyterians and Jewish schools. Methodists, Episcopalians, Baptists, Presbyterians, and Dutch Reformed opposed the Catholics, arguing that if Catholics wanted to operate schools they should pay for them.[34]

It is not the intent of this chapter to detail charge and counter-charge in the struggle over schooling in New York City in the early 1840s; Vincent Lannie, among others, has already done that effectively. Rather, it is to highlight some of the more important points of this controversy, and, in the process, demonstrate how Hughes indeed qualified as a "Dissenter."

One of those events was the "Petition" of the Catholics to the Board of Aldermen of New York City as a result of the meeting of the "Catholics of the city" on September 21, 1840. Authored by Catholic laymen, the petition called attention to the Society's own statement that it was "*aware of the importance of early* RELIGIOUS INSTRUCTION" and that "none but what is '*exclusively general and scriptural in its character should be introduced into the schools under their charge.*'" The kind of "*religious instruction*" was to be "*exclusively general and scriptural in its character.*" It described the effect of that instruction as follows: "*The age at which children are usually sent to school affords a much better opportunity to mould their minds in peculiar and exclusive forms of faith than any subsequent period of life.*"[35] The Society reports that the day is opened with Scripture reading and the books are such as "recognize and enforce the great and generally acknowledged principles of Christianity." They praise a deceased teacher for the "moral and religious influence exerted by her over the three hundred girls daily attending her school." And in all "these early religious instructions, religious impressions, and religious influence, essentially anti-Catholic," there is supposedly nothing "sectarian." But the Society contends that if the petitioners were to bring their influence on the minds of their "*own* children, in favor, not against, their *own* religion, then this society contends that it would be sectarian!"[36]

Many other points in the petition could be listed. For example, Catholics objected to the frequent use of the term "Popery" in the texts used, as prejudicial against Catholicism. They cited a passage from *Putnam's Sequel*, a book used in the PSS's schools, which described John Huss as follows:

> Huss, John, *a zealous reformer from Popery; who lived in Bohemia, towards the close of the fourteenth, and beginning of the fifteenth centuries. He was bold and persevering; but at length,*

trusting himself to the deceitful Catholics, he was by them brought to trial, condemned as a heretic, and burned at the stake.[37]

The Catholic petitioners made several other pleas on behalf of eight Catholic parish schools in the City, and following a guarantee that any public funds received would be used for the education of poor children, who were children of New York City residents, and assured the Aldermen that the "money will not be applied to the support of the Catholic religion"[38]

Bishop Hughes Enters the Fray

Hughes returned to New York City on July 18, 1840, and promptly took charge of the Catholic cause. He declared that Catholics were seeking support for their schools as a right of conscience, and as citizens, not as Catholics. He denied he was mixing religion with politics. The Society's schools were Protestant in their operation, and the society's denial of their sectarianism made them institutions of "deistic rationalism."[39] In a meeting on July 29, 1840 in St. Patrick's Church in New York City Hughes said the Society's textbooks were biased against Catholics, and he had to discharge his duty to the "Eternal Judge" by seeing that the abuses were corrected or Catholic parents would have no alternative but to withdraw their children from these schools.[40] He pointed to the problems the Church was having in Prussia and France with the government in education and claimed that the present path in the United States would lead to indifference in religion or "practical infidelity." Quoting George Washington who had warned "Beware of the man who attempts to inculcate morality without religion," Hughes said Catholics could not conscientiously approve the New York system. He was, he averred, upholding the sacred rights of conscience for parents. This right belonged to Protestants and Jews, too, not just to Catholics.[41]

In late August of 1840 Hughes wrote Bishop Anthony Blanc of New Orleans about the fight. While he was not sure of the response to the Catholic petition, he penned that "the effort will cause an entire separation of our children from these schools, and excite greater zeal on the part of the people" for Catholic education. Hughes, Lannie maintains, "would fight the good fight, and if he fell it would be in the thick of battle."[42]

Hughes next debated Theodore Sedgwick and Hiram Ketchum of the PSS and the Rev. Thomas Bond, a Methodist minister, before the New York Common Council on October 29, 1840. Basically, Hughes argued that Catholics were entitled to their fair share of the funds for poor children since the schools of the PSS were prejudiced against Catholic beliefs. Sedgwick denied that the schools were anti-Catholic, asserting that they were neither secular nor sectarian, but religiously nonsectarian. Ketchum agreed with Sedgwick and referred to Hughes as the "mitred gentleman" who ignited the passions of his flock. Ketchum said that a "foreign potentate," obviously the Pope, would not be allowed to interfere with education in the United States. He urged Hughes to "give his heart" to his adopted country and to have the children of his flock sit "side by side" with American children in school.[43]

The debate continued the next day, and the arguments demonstrated the impassable gulf between Hughes' Catholic views from those of the Society. The PSS representatives maintained that they did not teach sectarian dogmas but taught "common-core Christianity"; Hughes asserted that was in effect teaching Protestant sectarianism.[44]

The Society offered to remove anything offensive to Catholics in their texts and operation; Hughes volunteered to follow the guidelines set forth by the Society if Catholic schools were publicly funded, including using only approved (by the Society) teachers and limiting religious instruction to outside the regular school hours.[45] The Committee of Aldermen authorized to hold hearings on the matter reported to the full board on June 11, 1841. It rejected the Catholic petition, praised the Society's schools, and criticized the three Catholic schools it had visited as "lamentably deficient in accommodations, and supplies of books and teachers: the rooms were all excessively crowded and poorly ventilated; the books much worn as well as deficient in numbers, and the teachers not sufficiently numerous."[46]

Hughes had a right to complain. Some of the books used in the Society's schools were clearly offensive to Catholics, either as "openly disrespectful to Catholics" or "blatantly Protestant in sympathy." Catholics were portrayed as "inquisitional villains" and Protestants usually pictured as "righteous heroes." In the texts, Catholics suffered in comparison with Quakers who held that people have the right to worship God as they chose, a choice not given to others by Catholics. Additionally, students read the Protestant Bible, sang Protestant hymns, and recited Protestant prayers in the schools.[47] One book, *An Irish Heart*, asserted that if Irish immigration continued on the same scale to the United States the latter would be "appropriately styled the common sewer of Ireland."[48] It was not fair, Hughes argued, for Catholics to be taxed for schools they could not use.[49]

The State Arena

Hughes and the Catholics failed in their attempts to gain support for their schools from the New York City Common Council. The conflict next moved to the state level, where, due to the presence of some sentiment sympathetic to the Catholic cause, Hughes was more confident of victory. Following some initial discussions and the submission of the Catholic petition to the Senate, in April of 1841 Secretary of State and *ex officio* State Superintendent of Schools John C. Spencer reported that the Society was failing in its mandate to educate the children of New York City, when compared with the rest of the state. He claimed that of 592,000 children in the state between the ages of five and sixteen, 549,000 attended public schools. In New York City there were 62,592 children within this age bracket, and of these 30,758 went to private or public schools. The Society enrolled 22,955 of the 30,758 school attendees. Spencer asserted that the real number in attendance at public schools was only 13,189, and he concluded that the Society had failed in its principal purpose, for which "public funds have been so freely bestowed upon it."[50]

The conflict continued to simmer throughout the summer of 1841. In late October, shortly before the fall election in New York City, Hughes announced an independent ticket of ten Democrats who were "friendly to our alterations in the present system of public education." He was denounced in both the secular and Protestant press for "mixing religion and politics." Hughes responded that the Catholics had no choice, because both parties (Democrats and Whigs) had abandoned them.[51] The "Carroll Hall" ticket, as it was known, did well in the November election and showed Hughes' power, with the voters repudiating those Democrats who were viewed as not "really Catholic." Further, Hughes averred that the Catholics had no other choice, and it was the assailants, not the assailees, who had mixed religion and politics in the first place. Catholics, he said, objected to "vague, sickly semi-infidel Protestantism which prevails in the public schools." While he wanted all schooling to be under the domain of denominations, he preferred the secular version to the Protestant-oriented schools of the Society.[52]

The battle continued in the political arena in the state. Governor Seward's address to the legislature in 1842 called attention to the Society's "failure" to educate many of the City's poor. William Maclay was named chairman of the committee in the Assembly that dealt with educational matters in the state. On January 6, 1842 he reported to the Assembly that ninety-six percent of the eligible students attended public schools throughout the state at an annual cost of $1.04 per child, whereas in New York city the attendance rate was less than sixty percent and the per annum cost over $3.15 per student.[53] A bill, the Maclay Act as it came to be known, was a result. The bill called for qualified voters in each city election in the state to elect three commissioners and two inspectors of common schools, whose compensation would be determined by the Common Council. The voters would elect ward trustees at this election who would have the responsibility to "establish, maintain, and regulate common schools," who would function in their respective districts, subject to the commissioners. The commissioners were empowered to distribute local funds, equal to the state appropriations that were raised for each school in their districts on a pro rata basis. In New York City, the PSS's schools would remain intact under the general jurisdiction of the ward commissioners.[54]

Results of the Struggle

The Maclay bill passed. (In New York City a mob shattered the windows of St. Patrick's Cathedral and "stoned the Mulberry street residence of Bishop Hughes who was out of town," apparently holding him "culpably responsible" for the displacement of the Public School Society).[55] As Ravitch notes, the Hughes-led Catholics didn't win but the Public School Society lost (it was ultimately absorbed into the public school system in 1853), and a public school system resulted.[56] A ward system of public schools, which often fought with the central office, was established. Hughes then led the movement to establish a separate Catholic school system, a trend that had national implications.[57]

Hughes had proven to be a formidable adversary to the group of wealthy influential men who led the New York Public School Society. McCadden alleges that the struggle might be "more properly regarded as an extension of Old-World" conflicts that was "directed not by an understanding of the basic problems but, rather, by mutual distrust" and deep-seated emotions. The Society was Quaker-dominated, as was the society against which Daniel O'Connell, the famed Irish patriot, had fought for about twelve years in Ireland. Called the "Society for Promoting the Education of the Poor of Ireland," its goal was to make citizens of the "unlettered turbulent natives."[58]

Generally, Catholic commentators on the conflict have held that Hughes was a defender both of his people and their rights of conscience and of the Catholic faith. For instance, Gabel maintains that Hughes wanted a "just settlement" that would "recognize minority religious rights."[59] James Burns, enunciating the traditional Catholic interpretation of the struggle, argues that

Hughes' educational principle was that "parochial schools" should be "established and maintained everywhere; the days have come . . . in which the school is more necessary than the church." Carried out in practice, this meant that "the school is before the church."[60] The Catholic historian Harold Buetow looks on Hughes as the defender of Catholicism when there were few Catholics and when "bigotry against them stalked the nation."[61] One of Hughes' biographers, John Hassard, describes the results as "partially a victory":

> It utterly overthrew the rich and powerful Public School Society, but it left the Catholic schools as poor as they were before; it left untouched the fundamental vice of the system of State instruction—education without religion; and if it was the means of driving sectarianism out of the common schools for a time, it secured no guarantee that sectarianism should be kept out of them—and in point of fact it was soon introduced again. The bishop himself was conscious that he had not succeeded. Ceasing from further opposition, because he saw that it would be useless, he exerted himself to establish a system of Catholic education in the diocese, hoping that his people would soon be able to withdraw their children entirely from the public schools. He exhorted his priests to spare no labor in founding parish schools.[62]

Brann concurs with the notion of a partial victory, though he claims Hughes performed an "invaluable service" to the Church in New York, and thus his arguments on behalf of Catholic schools have survived over time. Nonetheless, he "failed to secure the blessings of religious education for the children of the public schools. But his arguments in this case live after him, and have never been answered."[63] Recognizing the authoritarian nature of Hughes' episcopacy, Henry Browne observes that it is no surprise that the steadfast opponent of lay trusteeism in the Church, John Hughes, took the lead in the controversy and New York's lay Catholics followed, or at best were occasional cooperators.[64]

The common Catholic interpretation holds that Hughes was committed to building Catholic schools after the "war" ended in 1842. A study of records reveals that Catholic school enrollment in New York City grew steadily after 1842, but the percentage of the total school enrollment attending Catholic schools declined. For instance, in 1842 Catholic school enrollment was twenty percent of the total school enrollment while in 1865 it had declined to sixteen percent. By 1890 only sixty-four percent of the parishes had schools.[65] Some have attributed this to the ward system, which led to the hiring of Catholic teachers in wards that were "densely Catholic." As one person put it, the appointment of non-Catholic teachers in those wards was "an idea too preposterous to be entertained."[66]

The common story of Catholic writers about this period is that Nativism was rampant in the land. Citing illustrations from Boston, Philadelphia, Louisville, and other places these writers see Hughes as a champion of the immigrant poor Catholics besieged in a hostile Protestant country. Gustavus Myers, in his widely acclaimed book, *History of Bigotry in the United States*, speaks to this issue. Myers argues that Nativism, at first anti-Catholic and by 1843 anti-Irish as well, was alive and well in New York City, as witnessed, for instance, by the use of the term "popery" in Hughes' time.[67]

But not all Catholic scholars agree with the traditional position espoused above. Catholic historian David O'Brien is critical of Hughes and the role he played in the school controversy, as well of the interpretations presented by some uncritical Catholic historians. He argues that the school controversy was "but one episode which demonstrates the inconsistency of Catholic policy and points up the weakness of Church history in dealing with sensitive questions." In his view, the controversy gave a "powerful stimulus to nativism."[68] This was so because Hughes' tactics led Protestant groups, who were at odds with the Public School Society, to rally to the Society's support "because they saw that Hughes' attack must eventuate in the removal of religious influence from public education." Then, once it became clear that "no concessions would appease Hughes and his followers the society's trustees gave free rein to nativists." Hughes' aim, O'Brien says, was to build support for parochial schools controlled by the hierarchy and the "unification of Catholics into a militant phalanx against the hostile Protestant majority." Only if one accepts these goals as "valid and worthwhile objectives can the bishop's policies be judged beneficial and wise."[69] O'Brien criticizes the scholarly standards of Catholic historians in their favorable assessments of Hughes' actions in the struggle:

> Catholic historians too long have taken for granted the anti-Catholic prejudice of other Americans, and, in a cause and effect relationship, the resulting self-consciousness of the Catholic ghetto. They have ignored the very real actions and statements of Catholics themselves which have confirmed and strengthened Protestant fears and suspicions.[70]

Another respected American Catholic scholar, the priest-sociologist Andrew Greeley, is of like mind. Greeley maintains that it is "very dubious whether Hughes was what New York and the American Church needed in the antebellum days but it's what they got."[71] Greeley cites Hughes' sermon in 1850 as evidence of Hughes' aggressive posture. In this sermon the bishop said that "The object we hope to accomplish in kindness is to convert all pagan nations and all Protestants, even England with her proud parliament and her imperial sovereign." There was "no secret" involved with this goal. "Everybody should know that we have for our mission to convert the world, including the inhabitants of the United States, the people of the cities, the people of the country, the officers of the Navy and the Marines, the commanders of the Army, the legislatures, the Senate, the Cabinet, and all."[72] Hughes, as described by Greeley, was essentially a "warrior, a fierce tongued battler, with little financial or administrative acumen."[73] Hughes' actions, Greeley believes, strengthened the Nativists. While calling Bishop Kenrick of Philadelphia "too mild," Greeley says that Hughes "was far too militant." He was, though, a "symbol around which the harassed immigrants could rally."[74] Greeley takes Hughes to task for his influence on the American Church which "was for the most part negative." He assumed a "position of pugnacious militancy vis-à-vis non-Catholics" in American society and could grasp no other relationship with his own people besides "authoritarian paternalism." Greeley contends that Hughes took his model from Ireland, and that "Despite his patriotism, he did not like American society, and he took it as his mission to protect his flock from being corrupted and injured by that society." Hughes, Greeley concludes, contributed to the "ghetto" mentality of American Catholicism, and "symbolized it, reinforced it, and worst of all, failed to provide a working alternative in precisely the time and the place where such an alternative could have been of critical importance."[75]

Conclusion

It is not within the scope of this chapter, which has as its purpose to see Bishop John Hughes as an important "Dissenter" to the majoritarian view of public schooling in the nation, to state what Hughes should have done in such turbulent times. Surely, Hughes was on occasion not merely aggressive but belligerent. One must consider, however, the times in which he lived. Consider, for example, the speech by a Protestant minister in the debate before the New York City Common Council on October 29, 1840:

> I do say that if the fearful dilemma were forced upon me, of becoming an infidel or a Roman Catholic, according to the entire system of popery, with all its idolatry, superstition, and violent opposition to the Holy Bible, *I would rather be an infidel than a papist.*[76]

The dangers involved more than mere words, or stories about runaway nuns and murders of infants fathered by priests of nun-mothers in convents, inflammatory and false as these were. The threat of violence was in the air. Hughes publicly declared that "if a single Catholic Church were burned in New York, the city would become a second Moscow." After determining that the City would not pay for the rebuilding of any Catholic Church destroyed by Nativists in 1844 (which had just taken place in Philadelphia), Hughes ordered between 1,000 and 2,000 fully armed men to protect every Catholic Church in the City. They were to keep peace as long as possible, but to defend the churches at all costs.[77]

Billington identifies Hughes as "ill-suited by temperament and training to any compromising policy," adjudging that he was "blindly loyal to the Catholic church and strove constantly to make that church stronger and better." There can be "no doubt of his success," Billington concludes, "but there can be no doubt too that his actions and utterances aroused considerable resentment among Protestants."[78] Michaelsen is of similar mind. He avers that Hughes' leadership that resulted in the defeat of the Public School Society was a "Pyrrhic victory" because it increased the secularization of public schools, something that Hughes could hardly have desired.[79]

Hughes was an ardent patriot, and was enlisted by the Union during the Civil War to keep Britain and France out of the conflict. He was denounced by the *Catholic Mirror* of Baltimore as a "champion of desolation, blood and fratricide" for his efforts.[80] Not an abolitionist, after the draft riots in New York City that followed the use of Black labor to break the longshoreman's strike in New York City, and which resulted in the lynching of some Blacks, Hughes attempted to evade criticism for what some felt was his unjustified inaction in the riots by saying that he was no "head constable."[81] Brann writes glowingly of Hughes as a churchman and a patriot in his biography:

> The free institutions of America were about as dear to him as his Christian faith. Take him all in all he was not only the greatest prelate the Catholic Church in America has ever had; but he was as great and good a citizen as ever deserved well of the American republic. Let her do him honor![82]

By virtue of his leadership on behalf of a poor, immigrant, besieged, and persecuted population in New York City in their struggle against the "establishment," the New York Public School Society, John Hughes has gone down in history as a man of courage and conviction. He is rightfully acknowledged as the prelate who stands out as the champion of American Catholic parochial education. He unhesitatingly supported the freedom of conscience of his flock in the issue of their children's education. He truly deserves the title of "Dissenter." Hughes died on January 3, 1864, receiving the respect which had "never been accorded to any other ecclesiastic in the country since the Declaration of Independence."[83] Perhaps the most fitting ending of this essay is to quote an old foe of his, James Gordon Bennett, editor of the *New York Herald*, on the occasion of Hughes' death: Hughes "stood as the champion of that Church and as the champion of its people, by whom he was so greatly admired. In his death the Catholic church of America has lost its best friend, . . . the country one of its best patriots."[84]

Notes

1. Neil G. McCluskey, *Catholic Viewpoint on Education*, Garden City, NY: Hanover House, 1959, 167.
2. Harold A. Buetow, *Of Singular Benefit: The Story of U.S. Catholic Education*, New York: Macmillan, 1970, 138.
3. Ibid., 142.
4. Vincent P. Lannie, *Public Money and Parochial Education: Bishop Hughes, Governor Seward, and the New York School Controversy*, Cleveland, OH: Case Western Reserve University, 1968, 8.
5. Richard Shaw, *Dagger John: The Unquiet Life and Times of Archbishop John Hughes of New York*, New York: Paulist Press, 1977, 13–14.
6. Henry Brann, *Most Reverend John Hughes, First Archbishop of New York*, New York: Dodd, Mead and Company, 1892, 13.
7. Lannie, *Public Money*, 8.
8. Shaw, *Dagger John*, 91.
9. Laurence Kehoe, ed., *The Complete Works of the Most Rev. John Hughes, D.D.*, I, New York: The American News Company, 1864, 8.
10. William O. Bourne, *History of the Public School Society of the City of New York*, New York: Arno Press and the New York Times, 1971, 3.
11. Ibid.
12. "Address of the Trustees of the Society for Establishing a Free School in the City of New York for the Education of such Poor Children as do not Belong to, or are not Provided for, by any Religious Society," in *History of the Public School Society*, by Bourne, 6–7.
13. Diane Ravitch, *The Great School Wars in New York City, 1805–1973*, New York: Basic Books, 1974, 10.
14. See Carl F. Kaestle, ed., *Joseph Lancaster and the Monitorial School Movement: A Documentary History*, New York: Teachers College Press, 1973.
15. Carl F. Kaestle, *The Evolution of an Urban School System: New York City, 1750–1850*, Cambridge, MA: Harvard University Press, 1973, 8–9.
16. "DeWitt Clinton's Address," in *History of the Public School Society*, by Bourne, 17.

17. Ibid., 19.
18. DeWitt Clinton, "To the Parents and Guardians of the Children Belonging to the Schools under the Care of the New York Free School Society," in Bourne, *History of the Public School Society*, 36.
19. Ibid.
20. Ibid., 37.
21. Ibid.
22. Ibid., 38.
23. Ibid.
24. Ravitch, *The Great School Wars*, 19.
25. Ibid., 20–21.
26. Ibid., 22–23.
27. Ibid., 26.
28. Ibid., 27.
29. Ibid., 31.
30. Lannie, *Public Money*, 18–19.
31. Shaw, *Dagger John*, 139.
32. Lannie *Public Money*, 21.
33. Neil G. McCluskey, "Pastoral Letters of the Provincial Councils of Baltimore" (1829–1849), in *Catholic Education in America: A Documentary History*, ed. Neil G. McCluskey, New York: Teachers College Press, 1964, 51–64.
34. Lannie, *Public Money*, 33–35.
35. Neil G. McCluskey, "Petition of the Catholics of New York for a Portion of the Common School Fund (1840)," in *Catholic Education in America*, ed. McCluskey, 65–69.
36. Ibid., 69–70.
37. Ibid., 71–72.
38. Ibid., 76.
39. Lannie, *Public Money*, 53–54.
40. Kehoe, ed., *The Complete Works*, I, 41–42.
41. Ibid., 43–44.
42. Lannie, *Public Money*, 74.
43. Ibid., 75–84.
44. Ibid., 90–91.
45. Ibid., 96.
46. Ibid., 97.
47. Ibid., 103–10.
48. Ravitch, *The Great School Wars*, 51.
49. Kehoe, ed., The *Complete Works*, I, 51.
50. Lannie, *Public Money*, 132.
51. Ibid., 172–78.
52. Ibid., 192–95.
53. Ibid., 206–11.
54. Ibid., 211–12.
55. Joseph J. McCadden, "Bishop Hughes versus the Public School Society of New York," *Catholic Historical Review* 50, 2 (July 1964): 207.

56. Ravitch, *The Great School Wars*, 76–77.

57. Ibid., 80.

58. Joseph J. McCadden, "New York's School Crisis of 1840–1842: Its Irish Antecedents," *Thought* 41 (Winter 1968): 561–63.

59. Richard J. Gabel, *Public Funds for Church and Private Schools*, Washington, DC: Catholic University of America Press, 1937, 723.

60. James A. Burns, *The Principles, Origin and Establishment of the Catholic School System in the United States*, New York: Arno Press and the New York Times, 1970, 374–75.

61. Buetow, *Of Singular Benefit*, 138.

62. John R. G. Hassard, *Life of the Most Reverend John Hughes*, New York: D. Appleton and Company, 1866, 251.

63. Brann, *Most Reverend John Hughes*, 13.

64. Henry J. Browne, "Public Support of Catholic Education in New York, 1825–1842: Some New Aspects" *Catholic Historical Review* 39 (April 1953): 27.

65. James W. Sanders, "Roman Catholics and the School Question in New York City: Some Suggestions for Research," in *Educating an Urban People: The New York Experience*, eds., Diane Ravitch and Ronald K. Goodenow, New York: Teachers College Press, 1981, 122–23.

66. Ibid., 124.

67. Gustavus Myers, *History of Bigotry in the United States*, New York: Random House, 1943, 167–68.

68. David J. O'Brien, "American Catholicism and the Diaspora," *Cross Currents* 16 (Summer 1966): 309–10.

69. Ibid., 311–14.

70. Ibid., 314.

71. Andrew M. Greeley, *The Catholic Experience*, New York: Doubleday, 1967, 113.

72. Ibid., 106–7.

73. Ibid., 113.

74. Ibid., 118–24.

75. Ibid., 124–25.

76. Quoted in Ray Allen Billington, *The Protestant Crusade 1800–1860: A Study of the Origins of American Nativism*, New York: Macmillan, 1938, 146.

77. Ibid., 231–32.

78. Ibid., 290.

79. Robert S. Michaelsen, *Piety in the Public School*, New York: Macmillan, 1970, 87.

80. James Hennessey, *American Catholics: A History of the Roman Catholic Community in the United States*, New York: Oxford University Press, 1981, 148–50; Brann, *Most Reverend*, 175.

81. Hennessey. *American Catholics*, 150.

82. Brann, *Most Reverend*, 178.

83. *New York Herald*, January 7, 1864, quoted in Shaw, *Dagger John*, 370.

84. Shaw, *Dagger John*, 371–72.

· 3 ·

INSTITUTIONALIZING
CATHOLIC DISSENT

The Nineteenth-Century Parochial School

The initiatives for Catholic parochial schools begun by Bishop Hughes in New York City spread throughout the land. Since Catholic educational policy differed sharply from American public school policy, Catholic parochial (parish) schools were the major dissenting institution from public education in the United States in the nineteenth century. In the eyes of the Catholic Church, education is a "mixed" matter, with several agencies, viz., the family, the Church, and the state all having legitimate rights in its conduct. In Catholic teaching, their proper roles are determined by the Church. Since many in the civil state did not agree with this position, the situation has been fraught with conflict. One such situation developed in the United States in the nineteenth century.

American Catholic Church Policy

The Catholic faithful constituted but a minute minority in the early United States. As such, they faced both formal and informal discrimination. Schooling was one place where discrimination occurred. This discrimination was the reason why Catholic bishops, responsible for the faith and morals of their followers, became increasingly critical of public school practices that dealt with religion.

The first official comment of the American hierarchy on education was made by Bishop John Carroll of Baltimore in 1792 in his "Pastoral Letter." His remarks, general in nature, pertained to the life-long benefits of a Christian education and reminded parents that, by properly raising their children, they were serving God by preserving religion and simultaneously benefiting the nation, "whose welfare depends on the morals of its citizens."[1]

In 1808 the Vatican created four new dioceses, joining the Archdiocese of Baltimore. Together they made up the Province of Baltimore.[2] The First Provincial Council of Baltimore met in 1829. Its "Pastoral" called on parents to become involved in the religious education of their children by reminding them of the words of Christ: "Suffer the little children to come unto me"; described Hell as "this is too frequently the necessary consequence of an improper education"; and warned parents that if they would not adopt the proper hierarchy of values, "what will it avail them to gain the whole world if they lose their souls?"[3]

The "Pastoral" of the Second Provincial Council in 1833 referred to the tremendous efforts put forth by the bishops on behalf of Catholic children to "provide schools . . . united to a strict protection of their morals and the best safeguards of their faith."[4] Four years later in 1837 the Province's bishops requested the faithful "to unite your efforts to ours for upholding these institutions which we have created for the education of your children."[5] The next Council held in 1840, termed the proper education of Catholic children a "dear subject," and after mentioning the general cooperation of the laity as regards Catholic schools, complained that the Catholic people "are not always so ready to aid in defraying the expenses which should necessarily be incurred in having them (the schools) secured and made permanent."[6] It is in this letter that the bishops referred explicitly for the first time to difficulties with the public schools. They complained of biased textbooks and even the system itself being directed against the Church, which, in their view, made it "no easy matter thus to preserve the faith of your children in the midst of so many difficulties."[7] The bishops also protested against the practice of Bible-reading in the schools, both because the version used—the King James—was not authorized by the Church and because the circumstances in which it was read led to contempt, rather than respect, for the word of God.[8]

The Catholic shepherds were more forceful in their indictment of public education in 1843. They exhorted Catholic parents to vigilance and reminded them of the seriousness of the obligations that resulted for their state of life:

We have seen with serious alarm, efforts made to poison the fountain of public education, by giving it a sectarian hue, and accustoming children to the use of a version
of the Bible made under sectarian bias, and placing in their hands books of various kinds
replete with offensive and dangerous matter. . . . Parents are strictly bound, like faithful Abraham, to teach their children the truths which God has revealed; and if they
suffer them to be led astray, the souls of the children will be required at their hands.
Let them, therefore, . . . see that no interference with the faith of their children be used
in public schools, and no attempt made to induce conformity in any thing contrary to
the laws of the Catholic Church. . . . [9]

In 1852, after further immigration of Catholics, mainly Irish, had swelled the
ranks of the Church to the point where there were now six ecclesiastical
provinces in the country, the bishops returned to Baltimore for their first plenary (national) council. They warned Catholic parents of the "terrible expec-
tation of judgment" that would befall parents whose children "perish through
his criminal neglect," or by their refusal to follow the "authority of God's
church." They could avert this evil by giving their "children a Christian education," and were told: "Listen not to those who would persuade you that religion can be separated from secular instruction."[10] What should be done? The
bishops instructed the faithful to "Encourage the establishment and support of
Catholic schools"; and to "make every sacrifice which may be necessary for this
object." They should spare the children from evils that were "too multiplied and
too obvious to require that we should do more than raise our voices in solemn
protest against the system from which they spring."[11]

By mid-nineteenth century there is little doubt but that official Roman
Catholicism was in dissent from American educational policy and practice.
Conflicts with what Catholic leaders perceived was the pan-Protestant nature
of public schools, as evidenced by the devotional reading of the King James version of the Bible, the use of textbooks with a perceived anti-Catholic bias, and
other religious practices that reflected the tenets of Protestantism had convinced Catholic leaders that the common public schools were no place for
Catholic children. The numbers of these children, due to immigration, were
growing rapidly as the nineteenth century progressed.

In 1800, approximately one percent of the nation's population was
Catholic.[12] Masses of immigrants from Europe came to the United States in the
nineteenth century. From 1821–1850 almost 2.5 million came, with 1,713,251
in the 1840s. More than one million of these were Irish, with 780,719 arriving in the 1840s.[13] Many of the Catholic clergy were of Irish descent, and they
held positions of leadership in American Catholicism. One of these was the
aggressive bishop of New York, John Hughes. His efforts to rid the schools of

the New York Public School Society of Protestant influence, including the read-ing of the King James version of the Bible, were unsuccessful, as were his later efforts to obtain a proportionate portion of the school fund for use by Catholic schools. According to the Catholic historian James A. Burns, even if the "Douay Bible were to be substituted for the King James version," Hughes would still have been dissatisfied. The only thing that would have satisfied him would have been if the Catholic creed were "taught, *in its entirety*."[14] No diplomat, Hughes sermonized in 1843 that:

> Everybody should know that we have for our mission to convert the world—includ-ing the inhabitants of the United States—the people of the cities, and the people of the country, the officers of the navy and marines, commanders of the army, the Legislature, the Cabinet, the President, and all.[15]

The temperament of the Bishop of Philadelphia, Francis Kenrick, was of a milder sort. He sought and obtained from the Philadelphia School Board per-mission in 1843 to use the Douay version of the Bible in public schools. A Nativist-inspired riot ensued, which resulted in two Catholic churches and dozens of homes burned down, and thirteen persons killed.[16] The anti-Catholic feeling continued until the Civil War, as illustrated by the success of the Know-Nothing party in the 1850s. For instance, in 1854 the Know-Nothing party elected seventy-five men to Congress, dominated politics in Massachusetts, and did well in several other states.[17]

Not faced with the language barrier as were the German immigrants, and often mired deep in poverty, the Irish were hardly unanimous in supporting parochial schools. Dorothy Dohen points out, though, that eventually many Irish became convinced that the public schools were dominated by Protestantism.[18] Their support of Catholic schools, as well as that of the Germans, was enhanced by the councils of Catholic bishops, both regional (Provincial) and national (Plenary).

Two of the five ecclesiastical provinces that were created shortly before the First Plenary Council of Baltimore were Cincinnati and St. Louis, which were to form the bases of the "German triangle" in the Midwest (Milwaukee was to be the apex). Cincinnati was to become, in a few years, the stronghold of advo-cates for Catholic education in the nation. Meeting in 1855, the First Provincial Council of Cincinnati admonished pastors to "strive by all the means in their power" to prevent Catholic children from attending schools that they cannot attend without "grave danger to their faith and morals." Simultaneously, they exhorted parents to "aid and sustain" parochial schools.[19] The bishops acknowledged with gratitude the tendency of the German parishes to establish parochial schools and they set them up as models to be emulated by their English-speaking brethren:

> Our excellent German congregations leave us nothing to desire on this subject. The children attend at Mass every morning, they sing with one accord the power of God, they go from the church to the school. They are accustomed to cleanliness and neatness of dress, to diligent and affectionate respect for their parents, the Reverend Clergy, and their teachers. We have nothing more at heart than that the pupils of our English schools should imitate their example.[20]

Three years later in 1858 the bishops of the Province met again and once more spoke out forcefully on education, this time putting the responsibility for Catholic schools squarely on the shoulders of the pastors, holding them under "pain of mortal sin" to establish schools in those parishes for which they were responsible.[21] The Fathers of the Third Provincial Council of Cincinnati criticized the public school system in the harshest of terms, calling it "plausible, but most unwise," and holding it responsible for the "rising generation" being educated without definite principles or with "false, at least, more or less exaggerated and fanatical principles." They accused the system, "if carried out," well-calculated to "bring up a generation of religious indifferentists, if not of practical infidels."[22]

The bishops of the young nation met again in Baltimore in 1866 for the Second Plenary Council. They reaffirmed the teaching of Baltimore I and added that "religious teaching and religious training should form part of every system of school education."[23] They called attention to what they described as a "prevalent error," i.e., parents consulting their children's wishes as to which school they would attend, and instructed parents to assume the responsibilities of their state in life.[24]

The question of the proper relationship between Church and state came up at Baltimore II. The bishops reminded Catholics that the principle of judgment for them was different than that of the sects, viz., that for the sects the individual was the "ultimate judge of what the law of God commands or forbids." Not so with Catholics, who have a "guide in the church, as a divine institution," that teaches what the law of God "forbids or allows." The state, the bishops contended, is bound to recognize this authority "as supreme in its sphere—of moral, no less than dogmatic teaching."[25]

Statements about the school issue were not the sole province of bishops gathered in councils. Individual bishops, in charge of a diocese, also made their positions known. (A Catholic bishop in charge of a diocese, called an "Ordinary," is the authoritative teacher for the Church in matters of faith and morals in that diocese.) A number of these individual American bishops made statements about school matters during the 1870s, demonstrating that they indeed were outspoken dissenters from the American public school. The Province of Cincinnati, with its heavy commitment to Catholic schools, was extensively represented by the positions of individual bishops on the school issue.

In 1872 Archbishop J. B. Purcell of Cincinnati proclaimed that the "Catholic school is the nursery of the Catholic congregation." He wondered how parents who "willfully and deliberately" neglect their duty of sending their children to Catholic schools can "worthily approach, or be conscientiously admitted to the sacraments."[26] Parents, he felt, would not sacrifice the souls of their offspring "while yet pure," for the "kind of education received in Godless or sectarian schools."[27]

Bishop St. Palais of Vincennes, Indiana, presented his dissent from the public schools in a series of objections:

1. We object to the public schools on account of the *infidel* source from which they originated.
2. We object to these schools because the teaching of religion is excluded from them, and such exclusion will *inevitably* produce religious indifference if not infidelity.
3. We object to these schools, because religious instruction which is necessarily connected with the acquirement of secular knowledge, cannot be introduced in them without interfering with the conscientious rights and wounding the most delicate feelings of the pupils.
4. We object to these schools again because the promiscuous assembling of both sexes of a certain age is injurious to the morals of the children, and because we dread associations which might, in time, prove pernicious to them and distressing to their parents.[28]

Two Ohio bishops, Rosecrans of Columbus and Gilmour of Cleveland, addressed the educational situation in their Lenten Pastorals for 1873. Bishop Rosecrans elevated support of Catholic schools to a par with the Real Presence of Christ in the Eucharist and the Divinity of Jesus in Catholic doctrine.[29] Bishop Gilmour advised that if a parish cannot build both church and school at the same time, they should build the school first and wait for the church, since there was "little danger of the old losing their faith, but there is every danger that the young will." On the school question there "can be, and must be, no division. Either we are Catholics or we are not." Gilmour authorized confessors to refuse the sacraments to parents who send their children to public schools "as these despise the laws of the Church and disobey the command of both priest and Bishop." Parents, he said, "*sin* who in their pride send their children to public schools," because we "cannot serve God and the devil."[30]

Archbishop Elder, Purcell's successor in Cincinnati, went on record that the Church's pronouncements on the school issue were so clear that "there is nothing for a Catholic to do but obey them or else renounce his religion. 'He that will not hear the Church, let him be to thee as the heathen and the publican'" (Matt. 18, 17).[31] Elder charged that the system by which the public schools operated was "false," and that the students' minds "are kept systematically excluded from the truths and practices of religion."[32] Across the Ohio River in Kentucky, Elder's contemporary Bishop Toebbe, was more critical of the public school system: "The public schools are infidel and Godless, and must therefore be avoided."[33]

In Indiana, Bishop Francis Chatard of Vincennes informed his flock that the "excuse of inferiority of the Catholic schools to the Public schools has little foundation."[34] His fellow Indianan, Bishop Joseph Dwenger of Fort Wayne, ridiculed non-Catholics with the regret that they were "so poor that they cannot support them (the public schools) without taxing the Catholics."[35] Catholic author Thomas Jenkins lauded the bishops of Indiana for their leadership on behalf of Catholic schools, noting that though New York State had nine times as many Catholics as did Indiana, the Hoosier state had half as many Catholic schools as did New York.[36]

Bishop John L. Spalding of Peoria qualified as one of the leading American prelates and Catholic educators of his time. He believed that "no better means" than the "godless public school system" could be found for the "diffusion of the spirit of unbelief." The public school educators wee "quacks" in his view, treating the child as "though he were mere mind," and using it for "low ends."[37]

The state of New York had a worthy successor to Archbishop Hughes in Bishop Bernard McQuaid of Rochester. The *Buffalo Courier* identified him as "the acknowledged exponent of the Catholic agitation against the present school system, or perhaps we should say, for the incorporation of sectarian schools into the system as it now exists."[38] McQuaid had begun his educational campaign in a talk at Auburn, New York in 1871, in which he complained that the state had stepped in as master of schools, instead of leaving control of the education of children to parents, both Catholic and Protestant, who should receive financial assistance from the state in educating their children.[39] It was not the union of Church and state that should be feared, in McQuaid's judgment; rather it was the "tyranny of no-religion, of open infidelity."[40] As citizens and taxpayers, McQuaid argued, Catholics had every right to complain about an educational system that featured Bible-reading, praying, and singing of hymns in its program.[41] He accused his opponents of fomenting discord in the nation when he asserted that it was a "favorite anti-Catholic trick to represent Catholics as plotting the destruction of the Public School."[42] All that Catholics wanted was justice, McQuaid claimed, which would be accorded them if they received their share of the tax fund to use for their own children in their own schools. Statements have been attributed to McQuaid that he had heard a Presbyterian minister openly avow "that the Bible and the Common Schools were the two stones of the mill that would grind Catholicity out of Catholics" and a Methodist minister boast that "in twelve years the Catholics had lost 1,900,000 children."[43]

In 1883 the bishops of New York State assembled under the leadership of Cardinal McCloskey of New York City, and addressed the school matter. They stated that "no Catholic of whatever rank or condition" could approve "any system of public instruction from which religion is totally excluded." Godless schools had resulted in "infidelity and impiety," and had led to "contempt for authority, self-seeking and dishonesty, complete disregard for moral obligation and other kindred evils." Schools without religion "have been in existence long enough for even the leas observant of men to be able to judge of their results. . . . 'By their fruits you shall know them!'"[44]

In 1873, while Bishop of Richmond (Virginia), James Gibbons had written his diocese that the "religious and secular education" of children cannot be *divorced* without "inflicting a fatal wound to the soul." This wound usually brings about a "spirit of indifference in matters of *faith*." The *"loss of Catholic faith"* is another evil that results from this separation. "If no provision is made for the Christian culture of the rising youth it is feared that twenty years hence, it will be much easier to find churches for a congregation, than a congregation for our churches."[45] Ten years later, speaking as the Archbishop of Baltimore, Gibbons proclaimed: "It may safely be asserted that the future status of Catholicity in the United States is to be determined by the success or failure of our day-schools."[46]

On the eve of the epochal Third Plenary Council of Baltimore in 1884, Gibbons wrote that among the dangers threatening the American nation was the "imperfect and vicious system of education, which undermines the religion of youth." As proof, Gibbons pointed to the increase of crime and other social problems that had occurred contemporary with the development of the nation's public school system.[47]

James Conway wrote of the consensus that existed among the American bishops in their dissent from the public school system in the 1870s and 1880s. As Conway put it:

> There is hardly a bishop living today in the United States who has not condemned the existing system of public schools in the strongest terms, and earnestly exhorted the clergy and the faithful entrusted to his charge to provide for Catholic schools for the education of the Catholic youth.[48]

The "Instruction" of the Propaganda de Fide (Propagation of the Faith) in 1875

The Catholic Church in the United States was classified as a mission country by the Vatican throughout the nineteenth century. Hence, it came under the jurisdiction of the Propaganda de Fide (Propagation of the Faith). This office of the Pope's Curia (or Cabinet) entered the school issue with an "Instruction" in 1875. Its origin lies in a request by a number of American bishops for a formal document from the Congregation, "to impress upon the faithful the seriousness of the matter and to strengthen their own authority in persuading pastors to build parish schools."[49]

The Congregation began its "Instruction" with the observation that it had been told many times that "evils of the gravest kind are likely to result from the so-called public schools." Its first specific objection was that the system itself was opposed to Catholicism since it excluded all religious instruction and thus constituted a great evil if children were allowed to be exposed to it. Second, since the schools were not under the control of the Church, teachers were selected "from every sect indiscriminately." Additionally, the practice of coeducation further endangered children's morals. Third, Catholics were told that the danger of perversion of faith must be rendered remote, for if the danger to the students' faith or morals were proximate then the natural, divine, and universal law dictates that Catholic children cannot in conscience attend such schools. Fourth, the bishops were directed to use every means to prevent Catholics "from all contact with the public schools," to establish Catholic schools and to improve existing Catholic schools. All Catholics, especially the wealthy and influential, were reminded that they had the duty of financially supporting Catholic schools. Fifth, there really was no obstacle preventing the Catholics of the United States from "averting, with God's help, the dangers with which Catholicity is threatened from the public school system," and having their own schools. Sixth, the existence of special circumstances that would exempt parents from sending their children to Catholic schools "is to be left to the conscience and judgment of the Bishop." Some examples of such cause in the Congregation's view were the absence of a Catholic school or an unsuitable Catholic school. But even then, the danger of perversion must be made remote. If it is not, then that public school "must be shunned at whatever cost, even life itself." Seventh, pastors and parents must make provision for the Christian training of children who attend public schools prior to their attendance at them. Among their responsibilities in this regard was to keep the children from contact with peers "whose company might be dangerous to their faith or morals." Eighth, parents who neglect to give Christian training, or who allow their children to go to schools "in which the ruin of their souls is inevitable," or those who send them to public schools without sufficient reason, and without rendering the danger of perversion remote, if obstinate, "cannot be absolved," which ought to be evident from the moral teaching of the Church.[50]

The "Instruction" was a clear-cut victory for the advocates of parochial schools in American Catholic life, lending, as it did, the weight of the Vatican to their side. Conway points out that the Propagation's teaching made it clear the "every effort" was to be made to "erect Catholic schools where such do not exist, or to enlarge upon them and make them more useful and efficient."[51]

The Position of the Catholic Press

The majority of the journalistic venture in the American Catholic world depended upon the approval, at least indirectly, of the Catholic hierarchy. Thus, the typical view expressed in the Catholic press rejected the public school, either because it was Protestant-dominated or godless. The solution presented was the erection of a denominational school system for both Catholics and Protestants, financially supported by public funds.[52] Eventually, Protestants would realize that the Catholic idea was a modification, not destruction, of the public school system, and as they witnessed the advance of atheism in the country they would realize that the true enemy of Protestantism was a combination of irreligion, pantheism, atheism, and immorality, otherwise known as secularism, and not the Catholic Church. One Catholic writer exhorted the Protestants to "Fight, therefore, Protestant, no longer us, but the public enemy."[53] Little could be expected of a beneficial nature from the civil state in education because it was by its nature "godless and material" and sought only those ends that were consistent with its nature.[54]

The proper changes in the educational system could be achieved if only the Catholic voter would assert himself, and become the "champion of faith, law, order, social and political morality, and Christian civilization," thereby arresting the "swollen current of corruption, crime and lawlessness which threaten to sweep away religion, morality, and liberty."[55] State-sponsored education was not only incomplete, what was worse was its pagan or godless character, which made it thoroughly incapable of producing good citizens. In fact, if the rights of Catholics were not acknowledged by the government, and if the state continued to act in its usurped role as educator, young Catholics, as well as other youth, bereft of the benign influences of God-centered education, will have no alternative but to end up as criminals and other pests of society.[56] The troubles of American society, and its school system, would be solved if only the American people would make every effort to ascertain the will of God, because "The Catholic Church is the medium and channel through which the will of God is expressed."[57]

Perhaps no Catholic book contains as much of the dissenting Catholic position on education in the latter nineteenth century than does *Public School Education*, authored by the Redemptorist priest, Michael J. Muller. His book, published in 1872, received the commendation of the then Rector of the St. Paul (Minnesota) Cathedral, John Ireland, who termed it "so well-timed, its doctrine so correct and precise, the arguments you employ so cogent, that I am confident it will, under God's Providence, do a great deal of good."[58] The book was a wholesale attack on the public school system in the United States. Among the accusations that it leveled at the system were it had produced the evils that were prevalent in the country; it failed to provide separate education for girls under "mature and pious women"; and it was more of a pagan system than any country's in Europe.[59] Muller accused the public school system of having all kinds of antireligious and sometimes antisocial aims as its goal "to bring about, namely, a generation without belief in God and immortality, . . . a generation that substitutes the devil for God, hell for heaven, sin and vice for virtue and holiness of life."[60] The system's success would be seen by a people without religion, and by the "substitution of the harlotry of the passions for the calm and elevating influences of reason and religion: How can it be otherwise," he asked?[61] Its evil effects were so pervasive that the "child even unlearns, in the society of the school, whatever principles of religion he may have learned from his parents," making it, in comparison with the ancient heathens "to our greater shame and confusion, and to their advantage."[62]

Its malevolent bent produced males that were "over-educated," "worshippers of the state," and "accomplished barbarians."[63] The harm the system did to boys was mild compared what it did to girls. These "mothers of tomorrow" have lost their divine calling in these schools where they "hear of a countless number of unnatural crimes, committed under the veil of marriage, that are becoming so common in the present day."[64] Worse, these schools have become, in some instances, "houses of assignation" where the older girls pass on their talents to the younger ones, where morals have sunk so low that "courtesans openly ply their trade."[65]

Little wonder then, Muller mused, that with a system inclined to such a vile end, that girls have lost their God-given mission and dignity and have become so frivolous that decent young men, afraid of sin, avoid them.[66] If people would only study history, Muller opined, they would realize that "*material civilization*" is nothing else than "*polished barbarianism*," and that with a public school system that sought to banish the very mention of God from its premises, "as sure as effect follows cause, every species of villainy and defilement will flood the land," if such a system were permitted to endure.[67] The nation, he warned, was in for a much more serious punishment than the Civil War if it continued to prepare its young for infidelity.[68]

Muller proceeded to attack the state in his diatribe, stating that this "wicked, detestable, irreligious system, diabolical in its origin, and subversive of all political, social, and religious order," is imposed upon all Christians whether they approve of it or not. The state, he contended, has "no right whatever to force such a godless system upon its subjects."[69] The "irreligious, godless system" turned the young of both sexes into the "worst kind of infidels," and made them "apostates" of "such secret societies as aim at the overthrow of governments and all good order, and Christian religion itself."[70] And what is worse, Muller declared, is that Catholics are forced to support this "*prolific mother of children of anti-Christ*," which places the government in the position of showing legal preference to nonbelievers, who themselves constituted a sect, which violates the United States Constitution.[71] If the present course is continued, Muller maintained, the public school system will deliver "hell upon earth," and once this is accomplished, Satan will be able to turn his attention elsewhere.[72]

Bible-reading in schools was impotent in the face of such an evil force and at best could only produce "dangerous speculation."[73] The only remedy was the teaching of the Christian religion in denominational schools financially supported by the government.[74] While this would work for Catholics it would be of little help to Protestants because the "infidel is the Protestant in full bloom."[75] The time for the application of the remedy for Catholics was now, he continued, because unless the current situation is rectified, the Catholic religion will "practically die out" after immigration ceases, unless Catholic youth are freed from contact with the contamination of the public schools.[76] With so much at stake, it is only just that Catholic parents be denied absolution if they don't care about a Catholic education for their children.[77]

Muller concluded his diatribe on the nation's public schools with a warning to Catholic pastors that they will be guilty of trampling on the blood of Christ if they fail to provide a school for their parish, and like the unprofitable servant in the Gospel, they will be found wanting on the day of judgment and will be cast outside by the Lord, whom they have so grievously failed, into the darkness where there will be the "weeping and gnashing of teeth."[78]

The Growing National Struggle over Catholic Schools

At the time Muller penned his commentary, public school advocates added to the controversy. They often associated public schools with patriotism, while denigrating private schools, particularly Catholic ones, with being divisive and "un-American."

For example, on September 29, 1875, the President of the United States, Ulysses S. Grant, spoke to the veterans of the Army of the Tennessee at Des Moines, Iowa. In his speech Grant called for the encouragement of "free schools, and resolve that not one dollar appropriated for their support" be given to any "sectarian school." Only the common schools, "unmixed with sectarian, pagan or atheistic dogmas," deserved support. "Leave the matter of religion to the family altar, the church and the private school, supported entirely by private contributors. Keep the Church and state forever separate," Grant urged. Then, wrapping the school matter in the blanket of patriotism from the late War, Grant said, "With these safeguards, I believe the battle which created the Army of the Tennessee will not have been fought in vain."[79]

Grant's speech was criticized in Catholic circles. One writer referred to it as "Bismarckian."[80] Archbishop Gibbons remarked that the "central government has no more right to dictate to the father when and where and how he must educate his children than it has to prescribe his food or the shape of his clothes."[81] Grant's speech was called "tyrannous," and Catholics pledged to continue their fight until they received equal rights as citizens, which meant tax money for their schools.[82] They charged that the aim of those who supported Grant's speech was "not to promote knowledge, but to destroy the religious conviction of our children and to keep us from growing in the land."[83]

A few months later Congressman James G. Blaine offered a constitutional amendment to the Congress that read:

> No state shall make any law respecting the establishment of religion, or prohibiting the free exercise thereof; and no money raised by school taxation in any State, for the support of public schools, or derived from any fund thereof, nor any public lands devoted thereto, shall ever be under the control of any religious sect; nor shall any money raised, or lands so devoted, be divided between religious sects or denominations.[84]

The "Blaine Amendment," as it came to be known, passed the House by a whopping vote of 180 to seven, but failed to achieve the necessary two-thirds vote in the Senate by a twenty-eight to sixteen count.[85] The vote reflected the mood of the country at that time, a mood that was reflected by the requirement passed by Congress that any state admitted to the union henceforth have a "system of public schools which shall be open to all the children of said State and free from sectarian control."[86]

Catholic Reaction to Criticism of Catholic Schools

Aware of the overwhelming mood in the country that opposed their position, nonetheless some Catholics pressed on. One writer attributed the existence of secular education to an alliance between the devil and the world in which Satan tells the world its "fundamental mistake" is to allow the Church to educate its children. "Very true, replied the world, but "it is not too late to correct the mistake, especially with your very valuable cooperation."[87]

Catholics saw the Masons as a powerful force against them in the educational conflict as well. One writer alleged that the public schools served the interests of the "worst of all sects—Freemasonry, and they are conspicuous for their sectarian intolerance and hatred of every form of religious belief."[88] As a result of the influence of freemasonry, the schools were so rotten that they frustrated the benign influence of Catholic parents by "giving to the children the practical example of religious indifferentism, which is sure to bear, sooner or later, its usual fruit of injustice, knavery and debauchery." These baleful consequences were inevitable, the "natural fruit of a bad system," and made the system a "disgrace to the country."[89]

Moreover, the Catholic press regarded the so-called "liberal theory" of public education as merely a scheme that "ignores parental rights and tends to transform the state into a Moloch, to which the children of the people ought to be sacrificed."[90] The public system, though it claimed to favor no sect, had favored Protestantism and presently was moving in the direction of secularism. Catholic parents were admonished that they could not abandon their children to such a godless system without endangering their eternal salvation. Their obligation, which included financial sacrifice, was to frequent and support the schools that ecclesiastical authorities had erected or ordered to be built. Simultaneously, Catholics should organize and cooperate with whatever groups were willing to obtain public funds for denominational schools. Thus, Catholics were opposed to irreligious or pagan schools and in favor of public denominational schools.[91] The columns of the *Catholic Citizen*, a moderate, lay-run Catholic newspaper published in Milwaukee, serve as an example of these ideas. In 1884, the *Citizen* requested a share of the tax fund for Catholic schools because the public schools had abandoned God.[92] The *Citizen* joined in the onslaught against public schools as godless institutions.[93] It proclaimed that as a result of this godlessness, "The parents of 600,000 American children do not believe in and will not patronize your schools."[94]

The publication of several articles on the benefits of parochial schools in the Protestant press were a welcome sight to some Catholics and led one Catholic author to speculate if the Protestants were "coming around" to the Catholic view on the school question.[95] Another Catholic writer was amazed at Protestant silence on what he considered the evisceration of Christianity in the common schools into their present "godless" status.[96]

To its enthusiasts, the Catholic school was not limited to providing religious benefits for its students. Its backers claimed that the best teachers were to be found there, because they were members of religious orders or clerics, and that due to these dedicated religious the atmosphere of the school was permeated by a virtuous spirit that could not help but surpass the public school in all areas, including patriotism.[97] The very presence and aid of God, and a thorough Christian training by His followers, could not but assist the student in all compartments of life, but especially that which was the most important, the supernatural. It was this belief that gave Catholics their zeal for their schools, despite what they considered unfair legislation that taxed them for schools that their consciences could not let their children attend, denied them a share of their own tax money for their children's education, and subjected them to hostile public opinion in addition.[98]

The school conflict led to vitriolic attacks on both sides, some of them very personal. For instance, some Catholics were highly critical of Protestant ministers. One writer wondered if the silence on the part of ministers to the "godless" nature of the public schools was due to the fact that so many Protestant "deacons and vestrymen are making their living" through the schools?[99] He felt that the ministers were hardly any better than the politicians and inspectors of public schools who "go around making speeches to win the admiration of female teachers who hold their places through political influence."[100] The *Catholic Citizen* compared the life of the priest with that of the minister, with the former far ahead. The priest worked harder, for less, and had given his life to the Church and his parishioners. The minister is "equipped with all the comforts of life," has only a little work to be done once a week in the preaching of a sermon "on some social or political topic, on how the law should be enforced to make people better, and thus lessen the work of the minister."[101]

The Civil State and Education

With the increasing participation by the state in education, the ideological differences between the backers of public education and the Catholic Church on the nature and function of state, Church, and parent came more to the forefront. Catholic authorities watched with alarm as the several states organized departments of public instruction, created county and city supervisors of education, laid down requirements for teacher certification, determined curricula, passed compulsory attendance requirements, and accredited schools. Aware of the recent setbacks the Church had suffered in Europe with civil governments over the control of education, they chose not to remain silent on what they considered similar developments in the United States.

According to conservative, and what may be labeled orthodox Catholic thought, the state's right in education should be limited to its own field, which meant it should operate as the promoter of education, and nothing beyond that.[102] To discover the state's proper sphere in education it is necessary to distinguish the essential from the nonessential. The only essential, Catholic teaching held, was knowledge of man's last end. Consequently the state, since it is not in any way involved with man's last end, has no right to compel parents to educate their children, since its legitimate area is confined to nonessentials. Further, the state must not interfere with the Church, which does deal with man's last end. It, as the promoter of education, must actively cooperate with the Church as it carries out its divine mandate.[103] Public education, as it existed in the United States, was founded on the deification of the state, contrary to the law of God, and surpassing in absolutism anything in the civilized nations of pagan antiquity.[104] In attempting to control education, it not only exceeded its proper boundaries but also was aspiring to be another Sparta.[105] The basic issue at stake in the educational controversy came down to the respective visions held by the advocates of "godless" and "religious" education on the relation of parents to children. The *Catholic Citizen* averred that the "assumption by the state of a right to educate or supervise and direct the education of children is an indefensible usurpation and a plain act of tyranny over parents."[106] Any act by the state in the area that belonged to parents was an intrusion and a "most impious and sacrilegious violation of the holiest rights of God and man."[107] Catholics based the grounds for the parental right and obligation in education on reproduction. Baptism elevated this duty to the supernatural level, because it made youngsters children of God by conferring supernatural life on them. The physical, moral, religious, and intellectual faculties of the person must all be developed if true education is to take place. The three Rs, given man's supernatural destiny, are the "least important part of education."[108]

While the rights of parents were called primary and paramount in education, in practice these rights were subject to the authority of the Church. The Church entered the field of education because of the command of Christ to teach all nations (Matt. 28:18). It possessed inalienable rights in the field because of the commission of Christ.[109] Parents receive instruction from their supernatural mother, the Church, who speaks to them with the voice and authority of the Son of God. At the time of their child's Baptism, parents commit themselves to listening to the voice of the Church as to how this child, who is now the Church's as well as theirs, should be educated. They have a moral responsibility to hear the Church, as Jesus told them to do. The Church's message embraces Christian doctrine and the moral and religious tone of the school, with anything that is related to man's last end, which can include secular instruction.[110] The Church has no choice but to fulfill her divinely mandated mission of teaching, of being the "earnest, constant and devoted foster-mother of education."[111] The Church's teachings were not intrusions but were sanctifying and the logical outcome of her divine mandate, to be neglected by Catholic parents at the cost of endangering their own and their children's eternal salvation. Such teachings underscored the importance of the Church's position on education, as emphasized in the influential Third Plenary Council of Baltimore in 1884 in which the nation's Catholic bishops highlighted the critical importance of Catholic schools in the life of the Church and individual to a degree not hitherto witnessed in the United States.

The Third Plenary Council of Baltimore

The acceptance of the public school as the foremost "American institution" in the years between the end of the Civil War and 1884 was immense. This acceptance posed problems for the Catholic Church in the United States. As the historian Peter Guilday has observed: "Step by step with that progress went an increasing abandonment of religious teaching and influence. There is no doubt that during these years the problem of Catholic children in these schools was the dominant anxiety of our prelates and clergy."[112]

The Catholic hierarchy, led by Germans and other conservatives, had labored indefatigably for the erection and maintenance of Catholic parish schools. They had successfully enlisted the Vatican on their side by means of the "Instruction" of 1875. The Vatican had heard of vast losses of Catholics to the faith in the United States, at least partly due to the secular public school.

It came as no surprise then that in 1883 three American archbishops were called to Rome where they were presented an agenda that the Propagation of the Faith wanted a new American council to implement.[113] The Americans were able to make some changes in the agenda, since it had been set by the Propagation and not by Pope Leo XIII directly.[114] The Vatican wanted an Italian to preside over the council, and it took a major effort by the Americans to have Archbishop James Gibbons appointed to that position.[115]

The council is best known for its treatment of education. After recalling the Church's ever-present devotion to education, the hierarchy declared that: "In the great coming combat between truth and error, between faith and agnosticism, an important part of the fray must be borne by the laity, and woe to them if they are not prepared."[116]

What the laity needed, the bishops decreed, was a moral and religious education if civilization were to survive, because civilization depends on morality and that, in turn, relies on religion.[117] It was civilization's duty to foster religion. The three agencies of home, Church, and school were intended to contribute to the fostering of religion, but this was impossible in the public schools of the United States that excluded religion by policy.[118] The school, the bishops held, ought to be under the "holy influence of religion," and when it wasn't, a "more false and pernicious notion" could not be imagined.[119] The bishops urged other denominations to look to Europe where the enemies of Christianity were "banishing religion from the schools" as a warning to what could happen here.[120] They recognized that the state was incompetent to teach religion in public schools and all friends of education should "simply follow their consciences and send their children to denominational schools, where religion can have its rightful place and influence."[121]

The bishops ended the education section of their Pastoral letter by setting down two goals for the laity, "to multiply our schools and to perfect them." The schools needed to be multiplied so that "every Catholic child in the land" would have one within their reach: "Pastors and parents should not rest till this defect be remedied." The hierarchy went on to say that "no parish is complete till it has schools adequate to the needs of its children." They concluded their message with the statement that "But then, we must also perfect our schools."[122]

The bishops of Baltimore III went further, not being content with issuing a "Pastoral Letter," and added decrees to implement the Pastoral's teaching. The decrees that bear on education were as follows:

> I. That near every church a parish school, where one does not yet exist, is to be built and maintained in perpetuum within two years of the promulgation of this decree, unless the bishop should decide that because of various difficulties delay may be granted.

> IV. That all Catholic parents are bound to send their children to the parish school, unless it is evident that a sufficient training in religion is given either in their own homes; or in other Catholic schools; or when because of a sufficient reason, approved by the bishop, with all due precautions and safeguards, it is licit to send them to other schools. What constitutes a Catholic school is left to the decision of the bishop.[123]

The centering of decision making on the bishop had several potential consequences for pastors and people. The bishop could transfer a recalcitrant pastor who did not want to build a school; he could impose canonical penalties on parents who did not send their children to the parish school; or he could transfer the pastor and leave the parish priest-less if the parishioners did not support the pastor in his efforts to erect a school.[124]

The bishops had set the "perfecting" of Catholic schools as their second goal. To this end, they charged pastors with the responsibility for supervising the schools. The bishops, however, were careful to remind pastors to observe the agreements that had been made with the orders of vowed religious women (nuns) who were teaching in the parish schools.[125] Finally, the Fathers of the Council granted discretionary powers as to what constituted a Catholic school to the bishop of the diocese (known as the Ordinary), to deal with private Catholic schools that were outside the parish structure.[126]

With the decrees of Baltimore III, the official leaders of the American Church had formally dissented from the public school system in the United States. Aware of the uneasiness that pervaded the atmosphere of the Church's relationship with the United States, and of the suspicion that a Catholic could not be a good American citizen, the bishops stated that "a Catholic finds himself at home in the United States."[127] They asserted that there was nothing in the "free spirit of American institutions incompatible with perfect docility in the Church of Christ," and that: "There is nothing in the character of the most liberty-loving American, which could hinder his reverential submission to the divine Authority of Our Lord, or to the like authority delegated by Him to His apostles and the Church."[128] Finally, in a protestation of loyalty to the Vatican, in which they attempted to allay the growing concern there of a separate American Church, they ended their official utterances at the Council with the statement that there was not in the United States an "American Church . . . but an integral part of the one, holy, Catholic, Apostolic Church of Jesus Christ."[129]

Pope Leo XIII on the Proper Relationship between Church and State

The dissenting nature of parochial schools was closely related to the "Americanization" of Catholics, which was highly suspect in many American circles, not all of them nativist. Could a sincere Catholic be a loyal American? What was the proper relationship between church and state, especially in "mixed matters" such as education? Was the American way of handling the separation of Church and state satisfactory to the Catholic Church? Did the parochial schools teach loyalty to the Pope and Church before that to the United States?

The Catholic position on the subject of the relationship between church and state had been a concern since the teaching of Pope Boniface VIII centuries before, a teaching that had never been retracted, in which the Pontiff had taught that the Catholic Church was necessary for salvation and that:

... there are two swords, the spiritual and the temporal. ... Both of these, ... are under the control of the Church. The first is wielded by the Church; the second is wielded on behalf of the Church. The first is wielded by the hand of the priest, the second by the hand of kings and soldiers but at the wish and by the permission of the priests. Sword must be submitted to sword, and it is only fitting that the temporal authority should be subject to the spiritual.[130]

This teaching had been reemphasized by Pope Pius IX in 1864 with his "Syllabus of Errors."

Pope Leo XIII had issued several encyclicals on "mixed matters" prior to Baltimore III. An encyclical has been defined as "a letter that the pope sends to all the bishops in communion with the Apostolic See in order to make known to the whole Church his mind and will on some point of dogma, morals or Church discipline."[131] Its binding force on Catholics, while not infallible in itself, is at least an exercise of papal jurisdiction and calls for both internal and external assent on the part of Catholics. Leo had published "Inscrutabili" ("On the Evils of Society") on April 21, 1878, in which he spoke of the removal of public institutions from the "salutary direction of the Church" as a source of the evils present in the contemporary world.[132] A consequence of the removal of the Church from her leadership position was the "unbridled freedom" of teaching and publishing all that is evil, but what else could be expected when the Church's "right to instruct and bring up youth is violated and obstructed in every possible manner."[133] As it presently existed, liberty provided only delusive civilization, and he instructed the world's bishops to make all education in accord with the Catholic faith.[134]

Later that same year he issued "Quod Apostolici Muneris" ("The Socialists"), in which he repeated the condemnation of secret societies, such as the Freemasons, and told the nations that they should restore the Catholic Church "to the condition and liberty in which she may exact her healing force for the benefit of all society."[135] On the tenth day of February in 1880 in "Arcanum" ("Christian Marriage"), he told parents that they were "bound to give all care and watchful thought to the education of their offspring and their virtuous bringing up" and complained that civil marriages performed by the state were a usurpation of the prerogatives of the Church.[136]

It was in "Diuturnum" ("On Civil Government"), issued on June 29, 1881, that Leo took up in greater depth the origin of the state and its authority, as well as the proper relationship that should exist between church and state. Judging that it belonged to him, as Vicar of Christ, to "publicly set forth what Catholic truth demands of everyone in this sphere of duty," he went on to say that: "men of more recent times . . . say that all power comes from the people, and that, by this rule, it can be revoked by the will of the very people by whom it was delegated. But from this Catholics dissent, who affirm that the right to rule is from God, as from a natural and necessary principle."[137] After identifying God as the ultimate source of civil authority, the Pontiff proceeded to set the limits of a civil ruler's authority, as defined by the will of God and then promulgated by the Church. In a reference to the past, the Pope recalled that when "the Roman Pontiffs, by the institution of the Holy Roman Empire, consecrated the political power in a wonderful manner," benefit to all had come from the "friendly agreement between these two powers."[138]

Suspicion remained on the part of many Americans as to the Vatican's, and hence American Catholics', position on church-state issues. That suspicion was not alleviated when Leo authored yet another encyclical that dealt with church-state issues, "Immortale Dei" ("The Christian Constitution of States") on November 1, 1885. One of the key points in this document dealt with the state's obligation to worship God and specifically to recognize the one true faith of Christ, which was to be found in the Catholic Church, and to allow the Church full sway in all those affairs which the Church considered to be its field. Humans' primary duty in life was to worship God, i.e., to practice religion. Not just any religion but the one God had enjoined and identified as the "one, true religion"—the Catholic faith. Since the state was composed of humans, the Pontiff asserted that it had the obligation of worshipping God as He wished to be worshipped. Because God had made the Catholic Church externally recognizable by means of identifying marks, "it cannot be too difficult to find out which is the true religion, if only it be sought with an earnest and unbiased mind, for proofs are abundant and striking." The Church, then, instituted by Jesus Christ, occupied a nobler place than did the state, because of its Divine Founder, its supernatural nature, its spiritual means and its eternal end. God had given the Church the "charge of seeing to, and legislating for, all that concerns religion . . . in short, of administering freely and without hindrance, in accordance with her own judgment, all matters that fall within its competence."[139]

The fruitful alliance between Church and state that had existed in Europe prior to the Reformation was beneficial to humans, he declared, because of the influence of religion in such an arrangement. It was the disruption of this union between the "kingdom and the priesthood" that had brought about so much evil in the world.[140] The cause of the discord in society could only be accounted for by the Protestant Reformation that had produced "tenets of unbridled license" and had reduced government to "Nothing more or less than the will of the people."[141] As a consequence, the state was freed from its divinely ordained duties that included the corporate recognition of the state's duty to God, which meant that the state should publicly profess the one religion that God had founded. Instead, he said, by being neutral in religious matters the state not only neglected its duty to God but also placed the Church in a position that was unjust to it, giving it "standing in civil society equal only, or inferior, to societies alien from it."[142]

With unmistakable clarity Leo authoritatively defined the Church's scope in morals: "The Church of Christ is the true and sole teacher of virtue and guardian of morals."[143] It was the task of the state to recognize the Church's unique place in this capacity: "Again, it is not lawful for the State, anymore than for the individual either to disregard all religious duties or to hold in equal favor different kinds of religion."[144] Leo dispelled any possible doubts about the binding force of his teaching or of any past or future occupants of the papacy on opinions concerning Church and state or on any other topic with the following statement:

> As regards opinion, whatever the Roman Pontiffs have hitherto taught, or shall hereafter teach, must be held with a firm grasp of mind, and, so often as occasion requires, must be openly professed . . . especially with reference to the so-called "Liberties" which are so greatly coveted in these days, all must stand by the judgment of the Apostolic See, and have the same mind.[145]

The Pope addressed Catholics on the duties incumbent upon them due to their Baptism. They were bound, he said, "to love the Church as their common mother, to obey her laws, promote her honor, defend her rights, and endeavor to make her loved and respected by those over whom they have authority." They must love her as more than individuals; they were also to "take a prudent part in municipal administration" and to do what they could to effect "public provisions for the instruction of youth in religion and true morality." Catholics were morally bound "to endeavor to bring back all civil society to the pattern and form of Christianity which we have described," that is, the union of Church and state in pre-Reformation days. He urged Catholics to stay united in believing and to reject all such movements as "Naturalism and Nationalism." Catholics, Leo declared, were morally bound to fulfill their duties as Leo had specified them, in both public and private life.[146]

The church-state theme continued to occupy Leo's attention. In 1888 he wrote to the world's bishops again, and through them to the world, this time entitled "Libertas Humana" ("Human Liberty") in which he took up the nature and extent of liberty in civil and ecclesiastical society. He first defined liberty as "the faculty of choosing means fitted for the end proposed."[147] Judgment must precede a choice of free will, which, in turn, necessitates law, the foremost of which was "natural law, which is written and engraved in the mind of every man," and is the same as the eternal law.[148] Human law was a derivation and application of the natural, eternal law, thus perfect liberty was found in obedience to the lawgiver par excellence, God.[149] Some contemporary humans, however, follow Lucifer and obstinately shout "I will not serve." Among these are the liberals in morality and politics, whose ideas would make every human a law unto himself, constituting an independent morality.[150] A consequence of such a theory is that the humanly organized state need not follow the laws of God, a ridiculous proposition, and one that leads to the "fatal theory of the need of separation between Church and State." Leo proclaimed that state authorities are obliged by God to consider the welfare of people's souls as well as their external well-being and convenience in enacting legislation.[151] Civil authority has no moral choice but to acknowledge and reverence God, for both justice and reason forbid that the state be godless.[152] The state must recognize the religion God had created to enable humans to reach the last end for which they were created—eternal salvation, which was the Catholic faith.[153]

The Impact of Leo's Teaching on American Catholic Education

Armed with the decrees of Baltimore III and the authoritative teaching of Pope Leo XIII, official Catholicism in the United States increased its efforts on behalf of Catholic schools, where the entire environment would be religious.[154] As far as some Catholics were concerned, the situation in the United States had deteriorated to a condition that approached Europe with its "God-hating European countries with God-eliminating systems of popular instruction."[155] If the trend persisted the nation would be entitled to the "ignoble distinction of being the newest thing in all history—a nation of Agnostics, Know-Nothings of God."[156] Observing the movement of the public schools from Protestant to secular that had occurred, Catholic author Thomas Jenkins wrote that the outcome would be a nation of agnostics because "creedless, neutral schools breed creedless children," and "indifference to God and virtue is the surest precursor to infidelity in practice."[157] The public system was in such a dilapidated condition that before long the public school buildings, deserted by Catholics and others also disgusted with the unchristian system, would be turned over to the churches for use as denominational schools.[158]

Jenkins' book, *The Judges of Faith: Christian versus Godless Schools*, published in 1886, was another in an assault on the "evil" public school system. It received approbation from the leading American Catholic cleric, Archbishop Gibbons of Baltimore, who wrote Jenkins, congratulating him on the manner in which "you have handled this vital question."[159] Gibbons, who denied that the Catholic clergy were "engaging in a systematic and general attack upon the public school system," was to state that the "second evil that bodes mischief to our country and endangers the stability of our Government arises from our mutilated and vicious system of public school education."[160] A leader in the Catholic dissent from public education, Gibbons explained why the Catholic school was necessary for Catholics: "The religious and secular education of our children cannot be *divorced* from each other without inflicting a fatal wound upon the soul. The usual consequence of such a separation is to paralyze the moral faculties and so foment a spirit of indifference in matters of faith."[161]

Some expression of why Protestants weren't alarmed with the secular drift in public education appeared in the Catholic press, and one writer questioned that if Protestants would acquire the sacrificing spirit of Catholics and if both groups could forget their mutual jealousies they could unite and obtain from the state a tax voucher plan by which a denominational school system could be set up.[162]

Nonetheless, the public schools continued to draw the fire of the Catholic press as the decade of the 1880s came to a close. They were accused of being "heartless," because they relied on a diet of "parched rationalism in science, on which the heavenly dew of religion does not fall"; of being "headless" because they were "heartless" and since they proposed to get along without religion they were also "Godless."[163] Catholics, then, had no alternative but to erect their own schools and assume the burdens connected, in order to "save their children from perversion."[164] The public schools, which have been advanced via the claim that they were the "mainstay of the republic,"[165] were, and must by the "ultimate decision of results, show their inferiority in all that constitutes moral excellence."[166] Catholics, in opposing public schools, found themselves alone in the familiar position of defending civilization against pagan onslaught. According to Baast, writing in *The Catholic World*: "The Catholic Church, which in the centuries of the past preserved society from the efforts of ruthless barbaric invasions, is determined to defend it now from greater and more destructive enemies—from irreligion and pagan infidelity. She will do this now, as in the past, by her schools."[167] Before long, one Catholic writer hoped, Protestants would come to the realization that the schools have failed "when Protestantism itself will be made a scoff in them, and with it all revealed religion," and join with Catholics in the battle on behalf of God and religion.[168]

Though the Catholic hierarchy continued to take the lead in the fight over the school question, in 1889 they were joined by the first Catholic Lay Congress that was held in Baltimore. The delegates recognized that education was "next to religion itself" in "forming the character of the individual, the virtue of the citizen, and promoting the advance of a true civilization." They committed to a "sound popular education," one that "demands not only physical and intellectual, but also the moral and religious training of our youth."[169] The delegates opted to "continue to support our own schools," since there is "no provision for teaching religion" in the state schools, and to do so until the "benefits of a Christian education may be brought within the reach of every Catholic child in these United States."[170]

The Congress' support came about the same time as Archbishop, later Cardinal, Gibbons repeated his theme that education had to include religion in order to deal with the whole person and that education without religion was "defective" and inflicted "a fatal wound upon the soul."[171] As a champion of the dissenting Catholics, Bishop Bernard McQuaid of Rochester made his voice heard on the topic as the year 1889 came to a close. McQuaid denied Catholics were trying to destroy the public school system, and said that such an accusation was simply an attempt to draw attention away from the defects of the system itself. It was a system, McQuaid stated, that was "liable to blunders innumerable, to inefficiency of accomplishments, and to the perpetrating of injustice."[172]

He leveled a new charge at the schools, maintaining that their underlying principle was "unadulterated communism." He accused the public schools of being an agent of "state paternalism," a denier of parental rights, rights that were being incessantly transgressed by the creeping tentacles of state authority.[173]

Catholics, unwilling to admit the "pagan and revolutionary claim that the educator of the people is the state," and believing that state education is "fatal to the personal independence of the citizen, destructive of national energy and character," pressed their request for what they termed "justice," that is, government-supported denominational schools.[174] At this time members of the hierarchy, as well as Catholic journalists, asserted the existence of an important distinction between education and instruction, a distinction that entitled Catholic and other denominational schools to government support.

Education, they said, means to draw out, and must necessarily include religion because it deals with the whole person; instruction, on the other hand, includes the passing on of information and encompasses only the intellectual component of humans. The civil state, by its very nature, is limited to the latter; the Church, by its very nature, includes the former.

Yet even with the tremendous effort put into the Catholic schools by lay and religious, Catholic schools educated only a little over one-half of eligible Catholic children in the late nineteenth century, and the percentage of parishes with schools increased only slightly in the decade following Baltimore III. Some Catholic parents simply resisted the pleas and edicts of their bishops; in other places, parishes were too poor to build and maintain schools, and sometimes when they did, some Catholics were too poor to attend them. Then there were those Catholics who dissented from the Church's educational efforts. One such was Father Edward McGlynn, a suspended New York City priest, who was an advocate of the public schools and urged Catholics to "Cherish your public schools."[175]

Protestant Reaction to the Catholic Position

Protestant reaction to the gradual secularization of the public schools and to the Catholic position varied. Julius Seelye, for instance, regarded religion as the mortar of society. He justified religious instruction in the schools on the grounds that it produced better citizens. In his view, the "greatest mistake any government is likely to commit regarding religious instruction is to have none."[176] A. A. Hodge took a different tack. He believed that it was impossible to separate religious ideas from the great mass of human knowledge. All history was the unfolding of Divine Providence, and a national system of education without religion was unknown. The elimination of theistic and Christian ideas from schools was contrary to the beliefs of the nation's founders, and Christianity was both an original and essential element of the law of the land. His concept of Christianity was that revealed in the Bible, not of any particular religious organization. The Christian character of the state required Christian theism in all value-laden subjects. Those with rival claims would simply have to be subjected to the dominant Christian culture.[177] As for the public schools, a Protestant-Catholic entente was needed for them to cling to their Christian nature, so that they can be kept in their sphere, "true to their claim of Christianity," or they must go "with all other enemies of Christ, to the wall."[178] Catholics generally did not accept Hodge's idea of a Protestant-

Catholic alliance; as one writer put it, what was necessary was for Protestants to "come back to the mother church."[179] Further, Catholics did not accept the role many Protestants accorded the public schools, that is, the "offspring of Christianity."[180]

There was a vast range in Protestant views toward the Catholic school phenomenon. One minister viewed it with alarm: "The determined efforts of Rome to undermine our public school system are already bearing fruit."[181] Another writer, observing the growing Catholic and Lutheran educational networks, wondered if "state supervision should not at once be extended to all schools."[182] Protestants were advised to be cautious, lest they play into the hands of the Catholic ecclesiastics by adopting courses of action that might tend to "solidify the Catholic population."[183] It was recognized that the Catholic Church simply did not have the resources to provide schools for all of their children; besides, some laity, especially the Irish, were not in agreement with the positions of their leaders.

The accusations made by some Catholics that the public schools were "infidel" and "godless" did infuriate some Americans, including Protestants. The *New York Times*, for instance, interpreted these denunciations as the means to get Catholic parents to send their children to Catholic schools because they had failed both in their attempts to get state aid for their schools as well as enlisting the voluntary cooperation of the laity.[184] This idea of a wedge between the Catholic hierarchy and the laity was exploited by some Protestant journals that recognized the laity as loyal, true Americans and not "Papists." According to an article in *The Andover Review*: "There is no authority in the Roman Catholic Church which can keep its members from becoming good citizens under the influence of sound institutions, broad methods of education, and the mutual respect of social classes and of religious denominations."[185] The Evangelical Alliance, an active Protestant organization, stressed this theme that the average lay Catholic who "renounced" the "ecclesiastical encroachments" on his religious freedom by representatives of a "foreign potentate," was a good citizen and supported common schools.[186]

There was some evidence of Protestant support of the Catholic effort. Frank Foxcroft, writing in *The Andover Review*, contended that the "parochial school movement is not without reason." It was the vehicle the Catholic Church has to teach between Sundays the religion it thinks is necessary for children's eternal salvation. He stated:

> Catholics are certainly not alone in feeling that the secular instruction of the public schools, supplemented by an hour a week in the Sunday School constitutes (for the

great multitudes of children who have little or no religious teaching at home) a very inadequate preparation for life, regarded in its highest and most serious relations.[187]

Foxcroft wondered if Protestants united as the Catholics had, "we might yet see a Protestant parochial school movement of large proportions."[188]

The NEA Addresses the Presence of Catholic Schools

The importance that the religious school question had generated in the United States is demonstrated by its inclusion on the agenda of the National Education Association (NEA) in its annual meeting, held in Nashville, Tennessee, in 1889. Four speakers were invited: two from the parochial side and two representing the public schools. James Cardinal Gibbons was the first speaker. He maintained that for education to be complete it had to involve the heart, as well as the head. This meant moral training, which was necessarily based on religion and had to be given consistently, not just once a week. The proper place for this complete education was in denominational schools.[189]

Bishop John J. Keane, a leading liberal Catholic prelate, followed Gibbons. Keane argued that denominational schools were the proper place for Christian training that was more important than the "three Rs," since it had as its object eternity whereas the "three Rs" dealt with worldly success. What makes a Christian school are the "moral atmosphere, the general tone, the surrounding objects, the character of the teacher, the constant endeavor, the loving tact, the gentle skill" by which the "light and spirit of Christianity" are made to "pervade and animate the whole school-life of the child."[190]

Keane agreed with Gibbons that there was no incompatibility between being a good American and a good Catholic. Denominational schools were as American as were the many denominational churches, for the school should not be a homogenizing unit since "we are not aiming at the communism of Sparta."[191] Keane promised more Catholic pressure for governmental aid, "until the good sense and the noble heart of the American people give the victory at last where it is rightly due," and all who believe in Christian education will "vie in guiding all the youth of the land in the gladness of Him who alone is or can be the light of the world."[192]

Edwin H. Mead was the first of the two speakers representing the public school position to address the Conference. He focused on the parental rights issue. After expressing his admiration for the Catholic appreciation of the many sides of humans and education, he faulted the Catholic Church for its policy of coercion of parents, while simultaneously claiming to be the champion of parental rights. In reality, he said the Church practiced the spirit of "compulsion," not of "family choice" and disregarded "liberty of conscience" to the point that family choice of school is "all pure fiction."[193] Mead doubted that there could be any real choice for Catholics who had been taught that "Outside the Church there is no salvation." He claimed that the Catholic Church was denying its members the rights of American citizenship when it coerced them as it did in education. He alleged that a "parochial school can never give anything else than a parochial education, whereas a public school, the conserver of democracy, brings the divergent elements of American society together."[194]

John Jay followed Mead on behalf of the public schools. He assailed the Catholics for their denunciations of the public schools as the hotbeds of immorality, ignorance, pauperism, vice and virtue, as well as being godless and heathenish. Rejecting what he termed the demands of ultramontanes, Jay asserted that the public schools represented two great features of the country: first, that our common law is broadly Christian, and second that as a result the nation affords the "fullest scope for the liberty of conscience and freedom of worship by a complete separation of church and state." The nation's history revealed that these "harmonious principles" have secured "peace, prosperity and strength by a popular government" based on the Bible that "all denominations of Christians prefer to recognize."[195] In his eyes the aims of the public and parochial schools were as antagonistic as "the constitution and the syllabus, as the doctrine of popular sovereignty and the dogma of papal supremacy." The parochial school aims to "form a subject of the pope, and not an independent citizen of the American Republic, and the character of the education is admirably fitted for that purpose."[196] To tax American citizens for schools such as these would be an "act of national suicide." Besides, the appeal for tax money for these schools had been made, not by the laity, American citizens, but by the hierarchy, who were directly subordinate to a foreign power, the Pope, and represented their interests.[197]

Leo Speaks Again:
The Encyclical "Sapientiae Christianae"

Shortly thereafter, Pope Leo XIII spoke out again on a controversial issue. This time, on the tenth day of January in 1890, he issued the encyclical "Sapientiae Christianae" ("On the Chief Duties of Christians as Citizens") for the purpose of teaching "Catholics their duties with all the clearness that we can."[198] That the encyclical would be a dissent, and a very controversial one, is clear from Leo's placing of love and defense of the Church ahead of love of country. This was so, because Catholics owe the Church the "life that will live forever" and "our duties to God have a much greater sanction than those which we owe to our fellow man."[199]

Any conflicts that occur between Church and state are the responsibility of the latter, Leo declared, and Catholics must with St. Peter "obey God rather than men."[200] Nor were Catholics free to decide for themselves if God's law had been broken by the state, for they "receive what they are to believe from the Church" and are to be "perfectly submissive and obedient to the Church and the Roman Pontiff, as to God."[201] This submission extended beyond the infallible teachings of the Pope to "assent to all that the Church teaches." Catholics, Leo said, were in God's plan to be "ruled and guided by the bishops, and particularly by the Apostolic See."[202] Catholics, Leo wrote, whenever the interests of Christianity were in danger in "mixed duties," were to "put aside party strife and undertake the defense of religion in full agreement."[203] Human laws should respect man's moral character, and if they didn't the Church had no choice but to publicly oppose them, especially if they "encroach on the right of the Church by passing due bounds."[204]

Opposing harmful legislation was not the only civic duty for Catholics. They should favor elected officials who were "of known honesty and are likely to deserve well of the Christian name." There was no reason why candidates should "be preferred who are filled with evil intentions against religion."[205] Indeed, Catholics should "accept religiously as their rule of conduct the political wisdom of ecclesiastical authority."[206]

Turning his gaze to education, the Pope reiterated Catholic teaching on the "natural right" of parents to "educate their children to the ends which God has given them." They should "repulse energetically all unjust violence done to them in this matter, so that they may guard their exclusive authority in the education of their children." In carrying out this obligation parents are bound to imbue their children with the "principles of Christian morality, and absolutely oppose their children frequenting schools where they are exposed to the fatal poison of impiety."[207] The Pontiff concluded his controversial encyclical with a plaudit for "Catholics of all nationalities" who "at the expense of much money and more zeal, have erected schools for the education of their children."[208]

The papal letter received considerable attention, including evoking much criticism. Bishop John J. Keane recognized the unfriendly reception it had received in some American circles when he commented that "few utterances of the great Pope have evoked so much hostile criticism from the Church's adversaries."[209] The *Chicago Tribune*, for example, cited it in the context of the ongoing strife between Church and state in Illinois and Wisconsin over educational matters, resenting what it felt was papal interference in American internal affairs, and called for the "defeat of such arrogance and presumption" by an "Italian priest living in Rome that he had the power to nullify" the "right of Americans to make their own laws" in issues between the "supporters and enemies of the American free schools."[210]

In essence the document had asserted the superiority of the Church over the state; had required Catholics to acknowledge such when necessary as defined by the Church; had prescribed acceptance of official Church teaching on anything, including politics, that was connected in any way with religion; had identified the Catholic response to laws that the Church declared to be against her interests; had spoken of the criteria for Catholics to follow in voting; had given the right of education to parents, but as instructed by the Church; had praised Catholic schools and those who built and frequented them; and had reminded Catholics that the common good rests on religion and morality, and that the Church is the guardian and interpreter of same. Considered intrinsically, there was nothing unusual in the pope's admonitions, but, as sources of potential application to particular contexts, they were fraught with tension-producing results. The encyclical was a model of dissent.

John Ireland: Dissent within the Dissenters

In stark contrast to Leo's proclamation, the liberal "Americanizing" Archbishop of St. Paul, John Ireland, was invited to speak at the 1890 meeting of the National Education Association that was held in St. Paul. Ireland worked to establish amicable relationships between the Church and American government at all levels and with all of Catholics' fellow citizens. He rejected assertions that the American government was anti-Catholic, saying that "The government in the United States is not a group of apostate Catholics banded by masonry in hatred of the Church."[211] His remarks would demonstrate that there was division within the ranks of the Catholic dissent; indeed, Ireland qualified as a "dissenter" from the ranks of the "dissent."

Education was one of the areas where Ireland sought compromise with his fellow Americans. In his talk to the NEA, Ireland backed parish schools, and said that he wished that all schools would be supported by the state. While he upheld parents as the primary educators of their children, he believed that the state had the right to intervene whenever parents failed to fulfill their basic responsibility. As he put it, "As things are, tens of thousands of children will not be instructed if parents remain solely in charge of the duty."[212] Then, in a statement that infuriated many of his fellow bishops, he praised the American public schools:

> Free Schools. Blest indeed is the nation whose vales and hillsides they adorn. And blest the generations upon whose souls are poured their treasure. No tax is more legitimate than that which is levied for the dispelling of mental darkness and the building up within a nation's bosom of intelligent manhood and womanhood.[213]

Ireland maintained that the state had to come forward as "an agent of instruction; else ignorance will prevail." Compulsory attendance laws were necessary, if universal instruction were to occur and universal instruction was a necessity for the welfare of the individual and society. The father who "neglects to provide for his child's instruction sins against the child and against society, and it behooves the state to punish him," said Ireland.[214] Ireland went on to praise the secular instruction given in the public schools as "our pride and glory," wished the public schools a long life and called for a curse on those who would destroy them, "The free school of America—withered be the hand raised in sign of its destruction."[215]

Turning to parish schools, Ireland said they were a necessity because state schools without religious instruction were unsatisfactory. Sunday schools were not a satisfactory substitute. Parents were not able to supply their children's need in this field, either because they lacked the time or were incompetent. As a result, "the great mass of children of America are growing up without religion." Ireland did not want the state to teach religion, but for the "sake of its people and for its own sake, it should permit and facilitate the action of the Church. It hinders and prevents this action." Ireland was a traditionalist in the sense that he believed morals could not be taught apart from religion, and that without religion in education the mind of a person could be an instrument for evil, not for good. He thought that religion and irreligion could live peacefully side by side in the schools.[216] Since the state could not teach religion, it should reimburse the denominations, all denominations, for teaching the secular subjects in denominational schools. Reimbursement would depend on the students in those schools passing examinations prepared by state officials.[217] Ireland concluded his compromise speech with a protestation of American Catholics' loyalty to their country, denying that Catholics were opposed to the public schools and with a request for the establishment of the "Christian state school."[218]

Ireland's address received widespread attention in secular and Church circles. For our purposes the emphasis will be on his fellow "dissenters." The *Catholic Citizen* of Milwaukee, in the midst of a recent state Supreme Court decision that had outlawed devotional Bible-reading in Wisconsin's public schools (and simultaneously caught up in a fracas between Catholics and Lutherans on the one hand and the State of Wisconsin on the other over the compulsory attendance Bennett Law), opposed Ireland's plan. It felt that Protestants, with whom Catholics would have to work in Ireland's ideas, were not trustworthy. The *Citizen* recommended no state supervision and no sectarian instruction in state schools. Ireland's speech, it opined, portrayed things as they "*ought to be*," not as they actually "*are*."[219]

The internal conflict among Catholic bishops was heated. Archbishop Corrigan of New York City and Bishop McQuaid of Rochester, among other bishops, complained to the Vatican about Ireland's speech.[220] The reactions were strong enough so that Ireland wrote a letter to Cardinal Gibbons explaining his position. He stated that his purpose had been to state plainly to the country the grounds of Catholic opposition to the state schools as well as to "allay the angry feeling which reigns between non-Catholic Americans and Catholics." In his view, the NEA meeting presented a "grand opportunity" in that "the country was my audience." Further, Ireland wrote that he sought to dispel the prevalent American idea that the Church was opposed to state schools "because she is opposed to the education of the children of the people."[221] He said that Archbishop Katzer of Milwaukee, who was currently embroiled in a conflict with the State of Wisconsin over the controversial Bennett Law, had contributed to the tenseness of the situation in a major way, because Katzer refused to acknowledge the state had the right to enact school laws, thereby allowing parents to raise their children in ignorance if they wished.[222] Ireland said he deplored the extent and frequency of the denunciations of the public schools by Catholic bishops and priests and regretted the spiritual harm that had been done to Catholics by episcopal anathemas for failure to send their children to Catholic schools. After all, he claimed, the mission of the Church was not to be found in "writing and ciphering." He denied the public schools were "*positively bad*," and "*hotbeds of vice*."[223]

Ireland's Catholic critics were numerous and vocal. "Strongly nationalistic German prelates and editors," involved in the Bennett Law controversy in Wisconsin were among them.[224] Ireland himself expressed how strongly the

Germans, Catholic, and Lutheran, felt about their language and how it drove their positions on education in a letter to Cardinal Ledochowski, head of the Congregation of the Propagation in Rome.[225] Bishop McQuaid of Rochester was especially critical of Ireland, believing that he was a leading bishop who was sacrificing the "spiritual interests" of Catholic children.[226] An Ireland ally, Monsignor Denis J. O'Connell, Rector of the American seminary in Rome, wrote Cardinal Gibbons in November of 1890 that the complaints about Ireland's speech were still coming in to the Vatican.[227] Evidently the criticism of Ireland was so strong that Gibbons wrote Pope Leo in December of 1890 defending Ireland, explaining to the Pope that Americans were proud of their public schools and considered an attack on them an assault on the country itself. The American bishops who had harshly criticized these schools had, in Gibbons' view, contributed to the polarized situation. Gibbons requested the Pope not to condemn Ireland for his NEA address because such an action would have a "disastrous effect" on the American Church.[228]

Ireland pressed ahead. In autumn of 1891 he turned the operation of the Catholic schools in Faribault and Stillwater, Minnesota over to the local school board for $1.00, following the precedent of Lowell, Massachusetts and Poughkeepsie, New York, earlier in the century.[229] The Board hired the teachers, including nuns, it judged competent. Only secular subjects were taught during the traditional school day. Ireland retained the right to terminate either agreement at the end of any school year.

The Faribault-Stillwater compromises generated considerable controversy. Conservative Catholics denounced the arrangements as "sell-outs." Archbishop Katzer of Milwaukee called Faribault the "surrender of a Catholic school to state authorities."[230] Some Protestants were equally irate, regarding the plan as a give-away to Catholic authorities. (The Faribault-Stillwater compromises lasted one year; their termination brought about by local non-Catholic opposition.)

In addition to Protestant pique, Ireland's plan accelerated the internal conflict within the Catholic Church over the school question. Spokesmen for the two sides were quickly identified, as a result of their writings on the subject. Dr. Thomas Bouquillon was a faculty member at the Catholic University of America. In December of 1891, he published a pamphlet entitled *Education— To Whom Does It Belong?*. Basically, Bouquillon argued that the civil government, as social authority, had the right and mission to educate, not merely instruct, along with the family and Church. Bouquillon's pamphlet enraged conservative Catholics.[231]

The response to Bouquillon was but a few weeks in coming. Rene I. Holaind, SJ, was the first to challenge Bouquillon. He argued in *The Parent First* that the state, especially the non-Christian state, did not have the authority to educate that Bouquillon gave it. In fact, Bouquillon's thesis weakened the authority of both the family and the Church.[232] Other writers followed. Sebastian Messmer, later to be Archbishop of Milwaukee, held that the state had only a substitutional right in education, to be exercised when Church and family abdicated their fundamental rights.[233]

Bouquillon defended his views in face of the widespread criticism within the Church.[234] Holaind and others, writing in *The American Ecclesiastical Review*, continued their attacks on the orthodoxy of his position.[235] Ireland vigorously defended Bouquillon at the Vatican, suggesting that the harsh denunciations of the public schools by some Catholic leaders might cause the Church to face a "formidable Kulturkampf" in the United States.[236]

Ireland also explained his Faribault-Stillwater plans to Vatican officials. He claimed that over one-half of eligible Catholic children were not in Catholic schools; that Catholics were about twelve percent of the American population; and that he and his programs were misrepresented by the combined attacks of the German and Jesuit presses throughout the world. Emphasis on what many Americans thought constituted "foreignism" could only lead to problems for the Church in the United States, which, he pointed out, was less Catholic than was Germany at the time of the Kulturkampf.[237]

The internal battle among the dissenters raged unabated. The bishops of the Province of New York wrote the Pope, urging him not to permit a decision to be made that would harm parochial schools nor to be threatened by a fear of persecution of Catholics in the United States over the school issue (a reference to Ireland's "Kulturkampf").[238] Leo replied, declaring his support for Catholic schools, "in which children are instructed in religion by persons whom the bishops know to be capable of such teaching." He also directed the bishops to see that nothing offensive to the consciences of Catholic children or opposed to their religion be permitted at schools conducted "at public expense."[239]

The Vatican Enters the Struggle

Cardinal Ledochowski, prefect of the Propagation of the Faith in the Roman Curia, exhorted the American hierarchy on behalf of "peace and Christian union" to replace "promptly the deplorable agitation which saddens us all" to no avail.[240] Archbishop Ireland, fresh from obtaining the Propaganda's permission to continue his Faribault-Stillwater experiment ("tolerari potest"), had returned to St. Paul.[241] The meaning of "tolerari potest" ("can be allowed") was heatedly disputed, ranging from Archbishop Corrigan of New York who said it meant Ireland's plan was condemned,[242] to one author who alleged it had received "official sanction,"[243] to Ireland himself who claimed it meant "fully allowed."[244]

The situation had deteriorated even further. For instance, Bishop McQuaid was quoted in the public press saying it was "time that the impudence of Archbishop Ireland should be checked."[245] Pope Leo then decided to send a personal legate, Archbishop Francis Satolli, to the United States with the intent that he settle the strife within the Catholic hierarchy. Satolli brought with him the express personal authority of the Pope himself:

> We command all whom it concerns to recognize in you, as Apostolic delegate, the supreme power of the delegating Pontiff; we command that they give you aid, concurrence and obedience in all things. . . . Whatever sentence or penalty you shall declare or inflict duly against those who oppose your authority, we will ratify. . . . [246]

The Americans expected a dialogue with the papal delegate.[247] Satolli, however, presented fourteen propositions to the American archbishops in a meeting on November 17, 1892 for that purpose. The propositions called for the American Church to erect Catholic schools and improve those that already existed and exhorted lay Catholics to frequent them. They allowed attendance at public schools if "the danger of perversion" of faith or morals was remote, as assessed by the bishop of the diocese. Proposition V was a bitter pill for the conservatives as it forbade anyone, "bishop or priest," to "exclude from the sacraments, as unworthy" parents who send their children to public schools. "As regards the children themselves, this enactment applies with still greater force." This proposition was the "express prohibition of the Sovereign Pontiff through the Sacred Congregation," and as such carried the weight of the Pope himself.[248] Satolli concluded with the reminder to the clergy that they should not "show less love for the children that attend the public schools than for those that attend the parochial schools."[249] Conservative bishops, who had been ardent backers of parochial schools, felt abandoned. Bishop McQuaid was the most vocal critic of the papal legate and his propositions, even extending his criticism to the Pope himself. "We are all in a nice pickle, thanks to Leo XIII and his delegate," he wrote Corrigan.[250] McQuaid even wrote the Pope, predicting vacant churches in a generation or two if Catholic children were not enrolled in Catholic schools and contending that those schools were the "necessary instrument" if the Gospels were to reach the children.[251] John Lancaster Spalding, the noted educator bishop of Peoria, Illinois, referred to "Faribaultism" after Satolli's presentation and predicted that "without parish schools there is no hope that the Church will be able to maintain itself in America."[252] The bishops of the entire Province of Cincinnati protested the undermining of Catholic schools by Satolli's propositions.[253] Bishop Healy of Portland, Oregon informed Cardinal Gibbons that seventy-five children, out of a school population of 500, had left one parish school in his diocese, confronting the pastor with Proposition V.[254]

As a consequence of this struggle at the leadership level, confusion reigned within the Catholic Church over just what was the Church's position on the school question. On May 31, 1893, responding to a plea from Cardinal Gibbons, Leo XIII wrote a letter to Gibbons that served to officially end the dispute. Leo wrote that the decrees of the Third Plenary Council of Baltimore were to be observed; that Catholic schools were to be "most sedulously promoted"; and that it was up to the "judgment and conscience of the ordinary to decide, according to the circumstances, when it is lawful and when it is unlawful to attend the public schools." He went on to say that the "public schools are not to be entirely condemned" and concluded his letter with an appeal for cooperation and unity among the diverse factions of the controversy. He stated: "Wherefore, we confidently hope that having put away every cause of error and of all anxiety, you will work together, with hearts united in perfect charity, for the wider and wider spread of the kingdom of God in your immense country."[255]

Conclusion

The internecine conflict among the American hierarchy over Catholic schools ceased with the Pope's intervention. Cardinal Gibbons wrote Cardinal Rampolla at the Vatican that he had "most gratefully" received the Pope's letter, which "thanks to Almighty God and the most Holy Father," had ended the school controversy and "brought longed for peace to the American church."[256]

Catholic schools continued to grow, due to the efforts of some American bishops, the dedicated service of nuns, who worked for scant compensation, and the support of Catholic laity. Some ethnic groups, especially the German and Polish, were ardent supporters of Catholic schooling. Catholic school enrollment increased steadily until it reached 1,701,219 in 1920 in 5,852 schools.[257] It survived external challenges due to prejudice and nativism, and some more internal strife due to several factors, a major one being ethnic strife related to movements such as Cahenslyism (named after Peter Cahensly, which alleged that the spiritual welfare of Catholic immigrants was not being adequately cared for and recommended that the Church be organized along ethnic rather than geographical lines).[258]

Despite the heroic efforts of lay, religious, and clerical Catholics, at no time did the percentage of Catholic children in Catholic schools go much beyond fifty percent. The Church simply did not have the resources. Catholic parochial schools of the nineteenth century provided a haven for the children of poor, beleaguered immigrants in this country and qualified indeed as the major dissenter to the dominant educational paradigm of the nineteenth century. Catholic schools, however, were not to have a secure existence in some parts of the United States as the next chapter reveals. Accused by some state government officials as being divisive and unconcerned with "good citizenship," the state attempted to regulate them and perhaps legislate them out of existence.

Notes

1. John Carroll, "Pastoral Letter" (1792), in *Catholic Education in America: A Documentary History*, ed. Neil G. McCluskey, New York: Teachers College Press, 1964, 48.
2. McCluskey, ed., *Catholic Education in America*, 51.
3. "Pastoral Letter," First Provincial Council of Baltimore (1829), in *Catholic Education in America*, ed. McCluskey, 52–53.
4. "Pastoral Letter," Second Provincial Council of Baltimore (1833), in *Catholic Education in America*, ed. McCluskey, 56.
5. "Pastoral Letter," Third Provincial Council of Baltimore (1837), in *Catholic Education in America*, ed. McCluskey, 56.
6. "Pastoral Letter," Fourth Provincial Council of Baltimore (1840), in *Catholic Education in America*, ed. McCluskey, 58.
7. Ibid., 61.
8. Ibid., 60.
9. "Pastoral Letter," Fifth Provincial Council of Baltimore (1843), in *Catholic Education in America*, ed. McCluskey, 63.
10. "Pastoral Letter," First Plenary Council of Baltimore (1852), in *Catholic Education in America*, ed. McCluskey, 79–80.
11. Ibid., 80–81.
12. H. Daniel Rops, *The Church in an Age of Revolution, II*, Garden City, New York: Doubleday and Co., Inc., 1967, 173.
13. *Report on the Population of the United States at the Eleventh Census 1890*, vol. I, part I, Washington, DC: US Government Printing Office, 1895, lxxx.

14. James A. Burns, *Catholic Education: A Study of Conditions*, New York: Longmans, Green and Co., 1917, 15.
15. Anson Phelps Stokes, *Church and State in the United States*, *II*. New York: Harper Brothers, 1950, 394.
16. Warren A. Nord, *Religion & American Education: Rethinking a National Dilemma*, Chapel Hill, NC: University of North Carolina Press, 1995, 73.
17. Ibid.
18. Dorothy Dohen, *Nationalism and American Catholicism*, New York: Sheed and Ward, 1967, 89.
19. "Pastoral Letter," First Provincial Council of Cincinnati (1855), in *A History of Catholic Education in the United States*, by James A. Burns and Bernard J. Kohlbrenner, New York: Benziger Brothers, 1937, 138.
20. Ibid.
21. "Pastoral Letter," Second Provincial Council of Cincinnati (1858), in *The Growth and Development of the Catholic School System in the United States*, by James A. Burns, New York: Benziger Brothers, 1912, 186.
22. "Pastoral Letter," Third Provincial Council of Cincinnati (1861), in *The Judges of Faith: Christian versus Godless Schools*, by Thomas J. Jenkins, Baltimore, MD: John Murphy and Co., 1866, 34.
23. "Pastoral Letter," Second Plenary Council of Baltimore (1866), in *Catholic Education in America*, ed. McCluskey, 82.
24. Ibid., 83.
25. "Pastoral Letter," Second Plenary Council of Baltimore (1866), in *The National Pastorals of the American Hierarchy 1792–1919*, ed. Peter Guilday, Westminster, MD: The Newman Press, 1954, 206.
26. Thomas J. Jenkins, *The Judges of Faith*, 82–83.
27. Ibid., 83.
28. Ibid., 89.
29. Ibid., 86.
30. Ibid., 84–86.
31. Ibid., 84.
32. Ibid.
33. Ibid., 87.
34. Ibid., 91.
35. Ibid., 92.
36. Ibid.
37. Ibid., 104–5.
38. Quoted in Frederick J. Zwierlein, *The Life and Letters of Bishop McQuaid*, *II*, New York: The Art Print Shop, 1926, 146.
39. Ibid., 120–22.
40. Ibid., 129.
41. Ibid.
42. Ibid., 145.
43. McCluskey, ed., *Catholic Education in America*, 86.
44. Jenkins, *The Judges of Faith*, 119–20.

45. Ibid., 121–22.
46. Ibid., 122.
47. James Gibbons, "The Necessity of Religion for Society," *The American Catholic Quarterly Review* 9 (October 1884): 681, 674.
48. James Conway, "The Rights and Duties of the Church in Regard to Education," *The American Catholic Quarterly Review* 9 (October 1884): 669.
49. McCluskey, ed., *Catholic Education in America*, 121.
50. "Instruction of the Congregation of Propaganda de Fide" (1875), in *Catholic Education in America*, ed. McCluskey, 122–26.
51. Conway, "The Rights and Duties of the Church in Regard to Education," 667.
52. "The School Question," *Catholic World* 11 (April 1870): 98–100.
53. Ibid., 106.
54. "The Catholics of the Nineteenth Century," *Catholic World* 11 (July 1870): 439.
55. Ibid., 437.
56. "The School Question," *Catholic World* 11, 104.
57. "The Catholics of the Nineteenth Century," *Catholic World* 11, 436.
58. John Ireland, "Letter to Michael J. Muller," in *Public School Education*, New York: D. J. Sadlier and Co., 1872, Appendix, 2.
59. Michael J. Muller, *Public School Education*, New York: D. J. Sadlier and Co., 1872, 15, 31, 41.
60. Ibid., 72–73.
61. Ibid., 74.
62. Ibid., 78–79.
63. Ibid., 85–86.
64. Ibid., 89–93.
65. Ibid., 106–8.
66. Ibid., 118–20.
67. Ibid., 129–32.
68. Ibid., 133.
69. Ibid., 140.
70. Ibid., 163.
71. Ibid., 164–68.
72. Ibid., 199.
73. Ibid., 200.
74. Ibid., 214, 237.
75. Ibid., 262–63.
76. Ibid., 349, 355.
77. Ibid., 369.
78. Ibid., 407–9.
79. "The President's Speech at Des Moines," *Catholic World* 22 (January 1876): 17.
80. James O'Connor, "Anti-Catholic Prejudice," *The American Catholic Quarterly Review* 1 (January 1876): 17.
81. Allen Sinclair Will, *The Life of Cardinal Gibbons, I*, New York: E. P. Dutton and Company, 1922, 161.
82. "The President's Speech at Des Moines," *Catholic World* 22, 442–43.

83. Ibid., 442.
84. Alvin W. Johnson, *The Legal Status of Church-State Relationships in the United States*, Minneapolis, MN: The University of Minnesota Press, 1934, 21.
85. Ibid.
86. R. Freeman Butts, *The American Tradition in Religion and Education*, Boston: Beacon Press, 1950, 144.
87. W. T. N. Marshall, "Secular Education in England and the United States," *The American Catholic Quarterly Review* 1 (April 1876): 279.
88. P. Bayma, "The Liberalistic View of the Public School Question," Part II, *The American Catholic Quarterly Review* 2 (April 1877): 242.
89. P. Bayma, "The Liberalistic View of the Public School Question," Part I, *The American Catholic Quarterly Review* 2 (January 1877): 12, 24–29.
90. Ibid., 1.
91. Pier Spaunhorst, 1877, in *The Social Thought of the German Roman Catholic Verein*, by Sister Mary Liguori Brophy, Washington, DC: The Catholic University of America Press, 1941, 53.
92. *Catholic Citizen*, August 30, 1884, 1.
93. Ibid., November 15, 1884, 4.
94. Ibid., October 7, 1882, 4.
95. Isaac T. Hecker, "Catholics and Protestants Agreeing on the School Question," *Catholic World* 32 (February 1881): 711.
96. H. O. Brann, "The Improvement of Parochial Schools," *The American Catholic Quarterly Review* 9 (April 1884): 239.
97. *Catholic Citizen*, May 17, 1884, 3.
98. William J. Onahan, "The Catholic Church and Popular Education," *The American Catholic Quarterly Review* 8 (January 1883): 264.
99. H. O. Brann, "The Improvement of Parochial Schools," *The American Catholic Quarterly Review* 9, 244.
100. Ibid.
101. *Catholic Citizen*, January 3, 1882, 2.
102. James Conway, "The Rights and Duties of Family and State in Regard to Education," *The American Catholic Quarterly Review* 9 (January 1884): 126.
103. Ibid., 125.
104. Ibid., 114.
105. Ibid., 105.
106. *Catholic Citizen*, July 21, 1883, 2.
107. James Conway, "The Rights and Duties of Family and State in Regard to Education," *The American Catholic Quarterly Review* 9 (January 1884): 117.
108. Ibid., 110.
109. James Conway, "The Rights and Duties of the Church in Regard to Education," *The American Catholic Quarterly Review* 9 (October 1884): 650.
110. Ibid., 657–59.
111. William J. Onahan, "The Catholic Church and Popular Education," *The American Catholic Quarterly Review* 8 (January 1883): 281.

112. Peter Guilday, *A History of the Councils of Baltimore (1791–1884)*, New York: The Macmillan Company, 1932, 237.

113. Thomas T. McAvoy, *The Great Crises in American Church History, 1895–1900*, Chicago: Henry Regnery Company, 1957, 28.

114. Thomas T. McAvoy, "Leo XIII and America," in *Leo XIII and the Modern World*, ed. Edward T. Gargan, New York: Sheed and Ward, 1961, 165.

115. McAvoy, *The Great Crises in American Church History*, 29.

116. "The Pastoral Letter of the Third Plenary Council of Baltimore," in *The National Pastorals of the American Hierarchy, 1792–1919*, ed. Peter Guilday, Westminster, MD: The Newman Press, 1954, 244.

117. Ibid.

118. Ibid., 245.

119. Ibid.

120. Ibid., 246.

121. Ibid.

122. Ibid., 246–47.

123. "Decrees of the Third Plenary Council of Baltimore," in *Catholic Education in America*, ed. McCluskey, 93–94.

124. Francis P. Cassidy, "Catholic Education in the Third Plenary Council of Baltimore," *The Catholic Historical Review* Part 1, 34 (October 1948): 305.

125. Francis P. Cassidy, "Catholic Education in the Third Plenary Council of Baltimore," *The Catholic Historical Review* Part 2, 34 (January 1949): 430.

126. Cassidy, "Catholic Education in the Third Plenary Council of Baltimore," *The Catholic Historical Review* Part 1, 303.

127. "Pastoral Letter of the Third Plenary Council of Baltimore," in *The National Pastorals of the American Hierarchy, 1792–1919*, ed. Guilday, 234.

128. Ibid., 235.

129. Ibid., 236.

130. Clarkson et al., eds., *The Church Teaches*, 73–74.

131. Pietro Parente, Antonio Piolanti, and Savatore Garofolo, *Dictionary of Dogmatic Theology*, trans. Emmanuel Doronzo, Milwaukee, WI: The Bruce Publishing Co., 1951, 86.

132. Leo XIII, "Inscrutabili," in *Social Wellsprings, I*, ed. Joseph Husslein, Milwaukee, WI: The Bruce Publishing Co., 1940, 3.

133. Ibid.

134. Ibid., 4–5, 9.

135. Leo XIII, "Quod Apostolici Muneris," in *Social Wellsprings, I*, ed. Husslein, 22.

136. Leo XIII, "Arcanum," in *Social Wellsprings, I*, ed. Husslein, 30, 33.

137. Leo XIII, "Diuturnum" in *Papal Thought on the State*, ed. Gerald F. Yates, New York: Appleton-Century-Crofts, Inc., 1958, 2–3.

138. Ibid., 8.

139. Leo XIII, "Immortale Dei," in *The State and the Church*, ed. John F. Ryan, New York: The Macmillan Company, 1922, 4–7.

140. Ibid., 11–12.

141. Ibid., 13.

142. Ibid., 13–15.

143. Ibid., 16

144. Ibid., 18.

145. Ibid., 21.

146. Ibid., 22–24.

147. Leo XIII, "Libertas Humana," in *Social Wellsprings, I*, ed. Husslein, 117.

148. Ibid., 118–19.

149. Ibid., 120–21.

150. Ibid., 123.

151. Ibid., 126–27.

152. Ibid., 127.

153. Ibid., 128–29.

154. James Conway, "The Rights and Duties of the Church in Regard to Education," *The American Catholic Quarterly Review* 9 (October 1884): 661.

155. Thomas J. Jenkins, *The Judges of Faith: Christian versus Godless Schools*, Baltimore, MD: John Murphy and Co., 1886, 6.

156. Ibid., 7.

157. Ibid., 8.

158. Ibid., 9.

159. Ibid., iv.

160. *Catholic Citizen*, October 22, 1887, 3, 1.

161. Ibid., 1.

162. George D. Wolff, "The Public School System and Protestantism," *The American Catholic Quarterly Review* 11 (October 1886): 733–34.

163. Patrick F. McSweeney, "Heartless, Headless and Godless," *Catholic World* 46 (January 1888): 435–37.

164. John Gilmary Shea, "Wanted—A New Text Book," *The American Catholic Quarterly Review* 13 (October 1888): 691.

165. Thomas Dwight, "The Attack on Freedom of Education in Massachusetts," *The American Catholic Quarterly Review* 13 (July 1888): 546.

166. Shea, "Wanted—A New Text Book," *The American Catholic Quarterly Review* 13 (October 1888): 696.

167. P. Baast, "Our Catholic Schools," *Catholic World*, 46 (February 1888): 609.

168. Shea, "Wanted—A New Text Book," *The American Catholic Quarterly Review* 13 (October 1888): 691.

169. Baltimore Catholic Congress, "For Social Reform and Americanization," in *American Catholic Thought on Social Questions*, ed. Aaron R. Abell, Indianapolis, IN: The Bobbs-Merrill Co., Inc., 1966, 185.

170. Ibid.

171. James Cardinal Gibbons, "Is Religious Instruction in the Public Schools Expedient? If So, What Should Be Its Character and Foundations?" *Public Opinion* 7 (July 13, 1889): 297.

172. Bernard J. McQuaid, "Religious Teaching in the Schools," *Forum* 8 (December 1889): 379.

173. Ibid.

174. Morgan M. Sheehy, "The School Question: A Plea for Justice," *Catholic World* 49 (August 1889): 651–52.

175. Edward McGlynn, February 24, 1889, in *Church and State in the United States, II*, ed. Anson Phelps Stokes, New York: Harper Brothers, 1950, 653–54.

176. Julius H. Seelye, "Should the State Teach Religion?" *Forum* 1 (July 1886): 430–32.

177. A. A. Hodge, "Religion in the Public Schools," *The New Princeton Review* 3 (January 1887): 30–36.

178. Ibid., 46–47.

179. Patrick F. McSweeney, "Christian Public Schools," *Catholic World* 44, 264 (March 1887): 788–89.

180. J. C. Greenough, "Morality and Religion in the Public School," *The Andover Review* 7 (June 1887): 645.

181. Isaac J. Lansing, *Romanism and the Republic*, Boston: Arnold Publishing Association, 1896, 29.

182. George Shipman Payson, "Laws Concerning Religious Instruction in Schools," *Our Day* 2 (November 1888): 185.

183. "The Public Schools and Roman Catholics," *The Andover Review* 7 (December 1888): 620.

184. "Parochial School Question," *The New York Times*, July 28, 1889, 4.

185. "The Public School and Roman Catholics," *The Andover Review* 7 (December 1888): 620.

186. Quoted in Stokes, *Church and State in the United States, II*, 686.

187. Frank Foxcroft, "Week-Day Religious Instruction of Children—An Experiment," *The Andover Review* 11 (April 1889): 368–69.

188. Ibid., 370.

189. James Cardinal Gibbons, "Should Americans Educate Their Children in Denominational Schools?" *National Education Association: Journal of Proceedings and Addresses* (Session of the Year 1889, held at Nashville, Tennessee), Topeka, KS: Kansas Publishing House, Clifford C. Baker, 1889, 111–13.

190. John J. Keane, "Should Americans Educate Their Children in Denominational Schools?" *National Education Association*, 117.

191. Ibid., 121.

192. Ibid.

193. Edwin H. Mead, "Has the Parochial School Proper Place in America?" *National Education Association*, 126–27.

194. Ibid., 143–45.

195. John Jay, "Public and Parochial Schools," *National Education Association*, 161.

196. Ibid., 165–66.

197. Ibid., 167–69.

198. Leo XIII, "Sapientiae Christianae" in *Social Wellsprings, I*, ed. Joseph Husslein, Milwaukee, WI: The Bruce Publishing Co., 1940, 144.

199. Ibid., 145.

200. Ibid., 146.

201. Ibid., 150–51.

202. Ibid., 153.

203. Ibid., 155.

204. Ibid., 156.

205. Ibid., 158.

206. Ibid., 159.

207. Ibid., 162.

208. Ibid.,

209. Bishop John J. Keane, "The Church and State," *The Bennett Law. Newspaper Clippings.* A Scrapbook in the Library of the State Historical Society of Wisconsin, Madison.

210. Quoted in Husslein, ed., *Social Wellsprings*, I, 140.

211. James H. Moynihan, *The Life of Archbishop John Ireland*, New York: Harper and Brothers, 1953, 92.

212. John Ireland, "State Schools and Parish Schools—Is Union Between Them Impossible?" *National Education Association: Journal of Proceedings and Addresses* (Session of the Year 1890, held at St. Paul, Minnesota), Topeka, KS: Kansas Publishing House, Clifford C. Baker, 1890, 179.

213. Ibid., 179–80.

214. Ibid., 180.

215. Ibid.

216. Ibid., 182–83.

217. Ibid., 184.

218. Ibid., 185.

219. *Catholic Citizen*, July 19, 1890, 4.

220. Neil G. McCluskey, in *Catholic Education in America*, ed., McCluskey, 141.

221. John Ireland, "Clarification to Archbishop Gibbons" (1890), in *Catholic Education in America*, ed., McCluskey, 142–43.

222. Ibid., 144.

223. Ibid., 146–48.

224. Sister M. Paschala O'Connor, *Five Decades: History of the Congregation of the Most Holy Rosary, Sinsinawa, Wisconsin.1849–1899*, Sinsinawa, WI: The Sinsinawa Press, 1954, 154.

225. Colman J. Barry, *The Catholic Church and German Americans*, Milwaukee, WI: The Bruce Publishing Co., 1953, 185.

226. McQuaid, quoted in *The Catholic Church and German Americans*, 489.

227. Denis J. O'Connell, "Letter to Cardinal Gibbons on November 24, 1890" in *The School Controversy, 1891–1893*, by Daniel Reilly, New York: Arno Press and the New York Times, 1969, 233.

228. "Cardinal Gibbons' Report to Pope Leo XIII, December 30, 1890," translated from the French by the Reverend P. H. Conway, OP, in *The School Controversy, 1891–1893*, by Reilly, 242–46.

229. Reilly, *The School Controversy*, 74–75.

230. Ibid., 138.

231. Thomas Bouquillon, *Education—To Whom Does It Belong?* Baltimore, MD: John Murphy, 1891.

232. Rene I. Holaind, S. J., *The Parent First: An Answer to Dr. Bouquillon's Query: "Education—To Whom Does It Belong?"* New York: Benziger, 1891.

233. Sebastian G. Messmer, "The Right of Instruction," *The American Ecclesiastical Review* 7 (February 1892): 104–18.

234. Thomas Bouquillon, *A Rejoinder to Critics*. Baltimore, MD: John Murphy, 1892.

235. Rene I. Holaind, S. J., "A Last Word," *The American Ecclesiastical Review* 7 (June 1892): 455–64; S. M. Brand, S. J., "The Touchstone of Catholicity," *The American Ecclesiastical*

Review 7 (February 1892): 89–97; and Bishop Francis S. Chatard, "Dr. Bouquillon on the School Question," *The American Ecclesiastical Review* 7 (February 1892): 98–103.

236. "Archbishop John Ireland's Address to the Cardinals of the Sacred Congregation for the Propagation of the Faith in Defense of Dr. Thomas Bouquillon," March 28, 1892, in *The School Controversy*, by Reilly, Appendix F, 267–70.

237. "Archbishop Ireland's Memorial," addressed to Cardinal Ledochowski, Prefect of the Congregation for the Propagation of the Faith, undated, presumably in the spring of 1892, in *The School Controversy*, by Reilly, Appendix E, 250–66.

238. Frederick J. Zwierlein, *The Life and Letters of Bishop McQuaid, III*, Rochester, NY: The Art Print Shop, 1927, 171.

239. *Catholic Citizen*, July 2, 1892, 1.

240. Reilly, *The School Controversy*, 134.

241. McCluskey, ed., *Catholic Education in America*, 151.

242. Ibid.

243. John Conway, "The Catholics and the Public Schools: The Significance of Tolerari Potest," *Educational Review* 4 (October 1892): 236–40.

244. Reilly, *The School Controversy*, 160.

245. *Catholic Citizen*, July 30, 1892, 4.

246. Ibid., March 11, 1893, 1.

247. Timothy Walch, *Parish School: American Catholic Parochial Education from Colonial Times to the Present*, New York: Crossroad Herder, 1996, 97.

248. McCluskey, ed., *Catholic Education in America*, 152–60.

249. Ibid., 158.

250. Ibid., 161.

251. "Bishop McQuaid's Letter to Pope Leo XIII on the School Question" (December 13, 1892), in *Catholic Education in America*, ed. McCluskey, 164.

252. David Francis Sweeney, *The Life of John Lancaster Spalding*, New York: Herder and Herder, 1965, 213, 216.

253. Reilly, *The School Controversy*, 211–12

254. Ibid., 218.

255. Ibid., 228–29.

256. Ibid., 230.

257. Harold A. Buetow, *Of Singular Benefit: The Story of U.S. Catholic Education*, New York: Macmillan, 1970, 179.

258. See Gerald Shaughnessy, *Has the Immigrant Kept the Faith?* New York: Macmillan, 1925, for a discussion of this issue.

· 4 ·

THE BENNETT LAW

A Source of Dissent

In the wake of the Civil War the federal government's role in national affairs greatly expanded. The war contributed to a nationalizing trend that affected the public schools, which came to be looked upon by many as the leading means whereby national unity could be achieved and maintained. States enacted a number of measures, including compulsory attendance laws, which were aimed at assisting the increasingly secular school to reach this patriotic goal. Concomitantly, parochial schools, mainly Catholic, were looked upon with growing suspicion as being divisive, fostering foreign loyalties, and thus causing dissent in the state. As Warren Nord has observed, "Public schools became the cultural factories of Americanization, transforming the raw material of foreign culture into good American citizens."[1] Wisconsin, with a large percentage of German immigrants, both Catholic and Lutheran, each with a major commitment to denominational schools, was a natural place for conflict between these religious/ethnic groups and efforts at using education to inculcate "good citizenship" by the civil state. The Bennett Law was such an attempt.

National Patriotic Sentiment and the Schools

Waves of nationalism were sweeping Europe in the 1870s, in Germany, France, Italy, and Great Britain. This nationalistic sentiment found considerable support in the United States. President Ulysses S. Grant, addressing the Army of the Tennessee in Des Moines, Iowa, in 1875, called on his hearers to: "Encourage free schools" and prohibit any financial support be given to "sectarian schools." Religion should be left to the "family altar"; Church and state should be kept "forever separate."[2] Archbishop Gibbons of Baltimore greeted Grant's remarks with the label of "Bismarckian."[3]

A short time later, Congressman James G. Blaine presented an amendment to the federal constitution to the United States Congress which supported Grant's remarks. Blaine advocated that no state should make "any law respecting an establishment of religion, or prohibiting the free exercise thereof." Nor could any money raised by school taxation for the "support of public schools" go to sectarian schools, or come under the "control of any religious sect."[4] Blaine's proposed amendment passed the House by a vote of 180 to seven, but failed to obtain the necessary two-thirds margin in the Senate where the vote was twenty-eight to sixteen.[5] The support for the amendment reflected the sentiment against parochial schools (the vast majority of them conducted under Catholic auspices) and for public schools. Congress did require any state admitted to the Union henceforth to have a "system of public schools which shall be open to all the children of said State and free from sectarian control."[6]

As immigration continued, and as the Catholic population in the United States grew, Catholic fears increased that the public schools would be instruments of the secular state that threatened the Church with loss of members and the members themselves with eternal perdition. Catholic opposition to these schools grew. The hierarchy, as one would expect with a hierarchy-dominated Church, led the way.

Wisconsin entered the union in 1848. Fifty-one of the sixty-nine framers of the Wisconsin constitution that year hailed from the Eastern United States, twenty-six from New England and twenty-five from New York, there were four Irishmen and one German.[7] As the nineteenth century progressed, the foreign-born population of the state grew rapidly, with much of that gain coming from Germany.

Likewise, state government activity in education increased in Wisconsin as the nineteenth century progressed. Fundamental questions arose concerning the relationship of the state to schools, especially those of the private nature. Some questioned their very right to exist; others raised questions as to the language of instruction used in the schools, and how they "fit" under compulsory attendance requirements.

In 1862, the State Superintendent of Instruction, Josiah L. Pickard, viewed the large number of private schools in the state as "serving a noble purpose," but felt that their existence would cease "when the people fully appreciated the capabilities of the Public school system." Denominational schools would be allowed to continue, but would need to "be made subservient to the general good." He advised that "it is better to bid them God speed, than to waste time in fighting them."[8]

Superintendent John McMynn was the first in his position to complain of the failure of private schools to report their attendance to his office. In 1865 he deplored their lack of cooperation. He wrote: "Indeed, there is little reliance to be placed upon the reports in regard to this class of schools. They, as a general thing, make no reports, and not being under the supervision of any school officer, it is difficult to obtain any information concerning them."[9] A. J. Craig, McMynn's successor, advocated school compulsory attendance laws on the grounds that the very preservation of the country's government and institutions could not be secured with a large percentage of its youth growing up in ignorance, which would occur without compulsory legislation.[10]

Samuel Fallows, the Methodist minister who succeeded Craig, contended that the state had the right to enact compulsory attendance laws because of the taxpayers, who had the right to insist that every child receive not only an education, but a good English education. This kind of education would fit every child for the duties of citizenship.[11]

Concern about the need for compulsory attendance was nationwide. The United States Bureau of Education had conducted a survey, which was included in Fallows' 1872 *Report*, which looked to Prussia as the model situation where "compulsory education has been most efficiently enforced, and its practical results can be easily computed."[12] Fallows, motivated by the statistics of the 1870 federal *Census*, wrote that the only solution was a "law requiring all children in the state to be instructed in the rudiments of the common English branches."[13] The legislature responded, directing Fallows to investigate the question of compulsory attendance and report back. Fallows did. He noted that "compulsory education" laws work, that they are legal and necessary.[14] The legislature then passed Chapter 276 that empowered cities to establish truant schools for children between the ages of seven and sixteen who have "no lawful occupation or business and are not attending any school."[15]

Several years later the Wisconsin legislature again addressed school attendance when it passed Chapter 121: "An Act to secure to children the benefits of an elementary education" in 1879:

Section 1. Every parent, guardian or other person in the state of Wisconsin, having charge or control of any child or children between the ages of 7 and 15 years, shall be required to send such children to a public or private school, for at least 12 weeks in each school year. . . . [16]

The public-private school question was not out of the public eye for very long. In his 1881 *Message* to the state legislature Governor William E. Smith spoke of the "healthy rivalry between public and private schools" and avowed that the educational field was "broad enough for all."[17] State Superintendent Robert Graham apparently did not share the Governor's feelings. In his 1882 *Report* he complained of the failure of denominational schools, especially "in the largest cities in the state, where it is well known there are large numbers of private schools," to report their attendance figures to his office (there were no reports filed from either Milwaukee or LaCrosse that year).[18]

Dissatisfaction with the law of 1879 resulted in the legislature's amending it and passing Chapter 298 of the Laws of 1882 in its stead. This new law empowered the district board to meet "for the purpose of hearing causes for the non-attendance upon the public school of all children in such districts between the ages of 7 and 15 years. And all parents, guardians or other persons having charge of such children, shall appear and show cause for such non-attendance."[19] Parents, or others in charge of the school-age children who did not attend public schools, were required to give the district clerk a written statement stating what school the child attended and the days of attendance. The power to determine if the child's non-attendance at public school was legitimate was placed in the hands of public school authorities.[20] Private school backers were opposed to this condition, considering it to be an infringement of parents' rights.

There were, in Wisconsin at this time, an increasing number of those parents. The Wisconsin Synod Lutherans reported 101 parochial schools in 1880[21]; Roman Catholics reported 200 schools with 21,727 students in 1882,[22] and those numbers increased to 251 schools attended by 24,495 pupils in 1884.[23]

The German "Problem"

Concerns related to private schools and lack of attendance at public schools and the failure to report private school attendance figures were not the only challenges facing public education in its first half century in Wisconsin. A large percentage of the immigrants to the state during this period were German, imbued with a love of their mother country, its customs and language. The language question arose as early as 1854. Responding to an appeal from a Milwaukee resident, Superintendent H. A. Wright replied that a school taught in the German language was not entitled to "any portion of the public fund, and is not a district school within the meaning of the law."[24] Wright went on to comment that English was "the language of our country; and I sincerely hope our German fellow citizens will feel the necessity and the importance of having their children well and thoroughly instructed in the English language."[25]

The issue endured, as the reply of Assistant Superintendent Stephen H. Carpenter to an appellant in 1859 shows. Carpenter averred that the required branches of instruction be taught in English, but perhaps a loose construction of the law was a more prudent course to follow, which would enable the courses to be taught in German as well.[26]

The Wisconsin legislature took note of the language question in schools and passed a law that gave district boards the power to permit instruction "in any of the foreign languages, not to exceed one hour each day."[27] Superintendent Craig remarked on the law's passing that its intention was "not to encourage but rather to limit the introduction of other languages than the English language into the common schools," thus making it state policy to have all state residents learn their country's common language.[28]

Wisconsin was not on its way to becoming a German state, but it did have a high percentage of German immigrants among its population. In 1880, native-born Germans and persons with both parents born in Germany totaled 410,653 or 31.2 percent of Wisconsin's 1,315,497 inhabitants.[29]

The Catholic bishops of the state, all German-Americans, were not reluctant to speak out on the school question. In 1872 John Martin Henni, the first Archbishop of Milwaukee, reminded the faithful in his Lenten Pastoral of 1872 of their religious duty on the school question. He asserted: "Every congregation, therefore, *is in duty bound—a duty its members owe both to God and to society*—to have its own *parish school* established; because the attendance at Public Schools *generally* results in the ruin of the tender soul."[30] Bishop Michael Heiss, destined to become Henni's successor in Milwaukee, while Bishop of LaCrosse publicly worried over the fate of Catholic youngsters in public schools: "We grieve in our inmost heart when we look on the children growing up in our diocese!—for, far the greater number of them are either without any school, or go to the Public schools, where so many of them imbibe in their tender souls the poisonous germs of infidelity and immorality."[31] After he was installed as Archbishop of Milwaukee, Heiss wrote that Catholic schools were a necessity for keeping the young in the Church, and equated calling this into question with "sinful opposition against the legitimate, divinely constituted authority of the Church."[32]

Heiss' successor in LaCrosse was Kilian C. Flasch, who like Henni and Heiss, had been born in Bavaria.[33] Flasch also believed in the necessity of Catholic schools. In his "Lenten Pastoral" of 1882 he wrote:

> The place where this divine right is secure to the children is the Christian school. There is no other chance for a sufficient Christian training and education of our youth. It is a mockery to say that the parents should instruct their children in catechism at home and prepare them for the holy sacraments. They have neither the time, nor the patience, and frequently not the ability, for such a task.[34]

The combined efforts of the bishops, the teaching orders of religious women, and lay Catholics resulted in the foundation and maintenance of many Catholic schools in the state. Undoubtedly, the German commitment to Catholic schools played a major part in this activity. As a result, by 1880 the Diocese of Green Bay had thirty-two schools with 3,371 students; LaCrosse had twenty-two schools with 2,500 enrolled; and Milwaukee reported 113 schools with 13,677 pupils.[35]

The Impact of the Third Plenary Council on National Educational Policy

In the wake of the Civil War, the American public school had made great strides in terms of growth and public acceptance. This progress caused problems for the Catholic Church not only in the United States including Wisconsin. As the Catholic historian Peter Guilday observed: "step by step with that progress went an increasing abandonment of religious teaching and influence. There is no doubt that during these years the problem of Catholic children in these schools was the dominant anxiety of our prelates and clergy."[36]

The conservative wing of the hierarchy had enlisted the aid of the Vatican Congregation, Propagation of the Faith, in the school question with its "Instruction" of 1875. The Vatican had heard of vast losses of faith by Catholic immigrants to the United States, occasioned at least in part by attendance at public schools.

It came as no surprise then when the Third Plenary Council of Baltimore was convened in 1884 that it became the scene of lively debate on a number of matters, educational affairs being the best known. After recalling the Church's long-standing commitment to education, the hierarchy declared: "In the great coming combat between truth and error, between Faith and agnosticism, an important part of the fray must be borne by the laity, and woe to them if they are not prepared."[37] What the laity needed, the bishops decreed, was a moral and religious education if a healthy civilization were to survive because civilization depends on morality, and that, in turn, relies on religion. The three educational agencies of home, Church and school must all take part in this task, but this was impossible in schools that excluded religion by policy. In the view of the bishops:

> To shut religion out of the school, and keep it for home and the Church, is, logically, to train up a generation that will consider religion good for home and the Church, but not for the practical business of real life. But a more false and pernicious notion could not be imagined. . . . Therefore the school, which principally gives the knowledge fitting for practical life, ought to be preeminently under the holy influence of religion.[38]

The bishops concluded the education section of their "Pastoral" by setting down two goals for the laity, to "multiply" Catholic schools, and "perfect" them. Recognizing that there were "thousands of Catholic children" in this country still "deprived of the benefit of a Catholic school," the hierarchy called on "pastors and parents" not to rest until this "defect be remedied." "No parish," the bishops maintained, was complete until it has schools "adequate for its children."[39]

The bishops followed up the "Pastoral" with decrees. Those that dealt with education were:

> I. That near every church, a parish school, where one does not yet exist, is to be built and maintained in perpetuum within two years of the promulgation of this council, unless the bishop should decide that because of serious difficulties a delay may be granted.

> IV. That all Catholic parents are bound to send their children to the parish school, unless it is evident that a sufficient training in religion is given either in their own homes, or in other Catholic schools; or when because of a sufficient reason, approved by the bishop, with all the precautions and safeguards, it is licit to send them to other schools. What constitutes a Catholic school is left to the decision of the bishop.[40]

Post-Baltimore III in Wisconsin

The Wisconsin hierarchy, thoroughly German and conservative, took the decrees of Baltimore III seriously.[41] They were unwilling to accept the educational ascendancy of the secular state. Kilian C. Flasch, Bishop of LaCrosse, had insisted on the absolute necessity of parochial schools at Baltimore III, spoke forcefully and often on the issue of Catholic school attendance in his diocese.[42] In his Lenten Pastoral of 1885, he advised pastors and parents that they should not rest until a religious education was within reach of every child, and that no parish could be considered complete until it had a school adequate for its children.[43] Three years later he wrote in another Lenten Pastoral "Let pagans send their children to pagan schools; infidels to infidel schools, but Catholic parents are bound in conscience to send their children to Catholic schools. . . ." Parents who don't do this, he charged, "are almost in every case, as experience proves, such parents as, either through ignorance or indifference, neglect their Christian duties toward their children at home."[44]

The scene was similar in Milwaukee. Archbishop Michael Heiss had lent his voice in support of Catholic schools in his messages to the people of the archdiocese. In his Lenten Pastoral of 1887, about one-third of which was devoted to educational matters, Heiss referred to the "hundreds of children not in Catholic schools" and said that "pastors and parents should not rest till this defect is remedied."[45] A year later he addressed parents on their duties of Christian education to their children; the Catholic Citizen editorialized that if parents would ponder his words there would be fewer instances of "children gone astray."[46]

Meanwhile, in Green Bay, the Austrian-born Frederick X. Katzer had been installed as bishop. Almost three quarters of his first Lenten Pastoral in 1887 was focused on education, the focus of which was set in the initial paragraph in which he stated that the "offspring of Catholic parents claim our principal attention and require the greatest vigilance." Katzer continued that a "thorough and perfect Catholic education—whatever others may say to the contrary notwithstanding—cannot be had in our state of affairs without a Catholic parochial school." Parental instruction of children at home, no matter how committed the parents were, was "not infrequently rendered useless and entirely subverted by their frequenting the public school." A "prominent cause" of fallen-away Catholics was a "more secular education."[47]

The growing Catholic school enrollment, abetted by German and Polish ethnic orientations, led to conflict with the state's educational authorities, especially in regard to reporting school attendance. Catholic authorities, regarding their schools as "altogether private enterprises," denied the right of supervision of these schools to the secular state.[48] Robert Graham, State Superintendent of Public Instruction in 1886 lamented in his Report that the private schools were "more and more neglecting to report their enrollment to the state superintendent." (Milwaukee was one city that made no report.)[49] Catholic sources reminded the state that Catholic schools, denied state financial aid, saved the state's citizens a considerable amount of money. It was estimated, for example, that in 1887 Catholic schools in Milwaukee saved the taxpayers $135,312.00.[50] Catholic sentiment was that the state had no right to insist on anything dealing with their schools.

The Battles Begin in Wisconsin

In 1888, the State Superintendent of Schools, Jesse B. Thayer, reported a decline in private school attendance of 3,825. From 1886 to 1888 there was an overall decrease of seven- to fifteen-year-olds in attendance at school of approximately eight percent from eighty-six percent to seventy-nine percent for that two-year period, which could only be accounted for by a lack of cooperation from private school authorities.[51] Thayer made a fervent appeal for legislation that would require private schools to report their attendance to his office He singled out the city of Milwaukee as being particularly uncooperative.[52]

Responding to Thayer's request, Republican Governor William Dempster Hoard emphasized the importance of citizenship in his 1889 *Message* to the state legislature. Being able to read and write English was a paramount concern of full citizenship. Consequently, Hoard asked for legislation that authorized local superintendents of schools to inspect all schools in their jurisdiction to see that such instruction was taking place.[53] A committed supporter of public education, Hoard looked upon the English language as an indispensable tool in bringing about a true American nationality among the state's residents, especially the foreign-born.[54] New York-born, Hoard was a lay Methodist minister who had served in the Union Army in Virginia during the Civil War; he believed that the lack of public schools in the South was responsible for the presence of slavery there.[55] Religiously committed to a broad version of Christianity, Hoard had little use for organized churches or for what he felt were the "narrow creeds and the dogmas of man-made religion."[56] During his tenure as Governor he would sign a controversial piece of legislation that would energize dissenters from the public school tradition.

The Bennett Law

Michael J. Bennett, a Catholic and a Republican from Iowa County who was chair of the Education Committee introduced what was to become the Bennett

Law into the Assembly on February 20, 1889.[57] It was signed into law by Governor Hoard on April 19, 1889.[58] Its key features required twelve weeks attendance at a school for children between the ages of seven and fourteen "in the town or district in which he resides," the precise time to be determined by the school board. It authorized the school board to levy fines on noncomplying parents and to legitimize exceptions. It prohibited child labor for children under thirteen years of age, unless allowed by legal authorities. It defined the school as one in which "there shall be taught therein, as part of the elementary education of children, reading, writing, arithmetic and United States history, in the English language."[59] The portions of the law that mandated attendance at a school in the town or district in which a child resided and the definition of a school as one in which certain subjects were taught in the English language were crucial in the view of parochial school adherents. They also felt that the law gave school boards, which sometimes were hostile to parochial schools, too much power over parochial schools.

Wisconsin's Lutherans were the first to respond. In a meeting of the Missouri Synod at Sheboygan, and of the Evangelical Synod at Portage, Lutherans promised to fight without flinching the English language requirement of the Law, regarding it as an assault on the German language and its use in schools.[60] The *Wisconsin Journal of Education*, through an editorial, had dismissed the Lutheran objections because the Law merely required what was necessary for good citizenship and did not interfere with either the faith or language of the Lutherans' tradition.[61] As the controversy blossomed, the Wisconsin teachers, meeting in Madison in December, saw fit to endorse the Law through a unanimous resolution:

> Resolved, That while we may entertain different views regarding the necessity or expediency of compulsory attendance laws, yet we see no injustice to anyone, but, on the contrary, great benefits both to individual and to the community from a just administration of the 'Bennett law. [62]

The Catholic Position

The *Catholic Citizen*, the English language newspaper published in Milwaukee, greeted Governor Hoard's "Message" to the legislature as looking "very much like a pretext to interfere." It felt time would "remedy the neglect" of teaching in English in some parochial schools. Given the hostility on the part of some school boards to parochial schools, the *Citizen* opined that "supervision of public school officials would be anything beyond a crusade of hostile criticism."[63]

The *Citizen* reported that the "instinct of parochial schools is that this whole movement is one of hostility and that suspicion is right."[64] While the *Citizen* rejected the claim that English was neglected in Catholic schools and held that voluntary progress was a "better remedy than legislation," [65] it did remonstrate with the *Columbian*, a Catholic newspaper in Milwaukee published in German, telling the German Catholics to "pay more attention to America than Germany."[66] The *Citizen* perceived the Bennett Law as an attack upon parental rights, which the state had no right to do, or to control private schooling beyond insuring that "no anarchistic or criminal teaching be permitted in any private school."[67]

Kilian C. Flasch, Bishop of LaCrosse, was the first member of the Catholic hierarchy in Wisconsin to speak out on the Bennett Law. He accused the Law of being opposed both to the Church and to his mother country.[68] A few weeks later he accosted both the secret societies, which want to "turn parochial schools into secular institutions," and "certain Catholic prelates" who, supported by some priests, with the "best of intentions," want to make the Church "American," with the "grand illusion" that they will "make all the *Americans* Catholic."[69]

On the tenth day of the year in 1890 Pope Leo XIII issued his authoritative encyclical, *Sapientiae Christianae*, in which he reaffirmed that it was the duty of every Catholic to uphold the position of the Church when Church and state clashed in "mixed matters," such as education.[70] Parents, he proclaimed, have "exclusive authority" in the education of their children. They are not free, however, to do as they please, but must oppose their children "frequenting schools where they are exposed to the fatal poison of impiety." The Pontiff concluded with praise of "those Catholics of all nationalities" who have "erected schools for the education of their children."[71]

Wisconsin was an apt place to apply the principles of Leo's letter. It had a recently enacted law that came under the papal proscription; its bishops had spearheaded substantial Catholic efforts, with considerable success, to erect Catholic schools; and there were a large number of Germans in the state, who were anxious to preserve their spiritual and cultural heritage via Catholic schools. In addition, there were others, also German, who maintained a substantial presence in parochial education in the state—Lutherans, who had similar goals for their educational system, and who also opposed the state's legislation. In fact the Census of 1890 reported that there were 249,164 Catholics and 160,919 Lutherans in Wisconsin in 1890, together constituting approximately seventy-five percent of the communicants of religious bodies of the state,[72] this in a state that had 32.98 percent of its residents listed as members of churches.[73] Further, Wisconsin ranked first of the north central states in private school enrollment with 66,065 students. Of this number there were 37,854 Catholic and 26,359 Lutheran school students comprising ninety-seven percent of private school enrollment.[74]

The Wisconsin Bishops' "Manifesto"

The turmoil over the Bennett Law had escalated to the point where Robert Luscombe, City Attorney of Milwaukee, thought it necessary to state on March 8, 1890, that the Law had been framed without any intention of attacking religion, parochial schools, or the German nationality. He asserted that copies of the bill had been sent to leading German Catholics and German Lutherans in the city; none of them had objected to it. He maintained that the purpose of the Law was to protect children from the "avarice of employers" and the "necessities of parents."[75] Whatever its purpose, and whatever the reason for the lack of opposition to it, including in the state legislature, it was fast becoming the touchstone of serious strife, to be heavily laden with emotional outbursts on both sides.

On March 12, 1890 the *Milwaukee Sentinel* announced that the Catholic bishops of Wisconsin would issue a "manifesto" on the Bennett Law the next day. It expected them to add their voices to the opposition to the Bennett Law because they were "not disposed to favor a system that is calculated to increase the strength and influence of the 'godless public schools.'"[76]

The *Sentinel's* prediction was accurate. The next day, Michael Heiss, Archbishop of Milwaukee; Kilian C. Flasch, Bishop of LaCrosse; and Frederick X. Katzer, Bishop of Green Bay, issued a document that protested the Bennett Law and what they believed were the religious and ethnic prejudices that motivated it. The text of their "Manifesto" revealed the influence of the recent encyclical, *Sapientiae Christianae*, of Pope Leo XIII.

The three men who authored the "Manifesto" had all been born overseas: Heiss and Flasch in Bavaria, Katzer in Austria. Heiss of Milwaukee was a very sick man, destined to die within two weeks of the issuance of the "Manifesto." The document has been described as his "last great work."[77] Flasch of LaCrosse had labored diligently and consistently on behalf of Catholic schools and urged the priests of his diocese to impress upon their people their duty of using the ballot box to "guarantee their rights as parents and to secure freedom of education."[78] Katzer of Green Bay, who was to succeed Heiss, saw the philosophy of Hegel and the schemes of the Masons behind the Law. He said the Bennett Law was similar to measures in Massachusetts, Germany, France, and Belgium and were "all children of one and the same family, Freemasonry." He asserted that the Law was an encroachment of anti-Christ in the form of an aggressive state on the rights of parents and the Church.[79]

The bishops began their protest with the allegation that the Law was not simply a political matter; rather, it touched upon "questions of the greatest interest to our Catholic church and our Catholic homes." Because of this, the bishops considered themselves "in duty bound to express and explain, even at some length, our opinion concerning" the Law.[80] The bishops then came to the heart of their objections: that the basic purpose of the Law was the destruction of the parochial school system in the state:

> After calm and careful study of the Bennett law we hold that it interferes with the rights of the church and of parents. We, moreover conscientiously believe that the real object of this law is not so much to secure a greater amount of instruction in and knowledge of the English language as rather to bring our parochial and private schools under the control of the state. And in this attempt, we cannot but apprehend the ultimate intention—gradually to destroy the parochial school system.[81]

Claiming that Catholic schools used English sufficiently, and that the parochial schools existed independently of the state, the bishops termed the Law "unnecessary, offensive, and unjust."[82] It was "unnecessary," because with few exceptions the Catholic schools of the state had voluntarily met what the Bennett Law required by way of the use of the English language. The gradual "Americanization" of the state's foreign-born residents would occur over the passage of time, not by coercive legislation. It was "offensive," because the state's Catholics had built and maintained their schools without "one dollar" from the state. Finally, the prelates addressed the "unjust" feature of the Law, their major concern. The Law, they claimed:

> . . . interferes with the sacred, inalienable rights of parents. . . . Indeed, we deny to the state the right to educate the children of those parents who are able and willing to do so themselves. . . . The state acts simply though delegated power. . . . If other parents, and they are thousands upon thousands, do not want to delegate the exercise of that right, they are perfectly free to retain it for themselves. . . . Now, whereas our Catholic parents provide an education for their children which not only not endangers but promotes the welfare of the state, their schools should not be molested by any interference on the part of the state.[83]

The bishops pointed out that the rights of parents were not "unqualified"; they were to be exercised in accord with the Church's teaching that children are to receive not merely a secular education, but a religious one, and this due to obligations "incumbent on Christian parents by the natural and divine law." This teaching was one from which no Catholic could dissent and remain a "true member of the church."[84]

The purpose of the "Manifesto" was not, the bishops averred, the retention of the German language. It was for the defense of the legitimate rights of parents and Church in education, as embodied in the parochial schools. They were unable to see the danger to the state in having another language taught, "be it German, French, Polish, Dutch, Bohemian or any other." The Wisconsin hierarchy concluded its protest with the assertion that it had been forced upon them by the aggressive action of the state. In their words, "We have never received one single cent of state help for our schools—we want no state interference with them either."[85]

Responses to the "Manifesto"

The "Manifesto" evoked, not surprisingly, a number of responses, both pro and con. The bishops of the Catholic Church in Wisconsin had informed the Catholics of the state that it was their Christian duty to work to repeal a certain piece of legislation, and to oppose all political candidates who were in favor of it. The bishops had declared that religion was involved; others decried their efforts as constituting an interference by the Church in the affairs of the civil state and its citizens.

The *Milwaukee Sentinel*, under the leadership of its editor, Horace Rublee, was the fiercest critic of the bishops. While admitting the defectiveness of the district clause for attendance, it accused the bishops of losing sight of "everything except the Catholic parochial schools," and of not caring about the 50,000 children who didn't go to school at all. The *Sentinel* charged that the bishops were using parental rights as a cloak to preserve the "power of the German branch of the Church," when these rights were really nonexistent since all they guaranteed was the obligation to follow the teaching of the bishops.[86] The *Sentinel* threw down the gauntlet to Catholics when it editorialized that the Catholics had a chance to win acceptance from their fellow citizens by rejecting the "Manifesto" of the bishops. If they supported it, Catholics could expect travail in the future from the bishops' "inexcusable interference."[87]

The *Sentinel* was quick to report any dissatisfaction among ethnic and Catholic ranks with the "Manifesto." Hence, it cited Assemblyman Slupenski of Milwaukee when he asserted that Polish Americans in that city were in favor of the Law and that they taught English two to three hours a day in "our parochial schools."[88] The *Sentinel* attempted to exploit ethnic differences among Catholics and play upon enmities brought from Europe when it editorialized in "A Talk to the Poles" that the "The Polish priesthood stands between them" and acceptance in American society, and "it will be a glorious thing if the Poles were ready now to declare for emancipation, ready to spit on the manifesto of the German Catholic Bishops."[89]

The tension spread to other religious denominations. For instance, Dean Babbitt of St. John's Episcopal Church in Milwaukee chastised the bishops for interfering in political matters and asked "The American schools, will they never be rid of the spectre of the monk?"[90] Two weeks later, in another sermon, he deplored the entrance of the Catholic bishops into politics. "Imagine," he remarked, "Uncle Sam kissing St. Peter's great toe at Rome." The struggle, he felt, pitted the Catholic Church against the public schools. Babbitt exclaimed: "Here stands the Romish Church facing with stern and determined brow the common schools of Wisconsin. . . . Have not the people reason to suspect the Romish Church when it strikes at their school system, reared at such expense, loved with so much ardor, so useful, so needful, so benevolent?"[91]

Catholics Reply

The *Catholic Citizen* headlined the "Manifesto" in its March 15 issue as follows:

> A Protest of the Catholic Bishops of Wisconsin Against a Law Which *Aims to Destroy* the Parochial School System.
>
> They Demand Its Repeal in the Name of 350,000 Catholics of the State. And Confidently Hope That Catholic Voters and All Friends of Parental Rights Will Do Their Duty.[92]

An accompanying editorial regretted the necessity of the "Manifesto" but alleged it was made necessary by legislation that was "in conflict with the better tradition of American politics." The "idea of the State interfering in any way with the management and course of study of private and parochial schools should never appear in any future legislation in this State," the *Citizen* opined.[93] Granting the state the right to educate, and the desirability of ending child labor, the *Citizen* opposed the district clause and the English language provisions of the Bennett Law. It centered its opposition on the Law's assertion of "supervision of parochial schools." It rejected the right of the state to specify a minimum amount of knowledge taught in the private schools, because such a power would make the state "an incipient master over the church schools."[94]

In its March 29 issue, the *Citizen* presented a sampling of support of the bishops' position from Catholic newspapers across the country. The *New York Freeman's Journal* alleged the purpose of the Bennett Law was to "destroy Catholic schools"; the *Boston Pilot* asserted that the Law "interferes with the sacred and inalienable rights of parents"; the *St. Louis Church Progress* said the Law was based on the "assumption that children belong to the state"; the *St. Louis Western Watchman* denounced the Law as "unnecessary interference of the State in the education of youth"; the *Philadelphia Catholic Standard* argued that, if left alone, the language question would work out naturally as it had with the "Pennsylvania Dutch"; the *Chicago Catholic Home* said their opponents wouldn't debate the question on its own merits (Illinois had a similar measure also recently passed, in the Edwards Law), but resorted to the use of "vile weapons of calumny and scurrilous language" such as "German bishops," and "ignorant priests" and the like; the *Philadelphia Freeman and Irish Review* saw in the Bennett Law an attempt to "revive and transplant the Penal Laws"; the *Minneapolis Irish Standard* declared that the parochial schools were none of the state's business; and the *Iowa Catholic Messenger* complained that the Law gave too much power to public school directors, who were "often too ignorant to examine a primary school and very often make up in prejudice and bigotry what they lack in educational requirements."[95]

Horace Rublee and the *Milwaukee Sentinel*

Horace Rublee, born in Vermont, a Republican who had been a Whig, was editor of the *Milwaukee Sentinel* at this time.[96] He kept the pages of the *Sentinel*, especially its editorial section, centered on the controversy. The paper's tone was offensive to Catholics and Lutherans.

On March 22, the *Sentinel* cited a number of the state's newspapers in defense of the Bennett Law. Collectively, these reports contended that the purpose of the Bennett Law was to make a good citizen. The *Sentinel* itself reported that it was the clergy, especially the German Catholic and Lutheran, who were stirring up the trouble.[97]

The *Sentinel* played upon the fears of English-speaking Americans by emphasizing the German nationality of the opposition to the Bennett Law. For instance, on March 27 it editorialized under the caption "Church against State" that the "3 German Catholic Bishops" were the aggressors and said they aimed at more than the Bennett Law. They sought, the *Sentinel* averred, to deny the state the right to compel education which amounted to "a denial of the right of the state to support the public school system." The paper maintained that the Irish American people and priests were for the Law, as were other English-speaking Catholics.[98]

The very next day the *Sentinel* reported that the suggestion of English-speaking Catholics for the appointment of an English-speaking archbishop of Milwaukee to succeed Heiss was resented by German priests. It felt that the request was reasonable, since all the other bishops of the state were German, although Catholics of other nationalities outnumbered the German Catholics in Wisconsin.[99] A day later the *Sentinel* brought up the ethnic issue again when it attempted to build upon the resentment of German control of the Catholic Church in Wisconsin on the part of other national elements when it averred: "It is safe to say that if there had been one English-speaking bishop in this state the impertinent manifesto would not have appeared."[100]

On March 30, it put together three quotations on its editorial page, by which it attempted to instill fear of a German Catholic takeover of Wisconsin's public institutions:

> "We confidently hope that our Catholic voters stand together for the repeal of this law" (The German Catholic Bishops of Wisconsin).
>
> "In politics, men ought always and in the first place to serve, as far as possible, the interests of Catholicism" (The Pope's Encyclical Letter).
>
> "Every Catholic who votes for George W. Peck (the Democratic candidate for Mayor in the upcoming mayoral election in Milwaukee), upholds the bishops' protest against the Bennett Law" (The *Catholic Citizen*, Authorized Organ of the Church).[101]

Another theme emphasized by the *Sentinel* was the "war" that the Catholic Church was waging against the state. On March 27, it said that the Catholic bishops had attacked the "foundation principle" of public education.[102] The next day it expanded on this idea when it posited its theory of the proper relations of Church, state and parents in education. It held that the state "has the right to employ measures necessary for its existence," because a "free republic is not compatible with popular ignorance." The state has the "right to prescribe this and to see that it is secured." The state's right is superior to that of the church when a "parent delegates his duty and function to the church," so if the "church does not teach the child that which the state considers essential to the welfare of the child and the state," it becomes the "duty of the state to provide for that teaching."

Then the *Sentinel* addressed what it considered the basic issue at stake, the right of the state in education to provide for its own existence and the Catholic denial of that right:

> This is precisely the point at issue. . . . Not whether a measure of instruction in English is essential to intelligent citizenship, but whether the state has a right to enforce instruction in English if it does consider that essential. The church schools say they will instruct in English or not, as it may please them. . . . But they also declare that if they do not choose to instruct in English, it is an infringement of parental rights, not to be endured, for the state to make other provisions for such instruction. . . . What the German Catholic prelates say in distinct terms, that parental rights are first and highest and that the public schools exist only by tolerance and not by any right lodged in the state. If this is conceded, everything is conceded. . . . If we admit that the state has no right to direct the education of its future citizens in any measure, then we admit that the state has no right to provide for its own existence.[103]

The Milwaukee Mayoral Election

The *Catholic Citizen* endorsed George W. Peck, a Democrat who opposed the Bennett Law, for Mayor, on the grounds of the school issue involved: "Every Catholic who votes for George W. Peck upholds the Bishops' protest against the Bennett Law. . . . No Catholic should vote for the Turner-Bennett Law."[104] The paper recalled a speech by Peck in which he endorsed private schools that "teach children their own religion, and may God bless them as long as they live." By voting for Peck, the *Citizen* declared, Catholics would preserve their churches and schools, currently under attack by bigots.[105]

Meanwhile, the *Sentinel* offered its readers its interpretation of the mayoral race: "If you like the un-American proclamation of the German Catholic bishops, then it is your business to vote for Peck." It forecast a gloomy picture for public schools and their advocates in the state if Peck won: "If the friends of the public schools can't vote together at this time, they will not be able to vote together when the next attack is made."[106]

Milwaukee was heavily populated by German immigrants in 1890. Some estimate that over one-half of the city's population was either born in Germany or born of parents who were.[107] With Catholic and Lutheran support, George W. Peck was victorious in the race for Mayor of Milwaukee.

The *Sentinel* recognized that the election had been a victory for the Catholic hierarchy but left no doubt that it considered the election results just a beginning: "The Catholic bishops have triumphed in the first set-to, and are to be congratulated on the discipline of their hosts."[108] The *Wisconsin State Journal* testified to the intense emotional level of the campaign by quoting William E. Cramer, editor-in-chief of the *Milwaukee Evening Wisconsin*, to the effect that in forty-three years of journalistic experience he had never witnessed anything like this before, that is, the "extraordinary combination" of Lutherans and Catholics uniting to win at the polls. The *State Journal* summarized the election as that "the fight is really against the English language, it is manifestly led by the extreme religious zealots of the two churches named."[109]

The *Milwaukee Journal*, on the other hand, warmly greeted the election results, calling it a "Verdict Against Paternalism" and said it amounted to a mandate to the government to keep its "hands off" the private schools. It approved the interpretation offered by the German paper, *Der Herold*, on the election:

> The democratic candidates were elected yesterday not so much as democrats than as the means used by the united opposition against the attempts to create by legislative enactment a permanent conflict between church and state. The Bennett law was the cause of the Republican defeat. . . . The church has rebuked the state in its attempts to encroach upon its rights in a way that even the blind and unbelieving in the Republican Party, who did not want to comprehend, must now concede their mistake.[110]

On April 3, the *Madison Democrat* laid the blame for the Republican defeat on the *Sentinel*, which it said had "Blained" the Law, in a reference to the Blaine Amendment.[111] The *State Journal* countered with the allegation that German Catholics and Lutherans "have made the issue that they shall dictate the laws of the state governing educational matters." If successful, the *Journal* wondered, would their alliance produce a "return to the darkness of middle ages and church rule the state?"[112]

On April 6, the *Sentinel* added a new twist to the clash. It recommended that the state examine and certify all parochial school teachers. Such a step was necessary because some parochial school teachers had no knowledge of English whatever and consequently were unable to teach the children of the state properly.[113]

The Impact of the Election

Shortly after the issuance of the "Manifesto," Governor Hoard had denied that the Bennett Law was an assault on parochial schools. Rather, it dealt with the parent, who he said, "is subject to the state in all matters pertaining to the necessities of the state."[114] Aware of the setback he had suffered in the Milwaukee mayoral election, Hoard remained steadfast in his defense of the Bennett Law. On April 2, speaking to the Southeastern Wisconsin Teachers Association, he announced that there were about 50,000 youngsters in the state between the ages of seven and fourteen who were not receiving any formal schooling. The state "says to the parent—not to the priest or parochial school" that you must not neglect to give your child an education, which is the right of the state to compel, whether that parent is found in a Lutheran or Catholic church or neither.[115]

Hoard referred to schools in the state, even public schools in several instances, where there was no English used. He reported: "Instances have come to my knowledge where the English language has been banished from the public school house and in one instance a German Catholic priest stripped the public school of its furniture and ordered the school closed."[116] The Governor wondered whether the "Lutheran and German Catholic clergy have suddenly become the only defenders of religion in the land." Where, he mused, are the "German Methodists, Baptists, Presbyterians, Scandinavian Lutherans and all that great body of English-speaking Protestants" who see no affront to religion? And have the Irish Catholics "suddenly become blind to the great danger that threatens their religious existence and integrity?"[117] He saw opposition to the rights of the state in education as the underlying cause for the opposition to the Bennett Law:

> The state asserts in the Bennett law the right to control the elementary English edu-
> cation of the child to the extent of at least twelve weeks in a year. The German
> Lutheran and Catholic clergy who are interested in parochial schools deny that right.
> That brings on a contest. The right of the state in educational matters is at stake, for
> if it has no right here it has none elsewhere, and thus the whole common school ques-
> tion becomes involved. It is simply a contest between church and state, and all men
> who believe in "rendering unto Caesar the things that are Caesar's and unto God the
> things that are God's" will take their sides with the state.[118]

The Governor argued that Catholic opposition was far from unanimous. "Irish and American Catholics," for instance, believe that "if the church was controlled by men who were warm and ardent American sympathizers" they would

not be opposed to the "true behests of the state in matters of education." Hoard singled out Catholic public school teachers, of "both Irish and German origin" for praise, who support the Bennett law and "everything that is distinctly American." The "state and nation have no more faithful workers on behalf of American civilization than these teachers."[119]

Catholic and Lutheran sources attacked Hoard's figures of children not attending any school as grossly distorted.[120] The *Milwaukee Journal* agreed, accusing Hoard of demagoguery in his reference to the "poor little German boys and girls" who were being kept in ignorance by their parents.[121] The *Madison Democrat* was of like mind, with its headline of "Hoard Watered His Stock" (a reference to Hoard's agricultural origins).[122]

The *Catholic Citizen* wanted the Bennett Law to be repealed. Yet, it separated its views from those who made "flagrant attacks" on public schools and felt that Catholics should not "begrudge" taxes paid for public schools, thus disagreeing with the German Catholic publication *Columbian*, which said that was "not the will of those who have the right to decide the Catholic position on the question."[123] The appropriate educational program for Catholics, according to the *Citizen's* editor, should center on: 1) the up-building and improvement of parochial schools; 2) opposition to state control or interference with private education; 3) avoidance of conflict with or opposition to unsectarian public schools; and 4) war with bigots and Know-Nothings who, because of the attitude of Catholics on the school question, impugn the civil capacity of Catholic citizens.[124]

The Wisconsin German Catholic Convention

The conflict brought about by the Bennett Law had alarmed Wisconsin's Catholic Germans. Sixty-seven German Catholic societies were represented at the state's German Catholic Convention, one object of which was "to go hand in hand wherever the Catholic cause is in danger."[125] Father Buechler, of St. Francis Seminary in Milwaukee, delivered the opening day sermon. In an emotional appeal he pictured the Bennett Law advocates as un-American and as enemies of Christ and those He redeemed. Any Catholic who refused to stand up and be counted in the struggle was charged by Buechler with the spiritual sin of apostasy.[126]

Buechler's sermon was an apt barometer of what was to come. He was followed by Bavarian-born Kilian C. Flasch, Bishop of LaCrosse. Flasch maintained that the Convention was well within its rights to stand against the

Bennett Law, because the issue was fundamentally religious and educational, not political. The "inalienable right" of the parents in education had been threatened. The Church was simply fulfilling its responsibility to "preach the gospel"; in this instance to see that children are instructed in the Catholic faith "at home and at school." Flasch described the coming months in military terms: "If Catholics are beat in their justified defense, they fall as a soldier does, in an honorable warfare. But do not stand there like cowards."[127]

The keynote address of the Convention was given by Bishop Katzer. Warmly received by the delegates, he outlined the proper order that should exist between individual, family, and state, with the latter last in creation and ordered by God Himself to the protection of the former two. The state has no right to "impair the rights of family and individual," since it was created to make "happy families protecting the rights of the individual and the people and thus to foster the growth of the state." Katzer then turned to the Bennett Law, delineating his conception of what the rights of the child were:

> What did the state do when the state created the—let us speak it right out—Bennett law? The father begets the child. The mother bears it and gives birth to it under unspeakable pain and sorrow. It belongs to them and to no one else.
>
> But here the objection is raised that the child also has some rights and that these must be protected by the state. . . . Now, what right does the child have that the state claims it is called upon to protect? That leaves the presumption that its parents had neglected these rights. These rights and prerogatives I do not deny for a moment. . . . But do they go as far as to allow the child to say to the parents: I want to be educated this way, and I must be clothed that way? No! They are entitled to such education and such care as will enable them to become good citizens and go through life with the possibility given them to find eternal salvation. Other material rights the child does not possess.[128]

Continuing, Katzer centered on the issue that most disturbed him—state influence, perhaps leading to control, of the curriculum of private schools. He speculated: "If the state is accorded the control of our schools, it can and probably will say that we must teach only English. Some foolish people say that the state may interfere with the family. Why, the next thing we shall hear is that the state appoints a commission to prescribe what your wives must cook for dinner."[129]

The man soon to succeed Heiss as Archbishop of Milwaukee ended his speech by urging the delegates to take to themselves the honorable and manly task of defending their schools. He proclaimed: "If we see somebody kick at our schools, the very heart-blood of our existence, then we Catholics must wake up and defend them. To do this is your highest duty and you must find it an honor. And if you do so, you may be sure that your opponents will also respect and honor you as men."[130]

The assembled delegates passed resolutions that it was by "divine and natural law" that parents are entitled and in duty bound to provide for the education of their children. If the parents "neglect this duty, the state is justified in compelling them by appropriate legislation to discharge their duty." This right justified compulsory school attendance upon parental neglect. The delegates made "no claim on the support of the state" for their schools but granted the state the right of interference in the operation of parochial schools only if "these collide with public order or the laws of morals." The Bennett Law, they contended, "unnecessarily and unjustly curtails our religious liberty," and therefore declared that, "without regard to former party connections, we will only vote for such candidates who pledge themselves to work for the repeal of the law."[131]

The *Sentinel* was the first to respond to the convention. It welcomed the concession made by the delegates that public schools were a necessity and that the state had the right to tax for their support. All that was needed now, it declared, was for the Catholics to admit that the state had the right to define what were the essential parts of education.[132]

Bishop Katzer's Position

Frederick Xavier Katzer's advance up the ecclesiastical ladder had been fairly rapid. By 1890, he was the acknowledged leader of Wisconsin Catholicism, a loyal churchman, a conservative, German, and thoroughly committed to parochial education. The views of the man destined shortly to be the next Archbishop of Milwaukee, who had charged the Masons with the onus for the Bennett Law and its aim of parochial school destruction, and who was reported to have said of himself in the summer of 1889 in Florence, Wisconsin, that "I am not a citizen, I am a Bishop,"[133] are most important in understanding the direction of Catholic educational policy in the Bennett Law strife.

Katzer's ideas received an airing by means of an interview with the *Wisconsin State Journal*, published on June 27, 1890. In his opinion, the Bennett Law was the entering wedge of the overall goal of the suppression of Catholic schools in the state. The Law's instigators, he averred, were "mainly if not solely motivated by intolerance." Those features that gave the school board power to decide what constituted a school and required attendance in the public school district in which the child lived were especially objectionable. There was no politics on the part of the Catholic Church, Katzer stated, and when asked his opinion of the effect the Church's opposition to the Bennett law would have on the upcoming gubernatorial election in November, he replied that he was not a politician but believed that "Catholics generally will pursue a course" of action that they "deem will best secure protection to the parochial schools against unreasonable and unwarranted encroachments upon their just rights and privileges."[134]

Superintendent Thayer at the NEA

In the meanwhile, Wisconsin school superintendent Jesse B. Thayer, the man who had asked for legislation that would compel the private schools to report their attendance to his office, addressed the NEA in 1890. He alleged that opposition to the Law came from the "ultramontanism, Jesuitical element" who felt strong enough to take on the American public schools. As Thayer saw it, the family "must be entrusted with early and infant education." The church, due to the "potency of religious life and sentiment," must be entrusted with "strictly sectarian instruction." That education that "relates primarily to the rights, duties and needs of sovereign citizens must be entrusted to the state." To deny the third, "is to abrogate the principles upon which our civil government rests."[135] Thayer argued that opposition to the Bennett Law was unpatriotic:

> When the German Catholic bishops, the German Catholic priests, and the German Lutheran clergy of Wisconsin unite in a political organization to secure the unconditional repeal of a compulsory law which has for its sole purpose instruction of all children of the state in the language and history of this their adopted country, I have a right to suspect that there is something in the movement that is not exactly American, nor in harmony with the principles laid down by the fathers of this republic.[136]

Thayer conceded that the state had no right to interfere with the freedom of worship of its citizens, but the church had no right to obstruct by means of parochial schools the legitimate interests of the state. Freedom of worship did not entitle a church to conspire against the government "nor conceal a plot to turn over the sovereignty of the state to the sovereign pontiff of the Vatican or the Mormon prophet of Utah." In referring to Wisconsin, Thayer questioned the "rights of parents" in the Catholic theory. He cited the Diocese of Green Bay, which under the leadership of Bishop Katzer had required its priests to build parish schools and its parents to send their children to them, unless they had the explicit permission of the bishop to do otherwise. Not only was this compulsory attendance, but it also was "decidedly un-American."[137] Finally, Thayer averred that there should be no conflict between church and state in education, but his view, when placed next to the "Manifesto," showed the impassable gulf that existed between the two agencies over education as it had been manifested in their positions over the Bennett Law:

> The secular state cannot impose upon the church the duty of instructing children in what pertains to the rights, duties and needs of citizens. That duty rests primarily with the parent, and involves the rights of the child and the right of the state. To impose this duty and secure these rights, just compulsory laws should be enacted and enforced. There is no other ground that the state can occupy and maintain an existence that will guarantee religious liberty and political freedom.[138]

The Bennett Law Revisited

As can be seen by the comments of Katzer and Thayer, the Bennett Law had stirred up the state of Wisconsin. Governor Hoard and the *Milwaukee Sentinel* had spoken of a Catholic-Lutheran alliance to overturn the Bennett Law. The Lutherans were, indeed, committed opponents to the Bennett Law.

Perhaps the most complete description of the Lutheran position on the Bennett Law is found in a position paper by Christian Koerner, the legal editor of the *Germania*, a Lutheran publication. Koerner charged the Law with being "unrepublican" and not in conformity with the nation's traditions that had not equated patriotism with use of the English language. If consistently applied, Koerner said the Law would destroy Lutheran parochial schools. Denying that the Lutherans were hostile to public schools, he declared the Law deprived people of freedom of religion and liberty of conscience. He claimed there were 137 Lutheran schools in which English and German were taught equally; 129 in which English was used more than German; and 108 in which German was used more than English. In some instances, he said, it was necessary to teach English by the use of German since some of the children were more familiar with the latter language. Koerner flatly denied that German was a "*foreign* language," since both English and German were "imported" to this country. According to Koerner, the Bennett Law constituted "slavery worse than negro slavery" and was nothing less than "warfare against the German language and parochial schools."[139]

The *Sentinel* regularly referred to a "German Catholic and Lutheran alliance" as the summer progressed. While there was no formal agreement between the two denominations, there were reports of joint meetings between them. Since both groups deemed their schools and native heritage at stake, they worked together as citizens, not as churches. Rasmus B. Anderson, a leading Wisconsin Scandinavian Lutheran of that era, commented that it was the "only time since the Reformation that Catholics and Lutherans had joined hands."[140] A letter to the editor of *The Nation* characterized the relationship in more sinister terms: "The children of Luther, and the children of the Pope, have for the first time made common cause, and, under a common flag, declared war against what they call an unjust, unnecessary, and unlawful enactment."[141] George W. Rankin, Governor Hoard's biographer, portrayed the alliance in a similar fashion. He wrote: "For the first time in the history of America, Protestants and Catholics made common cause, and misled by their spiritual advisors the great body of law abiding German-Americans within the state developed a religious fanaticism that swept everything before it."[142]

Christian Koerner addressed the Lutheran-Catholic relationship by asserting that while they were traveling the same road, "we don't exactly kiss and embrace each other." Thee reason for the kinship was "You see, the interests of the Lutherans and the Catholics are the same: their parochial schools are concerned just as ours are."[143] There was no compromise or union with Catholics possible, Koerner stated, it was the "school question" that "simply keeps us on a common footing."[144]

Composed of the Baptists, Congregationalists, Methodists and Presbyterians, what may be called the Protestant center or mainstream Protestants, were overwhelmingly in favor of the Bennett Law. Whether in their official state or local gatherings, or statements made by their clergy, these groups supported the Bennett Law as an indispensable bulwark for public schools as an "American" institution, featuring the English language as necessary for citizenship in the state and nation. They took exception to the entrance of the "Romish Church" into American politics. As one Methodist preacher declared, it was a question of "American schools for American children."[145]

This theme of "foreignism" was prevalent in the Protestant center's position on the Law. The schoolhouse "must stand along side of the church, for together they constitute the real protection of the republic," one speaker declared. The parochial school represented foreign interests, while the "common school system" was the "noblest product of American civilization."[146] The inculcation of foreign ideas was "hurtful" to the American way of life.[147] Indeed, these ideas were so dangerous that the "foreign element" had to be converted (and the public school was the chief instrument of this task for children), lest they drive Christianity out of the state.[148]

Likewise, Unitarians supported the Law and criticized the role of the Catholic hierarchy in the fray. For example, the Reverend Joseph Crooker of the Unitarian Church in Madison titled his sermon on Sunday March 30, 1890 "The Public Schools and the Catholics." The Catholic hierarchy, he said, "*claims to speak in the name of the Almighty with an higher authority than that of the state.*" The priest, by his position, was the "servant of the pope first and then an American citizen." There was "no question," he maintained, that the hierarchy means to use "every politic means to win America to the papal throne," and to achieve this goal was willing to "strike down the Public school, or any other distinctly American institution."[149]

The issue was crucial, he contended, and ultimately came to the point of "*Whether we shall maintain the modern state as a secular institution and its necessary function of secular education, or whether we shall surrender to the papacy and turn human progress back four centuries?*" The question of language was but a detail compared to what was at stake in the school question:

> We must recognize that the perpetuity of civil liberty and modern civilization depends on the maintenance of the district school with its free and secular instruction; and we must also recognize that the opposition to our system of secular education is deep-seated and far-reaching. Surrender to it means the extinction of American liberty, *and any compromise that shall impair the efficiency and sovereignty of American citizenship means an eclipse of humanity.*[150]

The state, he claimed, had the responsibility to protect its "citizens in embryo," its children.

Crooker concluded his remarks with a piece of advice to the Catholic hierarchy, advice which bears repeating in full. He admonished them to:

> Be wiser, be more modern, be more American. Stop reviling the public school. . . . Show that you are not Romish, but American. . . . Pray the good pope to send here no more encyclicals demanding that in politics the interest of the church be put higher than patriotism. Cease trying to coerce your families into opposition to the public school. . . . Finally, bind your people to you by love and true freedom rather than by fear, servility and bigotry.[151]

The Gubernatorial Campaign

In the midst of this highly charged rhetoric, Wisconsin citizens faced the task of electing a Governor. The Democrats, long out of office in Wisconsin, hoped the Bennett Law controversy would assist them to return to power. The Republicans, meeting in Milwaukee, promised to "modify the existing law" so it would conform to the parental right to select the school, "public or private," of attendance. The party's platform asserted that its educational policy was "to secure to all children" within the state's borders, "proper equipment for the discharge of the ordinary duties of citizenship," and to this end "invite the cooperation and aid of all broadminded and patriotic people."[152]

One week later the Democrats met in Milwaukee. First, they declared their loyalty to the public schools of the state that they had "created." Turning their attention to the Bennett Law, they averred that its "underlying principles were needless interference with parental rights and liberty of conscience." It was underneath this "tyrannical invasion of individual and constitutional rights" that the "shallow plea of defense of the English language" was advocated. Therefore, they denounced the Law as "unnecessary, unwise, unconstitutional, un-American and undemocratic and demand its repeal."[153]

As the November election approached, the tempo of the conflict increased. The *Catholic Citizen* asked its readers to take note of what the democratic Bennett Law League had to say about the Catholic Church. The document spoke of "plots and schemes of domineering prelates and ecclesiastical demagogues" and declared that the "Democratic party had crawled to the cross." Calling attention to the Church's "greed for power," the League asserted that "The *Church*, it is well known, has a BIG STOMACH." The authors, Hugh Ryan and John Nagle, Catholics, asked its readers to forget nationality and religion and to vote against the Democrats.[154] That same day the *Citizen* editorialized under the headline "The Impending Conflict" that the eyes of the nation would be on Wisconsin on November 4, election day.[155] "IRISHMEN OF WISCONSIN" headlined the *Citizen's* October 11 issue. The substance of the story was that the "British-Americans" had prevented the city of Boston from building a monument to "O'Reilly," and the editor asked "Will the Irishmen of the State Vote with Such Men to Sustain the Bennett Law?"[156]

The *Milwaukee Sentinel* reported a speech by Attorney Charles W. Felker of Oshkosh on October 18 in which he asserted that the "opinions of the Katzers and Koerners" were the "deadly enemies of the common schools." Claiming that the German Catholic priests "arrogate to themselves the right to dictate to the parent how his child shall be educated by denying absolution to those who do not follow their orders, Felker asserted that: "These priests assume the power that they deny the state, and clothe themselves with authority over parent and child that is above legislative control. Which is to govern, the law of the church or the law of the land?"[157]

On November 1, the *Sentinel* predicted that the "German Lutherans and Catholics will instruct their flocks tomorrow" (Sunday) for voting on November 4.[158] On election eve, it reported "Priests at Work Telling Their Congregations How to Vote."[159] On election day itself, it advised its readers to "Cast a Vote for Hoard and the Schools" and commented that the Lutherans had been told to "vote for those who will do Koerner's bidding."[160]

Meanwhile, in its last preelection issue, the *Catholic Citizen* asserted that Catholics "were free to vote as they please," and won't be branded as "traitors to Church" in the exercise of their free choice. The *Citizen* then qualified its position by observing that "The *Catholic Citizen* fails to see how any intelligent voter who happens to be a Catholic can treat the very evident desires of the Church authorities in this matter with levity." It urged Catholics to "follow the good example" of the twenty-two Capuchin monks who had registered to vote, and then to cast a "conscientious ballot."[161]

The election turned out to be a landslide victory for George W. Peck, the Democratic candidate, and a resounding defeat for the incumbent, Republican Governor Hoard. The *Milwaukee Journal* that had asserted that the Milwaukee mayoral election in the spring had demonstrated that there was no need for a compulsory attendance law now denied that the campaign had been a contest between the friends and foes of the public schools. In its words, "These politicians (Republican) decided that an onslaught on certain churches was the surest way to the favors of the rest of the people." They were guilty of "bigotry and intolerance," the *Journal* claimed, and as a result had been soundly defeated.[162]

The *Sentinel* took a different tack. After first announcing on November 5 that the election was "In Doubt,"[163] a chastened paper dutifully reported the next day that "PECK IS ELECTED," when it also informed its readers that Governor Hoard had been insulted by a mob at his Madison home. The McKinley tariff was one reason for the Republican defeat; the "opposition to the school law mainly created by flagrant misrepresentation of its character and purposes" was another. The *Sentinel* asserted that the German ethnic and religious forces, Catholic and Lutheran, had combined to bring out the democratic vote and thus had been victorious.[164]

The *Catholic Citizen* headlined its November 8 issue, "NO STATE INTERFERENCE." It attributed the victory to the Bennett Law alone, ignoring the tariff issue. It claimed that the "DECISIVE VICTORY" had been caused by "public revulsion toward the Bennett Law." It penned that the Law "drew all sectarian, bigoted, fanatical and crazy impurities in the Republican party, and some in the democratic as well. It had been assisted by the "Presbyterian conference and the lightweight 'educators.'" The German Lutherans had begun the agitation; they had been joined by German Catholics who brought other Catholics along with them.[165]

The Election's Aftermath

It is difficult to determine precisely the role the Bennett Law played in the Republican defeat. The populist movement, free silver, the opposition of farmers to the McKinley tariff, and the Progressive movement were other contributing factors.[166] Wisconsin's neighboring states showed similar Democratic victories in Congressional elections but not to the extent that Wisconsin experienced.[167]

Yet it is not possible to overlook the ethnic factor in the election of 1890, compared with the presidential elections of 1888 and 1892. As recorded in Milwaukee County, the 1890 "off-year" election returns reflect a strong trend to the Democrats, which was not present in the 1888 and 1892 elections.[168] The majority of German immigrants who had first come to the state around 1848 were Democrats and liberals.[169] Those who came to the state later were rather conservative. They included Lutherans who had left Germany to avoid being forced into union with the Reformed Church by Prussian leaders, and they sought religious freedom in the United States. Whole villages had left Germany, with their pastors, upon whom they were dependent. They implanted their native customs, including their commitment to parochial schools, in Wisconsin.[170]

The "foreign" element was a significant factor in the state. The Census of 1890 had revealed that 73.7 percent of Wisconsin's population was either foreign-born (30.6 percent), or with at least one parent foreign-born (43.1 percent). In Milwaukee 86.4 percent of that city's residents were either foreign-born or with at least one parent foreign-born. As for political strength, 52.9 percent of adult males in Wisconsin were either foreign-born or had a parent foreign-born. Wisconsin ranked third among the states in the union as to the percentage of eligible voters from foreign lands.[171] The German presence can be seen from the fact that 626,030 of Wisconsin's residents in 1890 were either born in Germany or had at least one parent born there. This in comparison to 113,349 from Ireland, and 64,716 from England. Since Wisconsin's population was 1,686,880 in 1890, approximately thirty-seven percent hailed from

Germany.[172] The Bennett Law appeared to have awakened a political consciousness among Catholic and Lutheran German-Americans who, as a result, "redoubled their support of the Democratic party."[173]

The Catholic and Lutheran German clergy in Wisconsin clearly viewed the Bennett Law as the "entering wedge" by which the state would ultimately destroy the German language schools and churches, and they were able to use this fear as a lever to intensify the national pride of Germans and to keep "Germandom" in America.[174] The Catholic hierarchy had recruited clergy from Germany with considerable success. A number of the religious orders that taught in the Church's parochial schools had emigrated from Germany to the United States. King Ludwig I of Bavaria had exhorted one group of these nuns "I shall not forget you, but stay German, German! Do not become English."[175] German Catholics followed the beliefs of Bishop Dwenger of Fort Wayne, Indiana, who said, "No schools now means empty churches later."[176] Bavaria, the homeland of Henni, Heiss, and Flasch provided the ideal model for church-state relations. There, in a country eighty percent Catholic, the libraries, normal schools and primary schools were under the supervision of the Catholic clergy.[177] As expressed by the editor of a German Catholic newspaper of Detroit, German Catholics took pride in their schools and the efforts they had put forth on their behalf, seeing them as a sign of their superiority to their "immigrant brothers from the green island." The "Germans, whenever a parish is formed, endeavor first to build a school, before they build a church." For if there is no school, the "church is only a passing thing," because when the parents die, the "children will no longer desire a church."[178] Catholic Germans in Wisconsin "looked naturally to German-speaking pastors, schools and newspapers to guard their faith."[179]

Commentary on the Election

Several writers laid some of the blame for the "bitterest" election "ever experienced in Wisconsin" on the *Milwaukee Sentinel*, which had "wrapped the law in the mantle of Americanism and patriotism."[180] It was the *Sentinel's* editorials and attitude that were "in a considerable degree to blame for the bitterness which was generated on both sides." The *Sentinel's* campaign had degenerated from opposing the lack of English instruction in the parochial schools to "Save the Public Schools," which had never been attacked.[181]

Colman J. Barry, the Catholic historian, questioned if the Bennett Law supporters, in their desire to "Americanize" the immigrants by forcing them into the main current of "American" secular cultural patterns, did not contribute to the resurgence of German nationalistic spirit.[182] Isaac Thomas came to a similar conclusion, when he wrote that a law wasn't always the remedy for a situation, and that the non-English-speaking people could not shut themselves off from the English-speaking people, even if they had wanted to.[183] J. J. Mapel opined that it was not surprising that, given their background, the German-Americans had followed the directives of Church authorities in voting. He contended that Americans had overestimated the assimilative powers of their country and underestimated the conservative influence of language and religion on the German immigrant.[184]

William F. Vilas, the "Bourbon" Democrat who was elected to serve as a United States senator in the Democratic election sweep in 1891 claimed that the "real controversy turned upon the right of the State to govern purely private schools, and to assume the education of children." He argued that it was "obvious that this denunciation [the English language requirement of the Bennett Law] was aimed at the private schools."[185] Vilas alleged that if the private schools had submitted to the legislation they would have recognized the principle of state control, for if public authority could prescribe some branches of study, it could forbid any, thus able to determine whether the private school was legitimate.[186] In effect, this is what the Catholic-Lutheran alliance had alleged, that the right of the state in education would have been both prior to and superior to the rights of church and parent. The language question, Vilas held, was but a pretext; at stake was the question of who decides what is desirable for the child to learn.[187] William Dempster Hoard was soundly defeated in his bid for reelection to the office of Governor in November of 1890. His ardent backing of the Bennett Law contributed to that defeat. His ideas on religion placed him at odds with the Catholic Church in Wisconsin.

During the gubernatorial campaign Hoard had been accused of paternalism toward and of nativistic prejudice against German-Americans. He had spoken of a conspiracy that existed between the "parents, the pastor and the church" to "darken the understanding of children, who are denied by cupidity and bigotry the privilege" of a free school education.[188] Accused of being a "fanatical enemy" of parochial schools and the German language, Hoard said the issue came down to the fact that "ignorance cannot control the destinies of our country." At stake in the conflict were the "progress of civilization and the perpetuity of our institutions."[189]

Perusal of a handwritten manuscript of his, entitled "The Farmer as Citizen," reveals why Hoard and the Catholic and Lutheran churches in

Wisconsin were on a collision course. He recognized religion's power, quoting Bismarck's advice to statesmen that it would be a "terrible mistake" for them to underestimate the force of religion. Hoard's interpretation of Bismarck's advice was that it was "through religious bias, prejudice and understandings, that a large majority receive their convictions of public duty." Religious feeling, not a "clear intellectual understanding," molds their ideas of citizenship.[190]

As a consequence of its ability to mold opinion in areas outside of its proper sphere, "ecclesiastical power has been used under the push of an ignorant, religious sentiment, to the great hurt of liberty and a broad true idea of citizenship." He predicted "severe battles will yet be fought in the republic, between ecclesiasticism and Republicanism." In the Bennett Law strife, he said the ecclesiastics have wisely directed their attacks on education, because "This being a republic and the school house being the most potent influence, whereby men are emancipated from ecclesiastical control." Ecclesiastics of all persuasions should steer clear of attempting to control education but should "Stand back; keep your place; that which belongs to Caesar or the state shall the state have."[191]

The man who called Jesus Christ a "magnificent democrat," felt that religionists were inimical to citizenship, since they placed their church ahead of the civil state. The intelligent person, Hoard contended, who was also truly religious, would advise the ecclesiastics to "build your citizenship and your religion each in its proper place," recognizing that "if you have no country where is your church."[192]

Years later, in 1917, Ellis B. Usher wrote Hoard that "you were ahead of your time" and said that he could now see that Hoard had been the victim of a "German conspiracy."[193] Hoard replied two days later, expressing his gratitude that he had lived long enough for Usher to see what the Bennett Law struggle had been about. There were three parties in the conspiracy, he claimed: 1) the German Lutheran and Catholic Churches who "strove for ecclesiastical domination over the minds of the young"; 2) the German language newspapers, who tried "to make the German language the principal vehicle of communication between themselves and all German-speaking peoples"; and 3) "A deep laid scheme of propaganda for the Germanizing of the state and nation as far as possible."[194]

In a letter to a leading Scandinavian American in the state, and a strong backer of the Bennett Law, Rasmus B. Anderson, Hoard had attributed the lack of knowledge of English among German Americans to the selfish policies of the institutional churches, Catholic and Lutheran, whose only purpose in education was the "perpetuation of ecclesiastical control over the minds of the young . . . with but little care for American citizenship."[195] A few days later, in another letter to Anderson, Hoard claimed that the "Bennett Law in its defeat was more powerful in the way of reflex effort upon the spirit of foreignism, than it could have been if victorious." This was so, he maintained, because the Catholic and Lutheran youth had become acquainted with the "baneful conspiracy against their American citizenship" and had rejected the views of their elders.[196]

The Catholic Postmortem

Humphrey J. Desmond, editor of the *Catholic Citizen*, commented that the Bennett Law was a manifestation of the hate against Catholics generated by bigoted groups such as the American Protective Association (APA).[197] Usher agreed with Desmond's assessment, saying that the Bennett Law controversy had "much inspiration" from the APA, an "anti-Catholic organization."[198]

Father A. F. Schinner, writing in Heming's *The Catholic Church in Wisconsin*, took an even harsher stance, arguing that the nativists attempted to destroy the successful Catholic schools via the Bennett Law. An "overt act of hostility" could not hurt the schools; rather a "measure was necessary that concealed hostile designs and gave color to them" such as the Bennett Law.[199] Claiming that at first glance the Law "seemed reasonable," Catholics and Lutherans later recognized its true intent. They regarded their parochial schools as their castles "as the Englishman does his home." Once they detected the true nature of the legislation, the bishops assumed leadership of protecting the parochial schools, the bulwark of Catholicism in Wisconsin, against state interference. The law:

> . . . seemed the narrow end of a wedge designed to lay the schools open to the chicanery of enemies; it was a blow aimed at religion; religion attacked by politics had a right to defend itself by politics. This the Bishops of Wisconsin recognized, and though reluctantly, from the bed of the dying Archbishop issued a combined protest. The blame, if there must be for this action, rests upon those who forced it upon them.[200]

Some Catholic thinkers argued that increased state activity, especially in education, would, unless checked, "ultimately culminate in a supreme state, fundamental in kind with old Rome."[201] The Bennett Law was viewed as the attempt by a tyrannical state to interfere with and control Catholic schools by legislating under what conditions private schools would be allowed to operate.[202] The Bennett Law was a measure that was constructed to "undermine altogether the liberty of education"; and loyal Catholics protested, "*in union with the Bishops*, from the love of *souls*, and the love of liberty."[203]

The Repeal of the Bennett Law

The election results of 1890 doomed the Bennett Law. In his *Message* to the legislature in 1891, newly elected Governor George W. Peck asserted that "The number of children in the state who do not attend school is in fact much smaller than has been represented in some quarters." The Bennett Law, he declared, has been "unwise and unnecessary" and a "source of much discussion and dissension." In some places it had resulted in "arbitrary and unjustifiable interference with parental rights, individual freedom and the liberty of conscience." Peck asked for its "prompt repeal" and charged that its "real underlying principle" was not "compulsory attendance at school, nor a wise advancement of popular education, but an assertion of the 'strong government' theory."[204]

His speech, by which he carried out the mandate of the November election, asserted that the Law would have destroyed "some of our private schools" and would "establish the right of the state as the dominant power in the state to dictate what, and what alone, all the children within its borders should be taught." A principle "more subversive of the most important protection of individual liberty, and the rights of conscience could scarcely be imagined." Schools "supported at private expense" should in no way "be interfered with by legislation." The "right of the citizen to educate his child in accordance with the dictates of his own conscience, without interference on the part of the state, should be recognized and defended."[205]

The legislature acted quickly. Humphrey J. Desmond, editor of the *Catholic Citizen*, and counsel for the Catholic plaintiffs in the Edgerton bible case, was chosen chairman of the Assembly's Education Committee.[206] On February 4, 1891 the legislature passed Chapter 4, "An Act to repeal Ch. 519 of the laws of the state of Wisconsin for the year 1889," which was entitled "An Act concerning the education and employment of children," known as the Bennett Law.[207] In its stead it enacted Chapter 187, entitled "An Act to promote school attendance and restrain truancy." This law eliminated the controversial district clause and the section that defined a school as one that taught specific subjects in the English language. It required twelve weeks attendance at a public or private school but did not apply to those who were "otherwise instructed."[208]

The bill to repeal the Bennett Law was the first bill to be introduced into the assembly in 1891.[209] Subsequently, Desmond recalled that there was considerable competition to repeal the Bennett Law. He stated that the drafting of the bill to replace it had been left to him, and he had proceeded by sending copies of his draft:

> . . . to various school officials, to the prominent Lutheran ministers who had taken an active part in the campaign, and also to prominent Catholic authorities, asking at the same time from all of these parties suggestions, and urging them to carefully examine the provision of the draft, to see that no personal rights were infringed. The draft came back to me from these various quarters with very slight and immaterial amendments.

The law that resulted from his efforts, Desmond declared, "is not what most compulsory laws are, and what the Bennett Law always was, a dead-letter law."[210]

Oliver E. Wells succeeded Jesse B. Thayer as Superintendent of Public Instruction in Wisconsin. Referring to private schools in his *1892 Report*, Wells wrote that it was the "tendency, though it may not be the purpose" of these schools, to "disintegrate and divide; to separate society into classes." He lamented the failure of parochial and private schools to report their attendance figures to his office and complained that "No private schools were reported from counties where they were known to exist." As a result, the State Superintendent was unable to accurately estimate the number of children in the state who were not receiving formal schooling.[211]

Catholics generally rejoiced in the repeal of the Bennett Law and the passage of the "Desmond Law" in its place. The *Catholic Citizen* said that the repeal made Wisconsin a "progressive state."[212] The nun-author, Sister Mileta Ludwig, remarked, with a certain finality, "With the passage of the 'Desmond Law' the parochial school system of the state was publicly vindicated and more firmly entrenched in the affections of Catholic people than ever before."[213] A long and arduous struggle was over. The Catholic bishops of Wisconsin and their Lutheran allies had emerged victorious. They had achieved a measure of independence for their schools, which they deemed absolutely necessary to their mission, from what they considered the unjustified onslaught of the civil state. They were, indeed, successful "dissenters," who objected to state efforts to regulate and perhaps eliminate their schools.

Notes

1.   Warren A. Nord, *Religion and American Education: Rethinking a National Dilemma*, Chapel Hill, NC: The University of North Carolina Press, 1995, 75.

2. "The President's Speech in Des Moines," *Catholic World* 22 (January 1876): 17.

3. Allen Sinclair Will, *The Life of Cardinal Gibbons*, I, New York: E. P. Dutton and Company, 1922, 161.

4. Alvin W. Johnson, *The Legal Status of Church-State Relationships in the Unites States.* Minneapolis, MN: The University of Minnesota Press, 1934, 21.

5. Ibid.

6. R. Freeman Butts, *The American Tradition in Religion and Education*, Boston: Beacon Press, 1950, 144.

7. Milo M. Quaife, ed., *The Attainment of Statehood*, Madison, WI: State Historical Society of Wisconsin, 1928, 931.

8. Ibid.

9. *Seventeenth Annual Report of the Superintendent of Public Instruction of the State of Wisconsin for the Year Ending August 31, 1865*, Madison, WI: Atwood and Rublee, 1865, 12.

10. *Annual Report of the Superintendent of Public Instruction of the State of Wisconsin for the Year Ending August 31, 1868*, Madison, WI: Atwood and Rublee, 1868, 6.

11. *Annual Report of the Superintendent of Public Instruction of the State of Wisconsin, for the School Year Ending August 31st, 1871*, Madison, WI: Atwood and Culver, 1872; *Annual Report of the Superintendent of Public Instruction of the State of Wisconsin, for the Year Ending August 31st, 1872*, Madison, WI: Atwood and Culver, 1873, 25.

12. *Annual Report of the Superintendent of Public Instruction of the State of Wisconsin, for the School Year Ending August 31st, 1872*, 287.

13. *Annual Report of the Superintendent of Public Instruction of the State of Wisconsin, for the School Year Ending August 31, 1873*, Madison, WI: Atwood and Culver, 1873, 31.

14. Ibid., 70–71.

15. Ibid., 71–72.

16. *The Laws of Wisconsin Passed at the Annual Session of the Legislature of 1879*, Madison, WI: David Atwood, State Printer, 1879, Chapter 121, 155.

17. *In Assembly. Journal of Proceedings of the Thirty-Fourth Annual Session of the Wisconsin Legislature, 1881*, Madison, WI: David Atwood, State Printer, 1881, 32.

18. *Annual Report of the State Superintendent of the State of Wisconsin, for the School Year Ending May 31, 1882*, Madison, WI: David Atwood, 1882, 11.

19. *The Laws of Wisconsin Passed at the Annual Session of the Legislature of 1882*, Madison, WI: David Atwood, State Printer, 1882, Chapter 298, 927–28.

20. Ibid., 928.

21. Personal correspondence from the Reverend Oscar J. Nauman, Wisconsin Evangelical Lutheran Synod, Milwaukee, January 28, 1971, 2.

22. *Sadliers' Catholic Directory, Almanac, and Ordo, For the Year of Our Lord 1882*, New York: D. J. Sadlier and Co., 1882, 570.

23. Ibid., 1884, 506.

24. *Decisions in Appeals. Wisconsin Superintendents of Public Instruction*, I, Madison, WI: State Historical Society of Wisconsin, February 17, 1854, 414.

25. Ibid.

26. *Decisions in Appeals*, II, June 6, 1859, 143.

27. *The Laws of Wisconsin 1869.* Chapter 50, Section 1, in *Laws of Wisconsin Relating to Common Schools, Normal Schools, and the State University*, Madison, WI: Atwood and Culver, Book

and Job Printer, 1870, 85.

28. Ibid.

29. Kate A. Everest, "How Wisconsin Came by Its Large German Element," in *Collections of the State Historical Society of Wisconsin, XII*, ed. Reuben G. Thwaites, Madison, WI: Democrat Printing Company, 1892, 308.

30. Thomas J. Jenkins, *The Judges of Faith: Christian versus Godless Schools*, Baltimore, MD: John Murphy and Co., 1886, 100.

31. Ibid., 99.

32. *Catholic Citizen*, April 22, 1882, 1.

33. James A. Biechler, "Kilian C. Flasch, Second Bishop of LaCrosse" (master's thesis, St. Paul Seminary, St. Paul, Minnesota, 1958), 1.

34. Ibid., 142.

35. *Sadliers' Catholic Directory, Almanac, and Ordo, For the Year of Our Lord 1880*, New York: D. J. Sadlier and Co., 1880, xxii.

36. Peter Guilday, *A History of the Councils of Baltimore, 1791–1884*, New York: Macmillan, 1932, 237.

37. "The Pastoral Letter of the Third Plenary Council of Baltimore," in *The National Pastorals of the American Hierarchy, 1792–1919*, ed. Peter Guilday, Washington, DC: The Newman Press, 1954, 244.

38. Ibid., 245.

39. Ibid., 246–47.

40. "Decrees of the Third Plenary Council of Baltimore," in *Catholic Education in America: A Documentary History*, ed. Neil G. McCluskey, New York: Teachers College Press, 1964, 93–94.

41. Sister M. Mileta Ludwig, *A Chapter of Franciscan History*, New York: Bookman Associates, 1950, 289.

42. Francis P. Cassidy, "Catholic Education in the Third Plenary Council of Baltimore," *The Catholic Historical Review* 34, Part 1 (October 1948): 303.

43. Biechler, "Kilian C. Flasch, Second Bishop of LaCrosse," 55.

44. *Catholic Citizen*, February 18, 1888, 1.

45. Ibid., February 26, 1887, 1.

46. Ibid., February 18, 1888, 4.

47. Ibid., February 19, 1887, 1.

48. Ibid., January 28, 1888, 4.

49. *Biennial Report of the State Superintendent of the State of Wisconsin, for the Two Years Ending June 30, 1886*, Madison, WI: Democrat Printing Company, 1886, 19.

50. *Catholic Citizen*, October 15, 1887, 4.

51. *Biennial Report of the State Superintendent of the State of Wisconsin, for the Two Years Ending June 30, 1888*, Madison, WI: Democrat Printing Company, 1888, 6–7.

52. Ibid., Appendix, 42.

53. William Dempster Hoard, *Governor's Message and Accompanying Documents of the State of Wisconsin, 1889*, Madison, WI: Democrat Printing Co., 1889, 18.

54. George W. Rankin, *William Dempster Hoard*, Fort Atkinson, WI: W. D. Hoard and Sons, 1925, 123–24.

55. Dwight L. Agnew, et al., eds., *Dictionary of Wisconsin Biography*, Madison, WI: The State Historical Society of Wisconsin, 1960, 172.

56. Rankin, *William Dempster Hoard*, 210.

57. *State of Wisconsin. Assembly Journal. Thirty-Ninth Session*, 1889, 34.

58. *Milwaukee Journal*, October 22, 1890, 4.

59. *The Laws of Wisconsin, Except City Charters and Their Amendments, Passed at the Biennial Session of the Legislature of 1889*, I, Madison, WI: Democrat Printing Company, State Printers, 1889, 729–33.

60. *Milwaukee Journal*, June 15, 1889, 1.

61. "Editorial," *Wisconsin Journal of Education* 19 (July 1889): 106–7.

62. *Milwaukee Sentinel*, December 29, 1889, 6.

63. *Catholic Citizen*, January 26, 1889, 4.

64. Ibid., April 6, 1889, 1.

65. Ibid., September 28, 1889, 4.

66. Ibid., January 4, 1890, 4.

67. Ibid., March 30, 1889, 4.

68. *Madison Democrat*, February 1, 1890, 1.

69. Kilian C. Flasch to Ludwig Missionverein, LaCrosse, February 20, 1889, in "Kilian C. Flasch, Second Bishop of LaCrosse," by Biechler, 61.

70. Pope Leo XIII, "Sapientiae Christianae," in *Social Wellsprings*, I, ed. Husslein, 144–59.

71. Ibid., 162.

72. *Compendium of the Eleventh Census: 1890, Part II*, Washington, DC: US Government Printing Office, 1894, 298–305.

73. *Report on Statistics of Churches in the United States at the Eleventh Census: 1890*, Washington, DC: US Government Printing Office, 1894, xx.

74. *Compendium of the Eleventh Census: 1890*, II, 120.

75. *Milwaukee Sentinel*, March 11, 1890, 4.

76. Ibid., March 12, 1890, 4.

77. John R. Beix, "Spiritual Values in the Life of Archbishop Michael Heiss" (master's thesis, St. Francis Seminary, Milwaukee, Wisconsin, 1935), 12.

78. Ludwig, *A Chapter of Franciscan History*, 291.

79. Benjamin J. Blied, *Three Archbishops of Milwaukee*, Milwaukee, WI: n.p., 1955, 51–54.

80. Harry H. Heming, *The Catholic Church in Wisconsin*, Milwaukee, WI: T. J. Sullivan, 1896, 263.

81. Ibid.

82. Ibid.

83. Ibid.

84. Ibid., 284–85.

85. Ibid., 286.

86. *Milwaukee Sentinel*, March 13, 1890, 4; March 14, 1890, 4; and March 15, 1890, 4.

87. Ibid., March 17, 1890, 4.

88. Ibid., March 15, 1890, 4.

89. Ibid., March 18, 1890, 4.

90. Ibid., March 13, 1890, 2.

91. Ibid., March 27, 1890, 2.
92. *Catholic Citizen*, March 15, 1890, 1.
93. Ibid., 4.
94. Ibid., March 22, 1890, 4.
95. Ibid., March 29, 1890, 1.
96. Agnew, et al., eds., *Dictionary of Wisconsin Biography*, 308–9.
97. *Milwaukee Sentinel,* March 22, 1890, 9.
98. Ibid., March 27, 1890, 4.
99. Ibid., March 28, 1890, 2.
100. Ibid., March 29, 1890, 4.
101. Ibid., March 30, 1890, 4
102. Ibid., March 27, 1890, 4.
103. Ibid., March 29, 1890, 4.
104. *Catholic Citizen*, March 29, 1890, 5.
105. Ibid.
106. *Milwaukee Sentinel*, April 1, 1890, 4.
107. Humphrey J. Desmond, "Early Irish Settlers in Wisconsin," *Wisconsin Magazine of History* 13 (June 1930): 370.
108. *Milwaukee Sentinel*, April 2, 1890, 4.
109. *Wisconsin State Journal*, April 2, 1890, 1.
110. *Milwaukee Journal*, April 2, 1890, 1.
111. *Madison Democrat*, April 3, 1890, 4.
112. *Wisconsin State Journal*, April 4, 1890, 1.
113. *Milwaukee Sentinel*, April 6, 1890, 11.
114. Ibid., March 19, 1890, 4.
115. Ibid., April 3, 1890, 4.
116. Ibid.
117. Ibid.
118. Ibid., April 6, 1890, 11.
119. Ibid.
120. *Catholic Citizen*, April 12, 1890, 4.
121. *Milwaukee Journal*, April 2, 1890, 1.
122. *Madison Democrat*, April 11, 1890, 1.
123. *Catholic Citizen*, April 12, 1890, 4.
124. Ibid., April 10, 1890, 4.
125. Heming, *The Catholic Church in Wisconsin*,1082.
126. *Milwaukee Sentinel*, May 28, 1890, 1.
127. Ibid.
128. Ibid.
129. Ibid.
130. Ibid.
131. Ibid.
132. Ibid., May 29, 1890, 4.
133. Frederick Xavier Katzer, *The Bennett Law.* Newspaper clippings, dated May 29, 1890. A bound scrapbook in the Library of the State Historical Society of Wisconsin, Madison.

134. *Wisconsin State Journal*, June 27, 1890, 1.
135. Jesse B. Thayer, "Discussion," *National Education Association Journal of Proceedings and Addresses* (Session of the Year 1890), 196–97.
136. Ibid., 196.
137. Ibid., 198–99.
138. Ibid., 199.
139. Christian. Koerner, *The Bennett Law and the German Protestant Parochial Schools of Wisconsin*, Milwaukee, WI: Germania Publishing Company, 1890, 9–18.
140. Rasmus B. Anderson, with the assistance of Albert D. Barton, *Life Story of Rasmus B. Anderson*, Madison, WI: n.p., 1917, 595.
141. Bradley C. Schey, "Letter to the Editor," *The Nation* L, 1290 (March 20, 1890): 2.
142. Rankin, *William Dempster Hoard*, 131.
143. *Milwaukee Sentinel*, May 31, 1890, 1.
144. Ibid., June 3, 1890, 1.
145. *The Bennett Law*. Newspaper clippings, dated April 3, 1890. A scrapbook in the library of the State Historical Society of Wisconsin, Madison.
146. *Milwaukee Sentinel*, July 7, 1890, 7.
147. *Minutes of the Wisconsin Annual Conference of the Methodist Episcopal Church, Forty-Fourth Session, 1890*. John Schuster, editor and publisher, 1890, 56–57.
148. *Minutes of the Synod of Wisconsin of the Presbyterian Church 1890*, Madison, WI: Tracy, Gibbs and Co. 1890, 8–14.
149. Rev. Joseph H. Crooker, *The Public School and The Catholics*, Madison, WI: H. A. Taylor, Printer and Stereotyper, 1890, 3.
150. Ibid., 4–6.
151. Ibid., 15.
152. "Wisconsin—Republican State Platform, 1890," in *The Blue Book of the State of Wisconsin. 1891*, compiled and published under direction of Thomas J. Cunningham, Secretary of State, 1891, 390.
153. "Democratic State Platform—Adopted August 27, 1890," in *The Blue Book of the State of Wisconsin. 1891*, compiled and published under the direction of Thomas J. Cunningham, Secretary of State, 1891, 393–94.
154. *Catholic Citizen*, October 4, 1890, 1.
155. Ibid., 4.
156. Ibid., October 11, 1890, 1.
157. *Milwaukee Sentinel*, October 18, 1890, 1.
158. Ibid., November 1, 1890, 3.
159. Ibid., November 3, 1890, 8.
160. Ibid., November 4, 1890, 3.
161. *Catholic Citizen*, November 1, 1890, 4.
162. *Milwaukee Journal*, November 6, 1890, 6.
163. *Milwaukee Sentinel*, November 5, 1890, 1, 4.
164. Ibid., November 6, 1890, 1, 4.
165. *Catholic Citizen*, November 8, 1890, 1, 4.
166. William F. Raney, *Wisconsin: A Story of Progress*, New York: Prentice Hall, 1940, 272–73.

167. Ibid., 273; Roger E. Wyman, "Wisconsin Ethnic Groups and the Election of 1890," *Wisconsin Magazine of History* 51 (Summer 1968): 289–90.

168. *The Blue Book of the State of Wisconsin. 1889*, compiled and published under direction of Ernest G. Timms, Secretary of State, 1889, 227–29; *The Blue Book of the State of Wisconsin. 1891*, compiled and published under direction of Thomas J. Cunningham, Secretary of State, 1891, 255–57; *The Blue Book of the State of Wisconsin. 1893*, compiled and published under direction of Thomas J. Cunningham, Secretary of State, 1893, 239–40.

169. William F. Whyte, "The Bennett Law Campaign," *Wisconsin Magazine of History* 10 (June 1927): 366.

170. Kate Everest Levi, "Geographical Origin of German Immigration to Wisconsin," in *Collections of the State Historical Society of Wisconsin, XIV*, ed. Reuben G. Thwaites, Madison, WI: Democrat Printing Co., 1898, 344–47.

171. *Reports of the Immigration Commission. Statistical Review of Immigration, 1820–1910. Distribution of Immigrants, 1850–1900*. III, New York: Arno Press and the New York Times, 1970, 471, 484, 430.

172. Ibid., 522.

173. Herbert F. Margulis, *The Decline of the Progressive Movement in Wisconsin, 1890–1920*, Madison, WI: The State Historical Society of Wisconsin, 1968, 3.

174. Kellogg, "The Bennett Law in Wisconsin," 11–12.

175. Colman J. Barry, *The Catholic Church and German Americans*, Milwaukee, WI: The Bruce Publishing Co., 1953, 11.

176. Edward Wakin and Joseph F. Scherer, *The De-Romanization of the American Catholic Church*, New York: The Macmillan Company, 1966, 60.

177. *The New York Times*, June 20, 1890, 1.

178. Barry, *The Catholic Church and German Americans*, 36–37.

179. Sister M. Mileta Ludwig, *Right-Hand Glove Uplifted: A Biography of Archbishop Michael Heiss*, New York: Pageant Press, Inc., 1967, 503.

180. Wyman, "Wisconsin Ethnic Groups and the Election of 1890," 269–71.

181. Whyte, "The Bennett Law Campaign," 337.

182. Barry, *The Catholic Church and German Americans*, 202–3.

183. Isaac Thomas, "The Bennett Law: Compulsory Education in Wisconsin," *The New Englander* 54 (February 1891): 137.

184. J. J. Mapel, "The Repeal of the Compulsory Education Laws in Wisconsin and Illinois," *Educational Review* 1 (January 1891): 56–57.

185. William F. Vilas, "The 'Bennett Law' in Wisconsin," *Forum* 12 (October 1891): 198–99.

186. Ibid., 199–200.

187. Ibid., 205, 201.

188. Whyte, "The Bennett Law Campaign," 388.

189. Ibid., 389.

190. William Dempster Hoard, "The Farmer as Citizen," in the Hoard Papers, in the Archives of the Library of the State Historical Society of Wisconsin, Madison.

191. Ibid.

192. Ibid.

193. Letter from Ellis B. Usher to William Dempster Hoard, dated August 27, 1917, in the Hoard Papers, in the Archives of the Library of the State Historical Society of Wisconsin, Madison.

194. Letter from William Dempster Hoard to Ellis B. Usher, dated August 29, 1917, in the Hoard Papers, in the Archives of the Library of the State Historical Society of Wisconsin, Madison.

195. Rasmus B. Anderson, with the Assistance of Albert D. Barton, *Life Story of Rasmus B. Anderson*, Madison, WI: 1917. Appendix: Letter from William Dempster Hoard to Rasmus B. Anderson, dated December 23, 1915.

196. Letter from William Dempster Hoard to Professor Rasmus B. Anderson, dated December 31, 1915, in the Hoard Papers, in the Archives of the Library of the State Historical Society of Wisconsin, Madison.

197. Humphrey J. Desmond, *The A.P.A. Movement*, Washington, DC: The New Century Press, 1912, 11–13.

198. Ellis B. Usher, *Wisconsin: Its Story and Biography, III*, Chicago: The Lewis Publishing Co., 1914, 544.

199. Heming, *The Catholic Church in Wisconsin*, 281.

200. Ibid., 282.

201. Conde B. Pallen, "A Conservative View of the Church's Social Mission" (1890), in *American Catholic Thought on Social Questions*, ed. Aaron A. Abell, Indianapolis, IN: The Bobbs-Merrill Co., Inc., 1968, 206.

202. E. A. Higgins, "The American State and the Private School," *Catholic World* 52 (July 1891): 527.

203. Joseph Schroeder, "The Catholic German Congress at Pittsburgh," *Catholic World* 52 (December 1890): 269.

204. George W. Peck, "Governor's Message," in *Governor's Message and Accompanying Documents of the State of Wisconsin, 1891, I*, Madison, WI: Democrat Printing Company, State Printers, 1891, 12–13.

205. Ibid., 13–14.

206. *The Blue Book of the State of Wisconsin, 1891*, 559.

207. *The Laws of Wisconsin, Passed at the Biennial Session of the Legislature of 1891, I*, Madison, WI: Democrat Printing Company, State Printer, Chapter 4, 3.

208. Ibid., Chapter 187, 217–18.

209. *State of Wisconsin. In Assembly. 1891.* January 20, 1891, No. 2A.

210. Heming, *The Catholic Church in Wisconsin*, 287.

211. *Biennial Report of the State Superintendent of the State of Wisconsin, for the Yeas Ending June 30, 1892*, Madison, WI: Democrat Printing Co., 1892, 13, 17–18.

212. *Catholic Citizen*, January 30, 1891, 1.

213. Ludwig, *A Chapter of Franciscan History*, 294.

· 5 ·

QUESTIONING THE
PREVAILING ORTHODOXY

Bible-Reading and the Edgerton Decision

The bitter conflict between the civil authority and backers of church-affiliated schools as witnessed in Chapter 4 over the Bennett Law was not the only educational strife in nineteenth-century Wisconsin. A group of Catholics in the city of Edgerton challenged the Protestant-driven practice of the devotional reading of the King James version of the Bible in that city's public schools. The conflict ultimately resulted in the decision of the Wisconsin Supreme Court in 1890 that has become known as the "Edgerton decision," the first of its kind in the nation, which outlawed that reading as constituting sectarian instruction.

The Bible in American Schools

The Bible held a cherished place in American society at the time of the Revolution. Its reading in schools was strongly advocated by leaders such as Benjamin Rush who wrote that "there is no book of its size in the whole world, that contains half so much useful knowledge for the government of state, or the direction of the affairs of individuals as the Bible."[1] Noah Webster, while he was opposed to the reading of the Bible in schools (he felt it would breed contempt for the word of God), nonetheless wanted it included in schools to be "used as a system of religion and morality."[2]

The Bible's use in the nation's schools received considerable support as the nineteenth century progressed. For instance, the American Bible Society, founded in 1816, stated its main purpose was to foster the Bible as a school book.[3] In 1839 and again in 1840 it pledged that the Scriptures would be read in every classroom in the nation.[4]

Conflicts with Catholics over the reading of the King James version of Scripture occurred in a number of locations. These clashes led one New York City minister to proclaim in 1840 that "I would rather be an infidel than a papist."[5] A Protestant leader of that era, the Rev. Horace Bushnell, pronounced that it was a "sacred duty" for all Christians to secure for the Bible a "proper place" in society and its schools.[6] Struggles with Catholics over the place of the Bible in schools led the Ohio Presbyterian and Congregational Convention to state in 1844 that the "liberty to worship God according to the dictates of conscience" cannot, "by any principle of legitimate interpretation, be construed into a right to embarrass the municipal authorities of this Christian and Protestant nation in the ordering of their district schools."[7] Perhaps the most notable of these conflicts was in Philadelphia, where Bishop Kenrick obtained permission of the Philadelphia School Board for Catholic children to read the Douay version of the Bible. Nativists rioted, with two deaths and considerable property destruction, in response to this decision.[8]

The King James version of the Bible, with its devotional reading and attendant practices, occupied a prominent place in the moral education of Horace Mann, often called the "Father" of the American common school. Accused of being nonreligious, the Unitarian Mann replied that he never had any thought to exclude the Bible, just to keep out the socially destructive presence of sectarianism. The Bible, as the "exponent of Christianity," makes known the "truths, which, according to the faith of Christians, are able to make men wise unto salvation." If this "Bible is in the schools, how can it be said that Christianity is excluded from the schools; . . . wherever the Bible might go, there the system of Christianity must be."[9] The practice of devotional Bible-reading epitomized the religious nature of the allegedly nonsectarian common school across the nation. With the passage of time, however, conflicts arose over its use in schools. It was to be in the state of Wisconsin where that conflict reached the Supreme Court for an official judgment of its constitutionality. Catholics were to be legally successful in their dissent from the majoritarian view of the practice.

Wisconsin at the Time of Statehood

In the 1840s, as the Wisconsin Territory became more inhabited and more organized, a movement toward the establishment of common schools took root and
began to grow. Reflecting the ideas of Mann, one approach looked on such
schools as the vehicle by which the heterogeneous elements of the area's population could be assimilated.[10] The Constitutional Convention of 1846 sought
to establish free schools. Its Education Committee, in an "Article on education,
schools and school funds," reported on November 25, 1846 as follows:

> Section 4. The legislature shall provide for a system of common schools, which will
> be as nearly uniform as may be throughout the state, and inasmuch as the public schools
> should be equally free to children of all religious persuasions, no book of religious doc-
> trine or belief and no sectarian instruction shall be used or permitted in any public
> school.[11]

The ensuing discussion resulted in a revision of Section 4, with the words "No
book of religious doctrine or belief" being deleted, "after some discussion,"
according to one participant.[12] Subsequent comments by government and educational leaders bolster the argument that the elimination of the words "no book
of religious doctrine or belief" meant that reading the Bible in public schools
was not considered sectarian instruction. In this way, one writer reasoned,
"The sectarian disputes which distracted and disgraced New York are forever
obviated."[13]

The 1846 Constitution was rejected by Wisconsin voters. Two years later,
however, they approved a revised constitution. This document proclaimed
religious liberty in Article I, Section 18, which, among other points, prohibited the use of public funds for religious purposes.[14] Article X, Section 3, prohibited any "sectarian instruction" to be used in the common schools.[15] The
words "no book of religious doctrine or belief" were omitted, H. C. Whitford
claimed in his commentary on the constitution, because they would have
"excluded the Bible."[16] The reading of the Bible, thus, was not considered to
be sectarian.

In 1850, two years after statehood had been attained, the population of
Wisconsin stood at 305,391. Of this number 54,332 were natives of the state;
139,366 had been born elsewhere in the United States, and 110,471 were of
foreign origin.[17] Catholic sources reported "about 40,000" members in 1848,[18]
and "about 100,000" in 1855.[19] *The Catholic Directory* for 1855 testified to the
inaccuracy of its statistics when it stated that the "figures of population" were

those "reported by the Bishop, but as they are not complete, we forebear any estimate of the total number of Catholics in the United States, in regard to which there exists so vast a difference of opinion."[20]

State documents of that period also help identify the religious tone of the age. For instance, Chapter 51, Section 8 of *The Revised Statutes of Wisconsin* of 1849 held masters responsible "for teaching the apprentice to read and write, . . . and that the master will give to such apprentice, at the expiration of his or her service, a new Bible."[21] Chapter 153, Section 8 of those *Statutes* mandates that prison-keepers will "provide, at the expense of the county," a Bible for each prisoner who is "able and desirous to read" during his confinement, and the prisoners will have "access" to ministers at "seasonable and proper times."[22] Section 5 of Chapter 102 lists the "family Bible" first among the articles of personal property that are exempt from seizure by public authorities on the occasion of a person's execution.[23]

The *Statutes* also addressed the matter of sectarian instruction in common schools. Section 48 of Chapter 9 held the state superintendent of public instruction responsible to "discourage the use of sectarian books and sectarian instruction in the schools."[24] Chapter 19, Section 39 said that the District Board "shall have the power, under the advice of the state superintendent of public instruction, to determine what school and text books shall be used in the several branches taught in the school of each district."[25]

The Constitution designated the state superintendent of public instruction as the chief educational officer of the state. Hence, their *Reports*, and their *Decisions in Appeals*, are of considerable weight in educational matters. Cumulatively, these documents support the contention that in the early years of statehood the Bible not only occupied an exalted place in the schools but also that its use was not considered sectarian instruction.[26] State Superintendent Eleazar Root decided that it was permissible for a teacher to pray in public schools, terming this practice "one of the most beneficial exercises that can be introduced."[27] "Religious education," as distinguished from sectarian instruction, rested on the fact that "all religions are grounded upon simple and universal truths and reinforced duties of which the human mind has an intuitive perception."[28] Schooling would be incomplete if it neglected a "just knowledge and love of those wholesome truths which form the basis of all religions."[29]

Azel P. Ladd, a New Hampshire native, succeeded Root.[30] Responding to an appeal in 1852 Ladd averred that "there can be no doubt, under our laws, of the Bible being a lawful book to be read in common schools."[31] Sectarian books, on the other hand, were not to be placed in school libraries and if present, should be replaced with books "adapted alike to the use of all religious per-suasions."[32] Ladd presented his view of the nonsectarian role of the common school in his 1853 *Report*. It offered education on "common ground upon which all sects and parties can meet," apart from sectarian rivalries, and free of ecclesiastical and political control.[33]

A Trend Toward Religious Heterogeneity

Based on the advice given an appellant in 1854, it is evident that some Wisconsin citizens were voicing opposition to the religious programs in com-mon schools as the 1850s progressed. H. A. Wright, state superintendent, advised prudence and to "discontinue the use of the Bible and the exercise of prayer" in schools if "such book and exercises are objected to by the parents or guardians of any child attending such school." Wright regretted that family ill-ness prevented him from giving an elaborate opinion on the subject, which he stated was "assuming more prominence."[34] Several months later he admitted that his predecessors had felt the Bible to be a lawful book for school use, but in his opinion it "should be subject to many restrictions," since the "common English version is wholly repudiated by a very large class of our population."[35] He declared that because of the strained situations that could develop in the classroom the teacher could not require the Bible to be read as a matter of school discipline, and wondered if "it is right that the scholars should be com-pelled to listen to that which their consciences tell them is repugnant to the doctrines of their Church." Wright wanted the school to be neutral in religious matters, limiting instruction to the intellectual and to the propagation of prin-ciples that all sects and no sects can equally agree on. What these were, how-ever, he did not state. Religious instruction should be limited to the family, Sabbath school and church.[36]

Wright's successor was A. Constantine Barry, a New York native and Universalist minister, who came to the position following a stint as Racine, Wisconsin's first school superintendent.[37] Believing that "too much attention cannot be paid to the development of the moral nature," Barry called on the schools "to be nurseries of goodness as well as learning."[38] Barry opined that learning was of no benefit at all, in fact it could be directed towards evil, unless it was "under the guidance and control of moral principles." Man's moral nature, he held, was his "divinest part."[39]

The Bible-reading issue surfaced again in 1858 during the term of Lyman C. Draper. Originating in Watertown, it resulted in the banning of the Bible from the public schools there. Draper had contended that the recitation of the Lord's Prayer and the reading of the Bible were not sectarian practices, believing that the people of Wisconsin would not consent to the banishment of the Bible from their schools:

> . . . and thus virtually repudiate its unequalled teachings of virtue and morality as unfit for the instruction and guidance of the children of their love—children who, at no distant day, must become the rulers and law-givers of the state, and custodian of all that we now hold dear and sacred, our homes, our country, Christianity and the Bible.[40]

Draper maintained that the teacher's most ennobling act was to teach moral virtue, but she was to take care not to make any sectarian comments in the process. It was up to the District Board to determine which version of the Bible to read, either the "common version" or the "Catholic edition," but at all costs "let the Bible be read, whatever be the version, reverently and impressively, and the blessing of the God of the Bible will never fail to attend it."[41] The use of the Bible in schools was "pre-eminently first in importance among textbooks for teaching the noblest principles of virtue, morality, patriotism and good order—love and reverence for God—charity and good will to man."[42] On the eve of his retirement, Draper defended his position on the role of the Bible, advocating for "moral, and as earnestly deprecating sectarian, instruction in our public schools, and pleading for the sacred preservation of the school fund, consecrated to the education of our children."[43]

Implications of the Changing
Population Patterns in Wisconsin

The Bible retained its prominent role in the schools of the state. Rev. Charles Brooks, writing in the *Wisconsin Journal of Education*, penned that "God is our teacher and the Bible our class book" in 1856.[44] Addressing the Wisconsin teachers Convention in 1859 the Rev. M. P. Kinney claimed that the Bible, the "book of God," belongs "by divine grant" to every human. It has an "equal right to the school-room with the air which the same God has made."[45]

Josiah L. Pickard occupied the post of state superintendent from 1860–1864. His memoirs, published posthumously, contain the statement that "The subject of religious exercises in schools was more frequently presented than any other."[46] During his term Pickard wrote that "bad morals and bad manners" were the "chief obstacles" to the progress of the common schools.[47] A year later he observed that the permanence of the nation depended on a "large, liberal and truly Christian basis" of the public schools.[48] As A. J. Craig, Pickard's assistant made clear, the superintendent's office ruled that Bible-reading could not be considered sectarian instruction.[49]

The Bible occupied a place in the "recommended textbook" section of the superintendents' *Reports* in the 1860s. It was listed, sometimes accompanied by Cowdery's *Moral Lessons*, under the textbooks to be used in "Moral Instruction."[50] The *Wisconsin Journal of Education* attested to the belief of the allegedly nonsectarian moral education role of the Bible in infusing Christian virtues in 1864: "There is enough—thank God there is enough—of common Christian ground in the Bible, for all sects to meet on and cultivate the spirit of Christian truth, love and brotherhood, without impaling themselves on sectarian points of irrevocably diverging into sectarian by-paths."[51]

John McMynn, who in 1861 had described the mission of teachers as "imparting moral and religious instruction, and in Christianizing the people," became superintendent in 1864.[52] The New York-born McMynn recommended Wayland's *Moral Lessons* for a textbook, which was an example of Protestant Christianity. For instance, it quoted Chillingworth's "The Bible, The Bible, The Religion of Protestants," and then stated that "What is contained here alone is binding upon conscience."[53] In Wayland's view, the New Testament was "intended for the whole human race," being a "final revelation of the will of God to man." It contained "all the moral precepts both of natural religion and of the Old Testament, together with whatever else" was important to "our salvation that we should know."[54]

The common schools, in McMynn's eyes, were the instruments Christianity demanded to save the republic and to promote morality and the good of all.[55] The common schools were to advance religion and morality, "without usurping the office of preacher, . . . by imparting the leading truths of the Bible, and thus laying the foundations for parent and minister of the gospel to build upon."[56]

Emerging Population Patterns in Wisconsin in 1870

The 1870 Census reveals the evolutionary trend in the composition of Wisconsin's population. Of the 1,064,985 inhabitants of the state, 364,499 were foreign-born, but even more noteworthy is that 717,832 had one or both parents foreign-born. Of those with foreign nativities, 162,314 hailed from

Germany.[57] To add to the diversity there was now a significant Lutheran presence in the state.[58] The Catholic population had grown to around 250,000.[59]

In 1870 Samuel Fallows was installed as state superintendent of schools. A Colonel in the "God and Morality" regiment in the Civil War, Fallows was a Methodist minister and the Secretary of the Wisconsin Methodist Conference for several years prior to 1870.[60] That same year the Methodists for the first time officially took note of the changing religious complexion of the state. They issued a forceful statement on the relation of the Church to the common schools. They declared that the common-school system was the offspring of the Bible; popular education existed only among Evangelical Protestants with Christianity alone capable of furnishing the inspirational base for the system's existence; Protestant Christianity, since it had founded and maintained the system had incurred duties to it, "It is especially bound to resist, and, if possible, to repel the assaults now made upon the system from whatever source or whatever pretext." There were two assailants. First, the atheists, who wanted to replace the "present healthy balancing and counterbalancing of various religious sects" with the "control of one great irreligious sect." Second, the Roman Catholics, who wished to make religious instruction in schools that "rigidly sectarian and exclusive type which is inconsistent with all freedom of thought or of conscience." The Catholics "demand the abolition of the system itself and the setting up in its place of denominational schools."[61]

Having identified the enemies of the common schools and their aims, the Methodists proceeded to attack these groups and their goals and to defend the Bible-based, but in their eyes, nonsectarian schools. They termed the effort to exclude the Bible a "very shallow one." They argued that the "cherished convictions of a great people" should not be "sacrificed to the abnormal prejudice and caprices of exceptional individuals, the majority of whom have come among us to avail themselves of advantages and privileges" which are the direct offspring of a system whose main features and essential elements they seek to destroy.[62] The moral and religious principles contained in the Bible are "indispensable to the formation of the manly and womanly character which is the true end of all education." The church's duty to the besieged common-school system, with so much at stake, was, the Methodists resolved, "totally obvious." It must "maintain and cherish the system," not forsaking it for any denominational schools. Methodists must insist that the "religious principles of the Bible," which have been the "basis and inspiration of the system from the beginning," must continue to "inform and animate it," in the interest of a "broad, Catholic, symmetrical culture."[63]

The Methodists were not alone in their defense of the Bible as the foundation of morality and allegedly nonsectarian Christianity in the common schools. In 1873 John B. Pradt, Assistant Superintendent of Instruction and an Episcopal clergyman responded to the query "Ought the Bible be read in the school, if any object?" He replied that the framers of the state's constitution did not consider the "judicious reading of the Bible in the school" to constitute sectarian instruction. Rather, it has been "customary from the earliest history of our common schools for the Bible to be read in them." For dissenters to the practice, Pradt counseled that their "rights and wishes" can hardly be considered to be of more weight than those who are upholding the tradition.[64]

There was, however, growing opposition to "Protestant" public schools in the decade of the 1870s. This view represented the growing number of persons in the state, still a minority, who looked to Republicanism rather than to Christianity as the spiritual foundation of public education.[65]

Furthermore, the 1880 Census revealed that the foreign-born population of the state had continued to increase significantly. Among the state's 1,315,497 residents, there were 405,425 who had been born in foreign countries, 184,328 of these in Germany.[66] The presence of these people led to conflicts with mainstream Protestants, i.e., Baptists, Congregationalists, Methodists, and Presbyterians, over the practice of the devotional reading of the Bible in public schools. Partially as a result of these clashes, and partially due to the growing secular spirit in the country in general and in education in particular, educators more and more began to speak of a distinction between morality and religion.[67] Religion was the province of home and church, while morality, separated from revealed religion, was in the sphere of the public schools. Disagreement mounted then, as to what constituted "sectarian instruction," with a consequent impact on school policy.

The laws and bills of the Wisconsin legislature during this period provide some supportive evidence for the secularizing trend in education. In 1878, Mr. H. Smith introduced Assembly Bill 91A in the legislature, "To prohibit religious instruction, prayers and the reading of the Bible in the Universities named, and the public schools of the state of Wisconsin."[68] This bill was defeated by a vote of forty-eight to thirty, with twenty-two members absent or not voting. [69] That same year a proposal by Senator Hudd, to "allow the right of conscience in matters of religious belief in State Institutions," was denied engrossment by a vote of sixteen to eleven, with six not voting.[70] The city of Milwaukee, home for many of the German immigrants, was the scene of conflict over the religious issue in education. (In 1880, Milwaukee's population was

115,587, of whom 46,073, approximately forty percent, were foreign-born.[71])
In 1878 the Milwaukee Common Council proposed that features such as "lectures by clergymen, reading the Bible, moral lessons, singing of hymns, etc." be
banned from the public schools by the state legislature in its next session.[72]

It is not surprising then, that when the state of Wisconsin was asked to
legally incorporate the German and English Academy in Milwaukee in 1880
that it did so only on condition that "no sectarian instruction whatever shall
be given, and no religious test required of teachers and scholars."[73] Several years
later the legislature enacted legislation that reflected the growing concern
over textbooks when it passed a law that read "But no text book shall be permitted in any free public school which would have a tendency to inculcate sectarian ideas."[74] While "sectarian ideas" and "sectarian instruction" remained
undefined at this time, it is well to note that state officials connected with the
common schools, especially the state superintendents, were counseling those
who asked questions about religious practices in schools to discontinue Bible-
reading, hymn-singing, and prayer if their practice caused strife in the
community.

Prelude to Edgerton

As the nineteenth century moved toward its end, district school boards, especially in a state like Wisconsin with such ethnic and religious diversity, found
less common ground in religion among their constituents and less agreement
as to what constituted "sectarian instruction." It should not come as a surprise
then, that Catholic petitioners Frederick Weiss, W. R. Morrissey, Thomas
Mooney, Jason McBride, J. G. Burns, and John Corbett brought suit on behalf
of their children who were pupils in the public school of the city of Edgerton,
Wisconsin against the District Board No. Eight of the City of Edgerton, over
the reading of the King James version of the Bible in that city's school.
(Hereafter the petitioners, Weiss, et al., will be referred to as the petitioners,
plaintiffs, or relators; the school board will be referred to as the school board,
the board, or the defendants; the case will either be called Weiss or Edgerton.)

The Edgerton case was not the first time that the reading of the Bible in
common schools had been the subject of litigation. Among the important
decisions made by other state courts on the subject prior to Edgerton were:
Donahoe v. Richards, 38 Me. 376 (1854), *Spiller v. Inhabitants of Woburn*, 94 Mass.
127 (1866), *Board of Education of Cincinnati v. Minor et al.*, 23 Ohio st. 211
(1872), and *Moore v. Monroe* 64 Ia. 367 (1884).

In *Donahoe*, the Maine Court upheld the right of the school to select the Bible as a textbook and to expel a student who refused to read it as such even though he claimed a violation of conscience.[75] In *Spiller*, the Massachusetts court said the school was within its rights when it required each student to bow his or her head during the daily reading of the Bible and the recitation of prayers. The court ruled that this was a reasonable rule, that the children were not required to take an active part in the exercises, and that the practice was neither a devotional nor a religious rite.[76] In *Minor*, the Ohio State Supreme Court reversed the lower Superior Court and ruled that religious instruction, including Bible-reading, was not required by the Ohio constitution. It did not, however, rule the practice unconstitutional.[77] In *Moore*, the Iowa court upheld the practice of the teacher reading the Bible in school, with no student compelled to be present, and it deemed the argument of "inconvenience" of children excusing themselves from the exercises of little weight.[78]

In 1883, the Wisconsin legislature enacted a law that forbade the use of textbooks in the public schools that would have a "tendency to inculcate sectarian instruction."[79] Court decisions that dealt with the issue at least indirectly, one before and one after the law was passed, were *Morrow v. Wood*, 35 Wis. 59 (1874), and *The State of Wisconsin ex. rel. John Kehoe v. Emma Freeman, Teacher, and the District Board of West Point, Columbia County*. In *Morrow*, the Wisconsin Supreme Court ruled that a pupil cannot be required to pursue a study when the parents request that he be excused from so doing.[80] In 1886 in *Kehoe*, Judge Stewart denied the school board the right to expel a student for refusing to abide by a rule that required pupils to keep their books closed during Bible-reading, and ruled that the "board and the teacher transcended their power in making and enforcing the order." The *Catholic Citizen*, in commenting on the decision, remarked that too many Catholic parents were "ignorant and timid," and should take heart in Kehoe's victorious fight over his bigoted opponents.[81] In the *Citizen's* eyes, the decision in *Kehoe* was a step in making the schools become what they said they were, "unsectarian—and not Methodist Sunday Schools under false pretenses." It felt a lasting settlement of the problem of religious practices in the schools, due to the frequency of occurrence, would come only with a "definitive prohibition of Bible reading, hymn singing and Methodist services in the public schools."[82] It was at this juncture that the *Citizen* received an offer of assistance from an unlikely source, a noted Milwaukee liberal, Robert G. Spencer, who volunteered the support of "free-thinkers and large body of Protestants" should "our Catholic fellow citizens inaugurate a movement in favor of legislation against the practice justly complained of."[83]

The *Citizen* reported that Judge Stewart had criticized the State Superintendent of Schools, Robert Graham, because he had not held a hearing in the case. Graham defended his actions in a letter to the *Citizen* with the assertion that the Constitution had placed the responsibility for those decisions on the district board, and for the courts to then judge their constitutionality. Graham wrote that if he had been asked for his opinion he would have declared that the rule requiring books to be closed during the reading of the Bible was unconstitutional, and that no student should be expelled for persistent refusal to comply with the order to close his or her book.[84]

The Edgerton Case Is Opened

In Edgerton, on Friday, November 12, 1886, the *Wisconsin Tobacco Reporter* referred to the case at West Point as "similar to the one brought by certain Catholic citizens" against the district board of the city.[85] This action by the Edgerton residents had been referred to several months earlier by the *Citizen* which offered its appraisal of the situation: "The liberal-minded citizens of Edgerton, Wisconsin, have been obliged to resort to the courts in order to protect their children from the sectarian inquisition at present established in the tax-payers' public school at that place."[86] The Edgerton school board had refused to halt several teachers who were reading portions of the King James version of the Bible in their classes in the free common school of Edgerton, although no disciplinary requirement was involved. Accordingly, Weiss, et al. sought a writ of mandamus from the District Court of Rock County, ordering the Board to stop the practice because, as Roman Catholics, they believed said version was incorrect and incomplete; that the Scriptures should not be read indiscriminately, that is, without the infallible interpretation provided by the divinely appointed Catholic Church; that such reading is likely to lead to errors of faith and worship, thus contrary to the rights of conscience of the Catholics and accordingly in violation of Section 3, Article X, of the Wisconsin Constitution.[87]

The Board, in its answer, admitted the Edgerton residency of the petitioners, the practice of Bible-reading by two teachers during school hours, and the presence of several of the relators' children in those classes. However, it stated that they were free to withdraw if they so desired. The Board denied that the Catholic Church is the sole interpreter of the Scriptures and asserted that each person had the right to read and interpret the Bible for himself, which, they said, made the claim of the petitioners sectarian. Further, the Board denied that the reading violated anyone's rights of conscience, that it constituted sectarian instruction, and that it was forbidden by Section 3 of Article X of the constitution. The Board also alleged that it had no authority to stop the practice. It asserted that the King James version of the Bible contained no provision that was not in the Douay, or Catholic version, but since both were merely translations of the Bible there were no material differences between them. The Board's response listed the actual verses read and declared these were not sectarian. It continued its response by alluding to the fact that the Board had the right to select textbooks for use in the school, and that the King James version of the Bible was on that list as recommended by the state superintendent. Thus, it was lawfully selected by the Board for the purpose of general instruction, not sectarian instruction. Further, the Board maintained that the vast majority of the people of the District were Protestant and desired the King James version to be used in school; that the Bible was a text unable to be replaced by any other book; and that it played an important part in the youngsters' education.[88]

When the case reached the Circuit Court, the *Tobacco Reporter* referred to it as "likely to interest Edgerton people."[89] In the summer of 1888, some Edgerton citizens apparently were upset with the $75.00 required to retain an attorney on behalf of the Board. In the "Annual School Report" the plaintiffs and the Board accused each other of precipitating the legal action. The Board, through the clerk, blamed the plaintiffs; the latter retaliated by charging the Board with "inaction and insolence in their official capacity" by which it "invited litigation and left the plaintiffs no other means of redress." The plaintiffs claimed that teachers had for years required children to listen to the reading of the Bible or be punished, and that their complaints had fallen on deaf ears, including a petition from forty taxpayers to the Board. They felt that "might made right" with the Edgerton School Board, and they intended to press their case to the State Supreme Court if they received an adverse decision at the Circuit Court level. The real culprits were the Board members, they charged, and they resented the attempts of the Clerk to place the onus of the cost to the taxpayers on them.[90]

Meanwhile the *Catholic Citizen* attempted to awaken the interest of Catholics in the state to the case. Calling it a "trial which may 'make law' for every school district in the state," it praised the role played by the Catholic pastor of Edgerton, Father Bowe, who advised the Catholics not to drop their suit during the two years it took to reach a decision in the circuit court.[91]

The Circuit Court Decision and Its Aftermath

John R. Bennett, born in New York of Puritan stock and a staunch Republican, was presiding judge over the 12th Circuit Court, Rock County, Janesville, Wisconsin.[92] His decision in the case included the following points: first, the Board did not transcend its powers in the selection of the Bible as a textbook; second, the Catholic children were not required to read the Bible or be present during its reading; third, and very important, the reading of the Bible did not constitute sectarian instruction; fourth, others, besides the Catholics, had "rights of conscience," and they made up the majority; fifth, Bible-reading was a part of the nation's history and did not make the school a house of worship; sixth, it was beyond the competence of the Court to decide which version of the Bible was correct, the differences between versions were but minor; and seventh, "sectarianism" came from "creeds which imperfectly define the great spiritual truths of the Bible, and which rituals only imperfectly express," and not from the Bible itself.[93] Judge Bennett referred to the Bible as a unique book, and rather nostalgically reminisced that it was the only book left in the schools since he was a boy. He described it as a "good, true and ever faithful friend and counselor." On November 19, 1888, he sustained the Trustees of the Board and overruled the demurrer of the plaintiffs.[94]

The *Catholic Citizen* headlined its November 24 issue with a question: "Wisconsin Catholics: Are You Willing That the King James Bible Be Read in the Schools You Are Taxed to Support?" The editor, saying that Judge Bennett had ruled in the affirmative, commented that Bennett's decision upheld sectarian bigotry in public institutions of learning from the "normal schools down."[95] Labeling the judicial outcome as "no small matter," the *Citizen* advised that steps should be taken to bring the case to the Wisconsin Supreme Court, complaining that it was the Protestants, not the Catholics, who were making the schools sectarian:

> Just as a pickpocket cries "stop thief" in order to distract the attention of the man whom he is robbing, so a respectable gang of sectarianism in and about the public schools are raising a howl that Catholics and the Catholic Church are plotting to make the schools sectarian. *At the same time they themselves are the parties who are insidiously introducing sectarian practices. . . . We believe that a sectarian ring is enthroned over our State school system.*[96]

A week later the *Citizen* exposed its plan to pay for the cost of taking the case to the Supreme Court, estimated at between $700–$800. The paper appealed for funds on behalf of the Catholics of Edgerton, "The 30 Catholic parents of the Edgerton school district and their pastor have exhibited the right kind of grit . . ." and it would not be fair for 300,000 Catholics to "shift the burden upon the few!" The *Citizen* stated that the appeal had the approval of Archbishop Heiss of Milwaukee although he did not personally write on the issue in its pages. Contributions were to be sent to the Reverend August Zeininger, Chancellor of the Milwaukee archdiocese.[97] The appeal was named "The Religious Equality Fund," and the *Citizen's* readers were both apprised of its progress and urged to lend a hand until the March 9, 1889 issue reported that it had reached the sum of $806.30, enough to carry the case to the high court.[98]

In the next several months the case received ongoing attention from the *Citizen*. On June 29, the paper said the questions should not read, "Shall the Bible be read in the Public Schools?" but rather "Shall the Protestant Bible be read in the Public Unsectarian Schools?"[99] A few months later it rejected the "majority rights" argument put forth by Judge Bennett, preferring to call it a "mob argument."[100] On September 21 the *Citizen's* editorial page "felt it necessary to rebuke Catholics who wanted an adverse decision in the case" because such would be a "boon" to Catholic schools, because parents would then withdraw their children from public schools and patronize Catholic schools.[101]

The Case Reaches the Supreme Court

Humphrey J. Desmond, a prominent figure in the state, had been educated in the public schools of Milwaukee. He was later to become the owner and publisher of the *Catholic Citizen* and was the author of a bill to replace the controversial Bennett Law in the Wisconsin legislature in 1891.[102] Desmond served as the principal attorney for the appellants.

Desmond and his colleagues argued that reading the Bible was sectarian instruction. It was so because reading the King James version showed preference to Protestants; reduced the religious equality of students to mere toleration; was the cause of recurring strife and controversy among the sects; had been used by the American Bible Society as a missionary textbook to combat "Romanism" in Latin America; excusing pupils from its reading was an admission of the sectarian nature of the practice; divided denominations over which version was correct and which books were to be included in it; Catholics and Protestants had conflicting ideas as to the "rule of faith" in interpreting the Bible; and Protestantism was known as the "religion of the Bible." The Court, counsel for the plaintiffs maintained, had no right to decide which view was correct in a theological controversy. Further, reading of the Bible made the school a place of worship; took money from the public treasury for same; and violated the rights of conscience of Catholics who were forced to support "religious societies" against their will. Desmond also averred that religious belief should be left to the family and the Church; the practice of Bible-reading forced children to act against the will of their parents; Christianity was not a part of the law of the land in the sense that its doctrines were to be enforced by civil government; and students who withdrew from the premises were being denied equality and were stigmatized in the eyes of their peers. The Bible, while it demonstrated Protestant ascendancy in the schools, was of little use in the character formation of the young, rather being a relic of colonial days and a futile exercise of bibliophilia. Morality was based on the natural law, a foundation more fundamental than the Bible.[103]

In the Respondent's Brief, A. A. Jackson answered for the District Board of Edgerton. He attempted to refute the contentions made by the counsel for the plaintiffs, mainly that the reading of the King James version constituted sectarian instruction and that its reading made the school a place of worship. Of particular interest was the emphasis he placed on the role of the Bible in the nation's history, and the allegations he made about the "record" of the Catholic Church as to liberty and freedom. He wrote:

> Their [the framers] purpose clearly was to decline to aid in creating or sustaining any priesthood or hierarchy, to rule and oppress the people, but to educate and make intelligent and independent the common people and leave them free to form their own religious opinions and choose their own form of worship.[104]

Liberty of conscience, he argued, meant reading and interpreting the Bible for oneself. The rights of conscience of the majority were at stake, and they were paramount as demonstrated by the maxim "Salus Populi Suprema Lex."[105] Quoting the "Syllabus of Errors" of Pope Pius IX, Jackson concluded that the Catholic Church was "opposed to our system of public schools under the control and direction of the civil power of the state."[106] Indeed, he asserted, the relators had no right to their own opinions since they were members of the Roman Catholic Church which maintains that it is the sole interpreter and infallible teacher of the Scriptures. Thus, the plaintiffs were inconsistent when they insisted on liberty for themselves under the constitution.[107] Jackson saw a sinister and secret purpose behind the suit, one inaugurated by the powerful force of Romanism, that had as its object the destruction of the common-school system.[108]

Jackson posited that this country was a distinctly Christian nation from its inception, one that had the Bible as its foundation. The Christian religion, in turn, was the common witness of the founders of the nation and of the public school system. The Bible could not be sectarian because it belonged to all humans and was responsible for civil liberty. The framers of the national and state constitutions intended that the Bible, its sublime truths and moral lessons, would ever be available to the youth of the nation through "places of education."[109] In fact, no one, including the district board, had the right to exclude the Bible from schools because it was "THE BOOK" to be used in teaching morals and the fundamentals of the Christian religion.[110]

Jackson concluded with a plea to the court not to abandon the Bible that had been of such immense value to the country and the individual, the banning of which would result in incalculable injury to both. He asked for a sustainment of the Circuit Court's decision:

> Shall this wonderful book that has commanded the admiration of men wherever it is known, whose teaching is the rule of action of people of this great nation, that has molded the form, and aided in a most remarkable degree the wonderful growth and development of this nation, and that has been, and is a guide in life, a consolation in death, be excluded from the schools where our children are taught.[111]

The Decision of the Wisconsin Supreme Court

In 1890, the Wisconsin Supreme Court, which adjudged that Bible-reading was unconstitutional by a five-to-zero vote, was composed of five men. Two of these, both native New Yorkers, Chief Justice Orasmus Cole, an Episcopalian, and David Taylor, a Congregationalist, did not write an opinion in the case.[112] William Penn Lyon, who wrote the chief opinion, was also from New York, a former Quaker, who had become a member of the Methodist Church.[113] John B. Cassoday, who also wrote an opinion, was born in New York and was a member of the Congregationalist faith.[114] The last member of the Court, Harlow B. Orton, was yet another native New Yorker whose two grandfathers had been Baptist ministers. Orton himself was a Presbyterian.[115] The pertinent parts of the Wisconsin Constitution that were involved were Article X, Section 3 that outlawed sectarian instruction in the common district schools and Article I, Section 18 that established freedom of worship and forbade compelling anyone to support a place of worship or using public money to support same.

Justice Lyon adjudged that Bible-reading in public schools constituted sectarian instruction and therefore violated Article X, Section 3 of the constitution. Lyon considered the Bible as a whole, and said that it was sectarian because its doctrines were not common to all religious sects. While he felt that it was permissible to teach the existence of the Supreme Being, to read the Bible to inculcate religious doctrine that not all sects believed in was sectarian. For Lyon, a sect was a group of people who believed in the same religious doctrines, who were more or less closely associated or organized to advance such doctrines and increase the members therein. The doctrines of one of these, not common to all the others, were considered sectarian. Lyon used as proof the testimony and practices of the American Bible Society in Latin America who used the Bible to gain converts from "Romanism." Study of the Bible in its literary and historical framework was permissible, as was its use as a text for moral instruction. Lyon argued that the Wisconsin Constitution had been written with the goal of guaranteeing religious freedom for the immigrants who were coming to the state, so the historical argument of the Bible's use was not a valid defense. Further, the decisions and opinions of the state superintendents were of no consequence in the matter at hand. The alleged hostility of the Roman Catholic Church to free institutions was set aside by Lyon as not germane to the issue at hand, because the Court was to decide on the basis of the Wisconsin Constitution, not supposed theological "errors." Equally inadmissible was the contention by the defense that pupils were not forced to participate in or listen to the reading, because the Constitution guaranteed equality to all that would not be the case if some students were forced to leave the room, thereby losing face with their peers. Further, if the practice were not sectarian, why allow the students to leave the room? In conclusion, Lyon declared that the Court was ruling on a case of first impression and alleged that the decision did not lessen respect for the Bible or its great truths, which should be the province of home and church to impart.[116]

Justice John B. Cassoday centered his attention on Section 18, Article I of the Constitution. He ruled that Bible-reading constituted worship in the proper sense of the term. He arrived at that conclusion after considering definitions of worship in several dictionaries and found that Bible-reading met the requirements of their consensus of worship. Bible-reading, in his observation, was an essential part of divine worship, whether done in public or private assemblies. It preceded prayer, and was the starting point for many sermons. Since the reading of the Bible was worship, the place where it was read was thus a place of worship—in this case the common school. This, in turn, compelled citizens to support places of worship from their taxes. Cassoday deemed the amount of time spent in the practice, and thus the outlay of money involved for this purpose, to be irrelevant. Further, the Constitution forbade drawing money out of the public treasury for the support of religious societies or seminaries, which was being done in the matter at hand. So, in his concurring opinion basing his reasoning on a different provision of the Constitution than did Justice Lyon, Justice Cassoday also ruled the practice of reading the King James version of the Bible in the public schools of Wisconsin unconstitutional.[117]

Justice Harlow S. Orton wrote the second concurring opinion, one that proved to be the bitterest pill for advocates of Bible-reading to swallow. In it, Orton asserted that the state was completely divorced, as a civil government and in all its civil institutions, "from all possible connection or alliance with any and all religions, religious worship, religious establishments or modes of worship, and with everything of a religious character or appertaining to religion." The name "common schools" not only meant the schools were free to all, Orton said, but also that they were completely secular. Consequently, religion as a system was ruled out of the schools, but religion as natural law was allowable in them. Calling the schools "Godless," Orton referred to religion in terms that religionists thought to be harsh, and had seldom heard, especially from the bench:

> There is no such source and cause of strife, quarrel, fights, malignant opposition, persecution and war, as religion. Let it once enter into our civil affairs, our government will soon be destroyed. Let it once enter into our common school, they would be destroyed. Those who made our constitution saw this, and used the most apt and comprehensive language in it, to prevent such a catastrophe. . . . That version [King James] of the Bible is hostile to the belief of many who are taxed to support the common schools, and who have equal rights and privileges in them. It is a source of religious and sectarian strife. . . .

Finally, Orton held that religion and government were both better off separated from one another, and that religion needed no support from the state. He felt that the case was timely, since it brought before the courts an apparently innocent entrance of religion into civil affairs, which was in reality a deadly assault into civil matters.[118]

Religious Reaction

The unanimous decision outlawing Bible-reading, with opinions written by three of the five Supreme Court justices, shook the Wisconsin religious world. Reactions were swift to follow. The state's Baptists, meeting in 1890, viewed the decision as creating an emphasis on the necessity of providing Christian schools of their own. The Court's decision, "that Christianity has no right in the public schools," had made that necessary.[119] (However, the Baptists did not follow up on their initial reaction. Nothing else appeared about Baptist schools in their subsequent state conventions.)

The Christian Education Committee of the Dane Baptist Association chided parents for not being awake and said that if they had been, their children would be "found in Christian schools, instead of being sent, as is often the case, into schools whose atmosphere is dominated by liberalism, so called, or infidelity." Parents, it said, had a "binding duty" to support schools "where they had a right to *ask* as to the moral and religious views held by those who teach."[120]

Wisconsin's Congregationalists saw the Edgerton decision as weakening the moral fiber of the nation. They adopted a resolution by Professor J. J. Blaisdell of Beloit College, which called for adherence to the traditional relationship of Christianity and the Bible to the nation and school, without which civilization could only decay. Arguing that the common school had its origin in the conception of the founding fathers, the Congregationalists proclaimed that the continuance of that tradition was indispensable, for without it the school "will not preserve society from disregard of government and from falling sooner or later into fatal confusion." Youth must be taught that they are "beholden to a Divine Ruler of the Universe . . . and taught by Jesus Christ, of obedience toward Him and of brotherhood toward man."[121]

The Congregationalists wanted the common schools as they had been, but opted for their own academies and colleges. They were active in support of common schools and sometimes occupied leadership positions in those schools. For instance, the Reverend Alberani Kidder was Superintendent of Schools in Eau Claire County in 1890.[122]

The most complete statement of the Congregationalist position is to be found in the paper read by Professor Blaisdell before the Beloit Congregational Convention at Palmyra on May 23, 1890 and accepted for substance by that body as an expression of its views. In his paper, Blaisdell attempted to refute, one by one, the key points of the decision. Calling for adherence to the spirit of the framers of the state's constitution, he quoted a Congregationalist survivor of the Wisconsin Convention, Almerin A. Carter that "it was not the most remote thought of any of the Convention that the Bible could be thought as improper for those schools."[123] Blaisdell also cited part of a letter from Michael Frank, hailed as the founder of public education in Wisconsin, in which Frank

doubted, as far as his memory could recall, that it was the Convention's intention to define the Bible as sectarian.[124]

Blaisdell called the decision "revolutionary," claimed that it had set aside
the Constitution, and asked that the question be referred to the people of
Wisconsin in a referendum. In a stirring appeal, he pleaded that the Bible be
retained in the schools for the safety of the Republic.[125] Speaking to the
Catholics, Blaisdell reminded them that "We live in the nineteenth century and
not the fifteenth." He worried lest the decision lead to a proliferation of
denominational schools that would separate the children from each other and
lead the people into "conflicting sects scrambling for support from the public
treasury."[126] Blaisdell concluded his paper with a reference to the traditional
Protestant position on the role of the Bible in society. He asserted: "But religion—the religion of the Bible—is provided for in the Constitution of our commonwealth as our birthright in the school-room, our birthright everywhere. The
Constitution recognizes it as the common atmosphere of our civic life. To that
birthright we make our claim."[127]

The reaction of Wisconsin's Presbyterians was closely akin to the
Congregationalists'. The Presbyterian General Assembly of the United States
declared its "unalterable devotion to the public school system as the most
effective agency, next to the Church of God, in laying the foundations of popular intelligence, virtue and freedom in the United States."[128] The delegates proclaimed their loyalty to the Bible as the "Magna Carta" of our best moral and
religious influences and stated that they would regard its expulsion from the
public schools as a "deplorable and suicidal act." They urged all Presbyterians
to "cooperate with all Christian people in maintaining the place of this Book
of God as an educating force among the youth of our land."[129]

The Synod of Wisconsin unanimously adopted a set of resolutions protest-
ing the decision. The group predicted dire calamities of social, moral, and
intellectual nature shortly to befall society as its result and sought universal
cooperation to ward them off.

It alleged the decision had been based on the "strained and unusual interpretation of language" and was in "direct contravention of . . . the framers of
the constitution and of the people who adopted it." The decision "logically
excludes all religious exercises . . . from all the public institutions" of the state.
It weakens the "schools as instruments of both intellectual and moral education" and leads to a "system of denominational schools promotive of class feeling and social alienation." It replaces the legislature with judicial decree foisted
on an "unprepared people" and "tends to weaken moral conviction" at a time

when the public conscience needs all the "quickening and invigoration" it can get.

Therefore it resolved that the decision gave a "false interpretation to the constitution"; called upon "our fellow citizens of every persuasion to unite with us in seeking to procure a reversal of this most ill-omened decision," and called on "ministers, Sunday School teachers, and heads of families" to make "widely known through sermons, books, and otherwise" the inestimable service "rendered to the cause of liberty, of civilization, of progress and of human welfare in general by the Christian Scriptures."[130] The Synod concluded its deliberations by thanking the Rev. W. A. McAtee for his pamphlet on the Bible; urged other ministers to follow suit; and formed a three man committee, of which McAtee was a member, to carry out the Synod's resolutions as far as possible.[131]

The committee gave its report a year later. It had found, first, no reason to abate the criticism of the decision that was "based on a strained and unusual interpretation of language; which was demonstrably contrary to the opinion and intentions of the framers of the constitution and the people who adopted it." Second, it claimed that "no serious attempt has been made in any quarter to support this decision against the assaults made upon it," a decision which has been shown to be "unhistorical, illogical, unprecedented, un-American, unpatriotic, and of immoral tendency." Indelicately hinting at professional coercion, the committee alleged "It is believed that the ablest lawyers of the state, were they free to speak, would condemn it with almost a single voice." The future did not look bright, however, for "no practical remedy" seemed available, but this was "not to be understood that we acquiesce in the decision of shaping permanently the policy of our public schools," because we serenely "await the return of a better mind both to the bench and to the enemies of the Book which made our commonwealth free and great."[132]

Unlike the Baptists, the committee refused to consider establishing Presbyterian denominational schools. It declared Presbyterians were "devotedly attached" to the public school system and would regard its "overthrow as disastrous to society and the state." While the committee acknowledged that the system would become "defective" if moral training, "based upon fundamental religious convictions" was excluded, it asked its fellow citizens to protest and "aid us in deriving means for its revival." Finally, the committee repeated the resolution of the previous year that all Presbyterians, especially their officials, do all in their power to restore the Bible to its deservedly exalted position in the schools.[133]

Rev. W. A. McAtee of Madison was the leading Presbyterian critic of the decision. In early April he wrote to the *Wisconsin State Journal* that when the Bible was thrust out of the New York public schools nearly all moral instruction went with it, and consequently "tens of thousands of children are being reared in ignorance of the moral law and its requirements." The civil state, for its own sake, needed to "teach reverence for God as the basis for morals." McAtee had little confidence in parents to instill virtue in their children, so without the Bible that meant that "thousands of our school children" will not be taught to be "clean, respectful, honest, and truthful." This was a most serious matter because: ". . . more than one-third of our school population does not attend any Sunday school whatever, *we have a generation of children coming forward to the responsibilities of government who have not been taught to reverence God, or love their fellow men, or at best, have had only slight and occasional instruction in these duties.*"[134]

He concluded this letter with the call to "all good citizens" to demand the return of the Bible to the schools, and with it the "theistic principles which are common to all sects and distinctive to none, which *are indispensable for good character and good citizenship.*"[135]

Three days later another letter from McAtee appeared in the *State Journal*. In this correspondence he featured the religious, but nonsectarian, role of the public schools. He alleged that this kind of religion was the "law of the land," and that "*Religion is the only solid basis of morals, and that moral instruction not resting on this basis is only a building upon sand.*"[136] But more was to be heard from McAtee. The Wisconsin Presbyterian Synod of 1890 had praised his position paper on the Edgerton decision and had urged other pastors to follow suit. His work, entitled *Must the Bible Go?*, was an attempted point-by-point refutation of the decision. It is interesting to observe that he referred to the Bible as the "chief foe" of sectarianism and asserted: "Keep the Bible away from the people, and they may be led almost at will by their religious guides. Put the Bible into their hands, let them read and interpret it for themselves, and ecclesiastical narrowness and intolerance will give way to breadth and liberality."[137]

While he rejected the reasoning of Justices Lyon and Cassoday, it was the opinion of Justice Orton that drew his wrath. "Orton," he wrote, "adds little except a more sweeping and radical application of the decision to all departments of life," and he abhorred Orton's contention that religion was the cause of strife. He rejected the Court's views on the separation of church and state, arguing that religion could not be shut out from society "without leading to most deplorable results." The effect on students would be catastrophic, informing them that the "Book home and Church teach them to revere as the Book of God, the state declares to be the book of sects."[138]

Wisconsin, McAtee said, now found itself as the only "Godless commonwealth" in the nation, unable to receive the blessings of a free government, which "can only be maintained by a firm adherence to justice, moderation, temperance, frugality, and virtue, and by frequent recurrence to fundamental principles." The decision deprived Wisconsin residents of the key to civilization by eliminating the Bible from the schools, and made the schools "*irreligious*" and unsatisfactory to Protestants as well as to Catholics. McAtee lamented that only eight of the 500 children in Edgerton were involved in the suit, making a minute minority, a "small proportion," supreme, at the expense of the vast majority.[139]

The anguish expressed by the Presbyterians was matched by the Methodists. The Wisconsin Conference of Methodists, while it did not desire that Bible-reading "be required by legal enactment," entered its "earnest protest against that part of the decision which declares the Bible a sectarian book." The Conference adopted a plan of interdenominational cooperation by resolving that a "commission of five be appointed to co-operate with other denominations in such action as may be thought necessary."[140]

The West Wisconsin Conference of Methodists first recognized the contributions of the American Bible Society that had been cited in the decision. It regarded the Society as "among the greatest institutions of our Christian country," and as a "bond of union among all Protestant Christians."[141] Turning to the decision itself, the Conference deplored it and regarded it as an "act emphasizing sectarianism and leading toward the much dreaded 'union of Church and State.'"[142]

Methodist ministers took up the cudgels in their pulpits. One of the leading clergymen was the Reverend Mr. Creighton of the Summerfield Methodist Church in Milwaukee. He accused the "Romish hierarchy" of being responsible for the decision. The Church of Rome, which had never had the scriptures until after the reformation and had kept the Bible from its own members, had labeled Bible societies a "most crafty, contagious invention which must be destroyed." Creighton predicted that the Catholics, encouraged by their victory in Edgerton that made the "whole school system itself sectarian with the Romish Church as the governing sect," would press on, hoping for the "downfall of public schools and the establishment of sectarian schools on their ruins." Why, Creighton wondered, would the Catholics want to drive God's word out of schools that they already called "godless and corrupting"? He concluded his sermon with a blast at Rome and a prophecy of redress.[143]

Other Methodist clergy took positions similar to that expressed by Creighton. An exception was the Reverend T. DeWitt Peake, pastor of the Methodist Church at Merrill, Wisconsin. Peake saw "nothing anti-Protestant, nothing un-American" in the decision. He felt it "will serve the better the cause of truth and the Christian religion," because the American state was neutral toward religion. Liberty is derived from the individual conscience, not from the civil power. The Court recognized this in the decision when it protected the Catholic conscience and their right to worship according to its dictates. It was not the business of the Court to determine whether the Catholic Church is friendly or inimical to the Bible or to public schools. Nor was it the right of any religious group to attempt to dominate public education. The Bible, he said, is a "sectarian book." Methodists should accept the decision as just and channel their energies into religious instruction of the young at home and at Church.[144]

The Protestant Episcopal Church in the state, in both the Dioceses of Milwaukee and Fond du Lac, did not mention the ruling of the Court in their 1890 meetings.[145] Bishop Cyrus F. Knight of the Milwaukee Diocese expressed "pain" in his observation of the judgment, but he saw no other alternative for the court in a "country where God is not recognized in the constitution" other than the "absolute secularization of the public schools." This will lead, he believed, to "all earnest Christians" realizing "the necessity of educating their children in religious institutions." Public schools, in his view, were a "rather poor substitute for the ideal school."[146]

Unitarians supported the decision. Generally, they believed that morality had a civil foundation and relied on a secular humanistic base, not a revelatory one. The leading Unitarian spokesman in this controversy was the Reverend Joseph H. Crooker of Madison. He became involved following a speech given by the former President of the University of Wisconsin, John E. Bascom. In a speech to the University's Law School, Bascom criticized the decision, saying that the public schools had "two enemies." The first of these was the "spirit of class" that manifested itself in private schools; the second was "sectarianism," which was found in the Catholic Church. Claiming that he was not appealing to the "hereditary antipathy" to Catholics, Bascom nonetheless saw a "menace to our liberties, to our national life, expressed in the unwillingness to train the children of this nation in one and the same system of schools, for one and the same end of good citizenship."[147]

Bascom, like the viewpoint expressed by the Protestant center, believed that Christianity based on the Bible could and should be taught in the public schools without sectarianism. He concluded his critique of the Court with the contention that in banning the Bible the Court was out of touch with humanity.[148]

It was this address by Bascom to which Rev. Crooker responded in his sermon on Sunday, June 29, entitled "Dr. Bascom and the Supreme Court." Initially, Crooker declared the nation to be a "completely secular state," and in this regard, the decision was "wise, practical, and helpful." Bascom, he said, was speaking from a three hundred year old Puritan context that was no longer applicable in American society. The sole question at issue was whether religious exercises in schools were lawful in a secular society. In reality, the Bible had not been outlawed, only the "formal, perfunctory, useless and unlawful use of the Bible" had to go, that a better use of it could come.[149]

Crooker defended the Catholic petitioners, said they had wanted to send their children to a perfectly neutral school, and if the "Catholic Church entrapped anybody it was the constitutional convention." He acknowledged that the Catholic record regarding free institutions was not spotless, but then neither was that of mainstream Protestantism; indeed while he feared "that policy and spirit sometimes shown toward our institutions by the Catholic hierarchy," he feared more "Protestant bigotry; and most of all I fear any possible curtailment of the freedom of American children. This decision has not given the victory to Catholics, but to American justice."[150]

Bascom erred, Crooker claimed, when he said that the country had a religion—Christianity. Rather, the "secular state, which Wisconsin is by manifest destiny and by the express declaration of its fundamental law" has no religion. Thus it follows that "its schools can rightfully and lawfully have no religious instruction whatever."[151]

Constituting but a minuscule percentage of Wisconsin's population in 1848, the number of Catholics in the state steadily increased over the decades. Some estimate that they numbered about 347,000 in 1890, the year of the Edgerton decision.[152] With their growing numbers, Catholics were not as willing to endure what they termed discriminatory practices in the state. The Edgerton case was one offshoot of this tendency.

A driving force in the Edgerton conflict was the Catholic newspaper based in Milwaukee, the *Catholic Citizen*. Although credit for "exposing the sectarianism in the Edgerton Bible Case" has been given to Archbishop Katzer of Milwaukee,[153] publicly at least, and unlike its role in the contemporary Bennett Law controversy, the Catholic hierarchy in Wisconsin was relatively inactive in the Edgerton case. The *Catholic Citizen*, which had spearheaded the drive for funds to get the case on the docket of the Supreme Court, celebrated the decision. The headline of its March 22, 1890 issue read, "Won the case," "Wisconsin Catholics Victorious in the Edgerton Bible Case."[154] An editorial in the same issue rejoiced that Catholics had struck a blow for liberty and religious equality of all in the state:

> It is no blow to the Bible or to religion. It is, rather, a conquest of the Golden Rule over un-Christian zeal and rancor. . . . The whip drops from the hand of the zealot and the parish child is emancipated. Out goes cant; out goes hypocrisy with its proselytism. It is a great victory and it is everybody's victory, who believes in Justice, Equality, and Good-will among men.[155]

The editor, Humphrey J. Desmond, who had been the lead attorney for the plaintiffs, credited the paper, contributors to the fund drive, the Catholics of Edgerton and their pastor, Father James Bowe, for the victory.[156]

Responding to Methodist critics, the *Citizen* suggested that if Bible-reading were so crucial to the education of the young, why didn't the Methodists establish their own schools, unless the editorial mused, they were too stingy.[157] A few weeks later it argued that the ousting of the Bible from the public schools served two purposes: "It compels the Protestants to be honest with their fellow-citizens, and it admits Catholics to an equality in school privileges."[158]

Reaction of the Press

The decision, the first of its kind in the nation, received national attention. The nation's press took note of it, from Edgerton, Wisconsin to New York City. For example, the *Wisconsin Tobacco Reporter* commented on March 21, 1890, that the decision was a blow to some in the community but provided cause for Catholic rejoicing.[159] The paper was more concerned with the costs of the case to the district than of the religious-constitutional issues involved but did see fit to place the responsibility for the rise of religious feelings from the case on the Catholics who made it a religious contest "after the case had been announced in the circuit court." It was a rather one-sided struggle, with the district board "singlehanded and alone" on one side arrayed against the "combined strength of the Catholic Church."[160]

In its April 18 issue, it reprinted a sermon by the Reverend A. S. Reid, Pastor of the Congregational Church in Edgerton in which Reid denied that the Bible was sectarian; that Bible-reading made the school a place of worship; and that religion was the cause of strife. Reid appealed to the people of the state for help in reversing the decision.[161] By that summer the decision had disappeared from the *Reporter's* pages.

The *New York Times* scathingly denounced "Protestant zealots who wish to convert the public schools into instruments of proselytism who do most to make it difficult to maintain the common school system against the Roman Catholics." Though "harmless" in itself, the practice was obnoxious to Catholics and should not be forced upon them. The *Times* saw the applicability of the case beyond Wisconsin. It thought the Court's ruling would lead to absolute separation of church and state in education by forcing the schools to be absolutely secular. Interestingly, it felt that it would put an end to any right a religious minority group had to ask for money for their schools, since the public schools no longer favored any group, including the religious majority.[162]

Implications of the Decision

No matter how deeply and sorely the decision rankled, no emotional outbursts, no appeals to the past, no calm reasoning could reverse it. Whatever it had been, Wisconsin was a different state than it had been in 1848.

In 1848, fifty-one of the sixty-nine framers of the Wisconsin constitution hailed from New York or New England.[163] In 1888, the Wisconsin senate had thirty-three members: nine were born in New York, three in New England, and eight were of foreign birth, of whom four came from Germany. Of the assembly's 100 members that year, nineteen were born in New York, seven in New England, twenty-two were born in Wisconsin, and thirty-seven came from foreign countries, ten of those from Germany.[164] The old stock Americans had simply lost some of their political power, which was reflected in their loss of dominance in the schools and now one of their most cherished policies—the reading of the King James version of the Bible in the schools was outlawed.

Legally, the decision was the first of its kind at the state Supreme Court level to adjudge that Bible-reading, without note or comment, was unconstitutional. Judge John R. Bennett, who had upheld the practice in Circuit Court, described the Supreme Court's decision as "devoid of law as hell is of hope."[165] Other writers testified to its importance, one noting that with it "the pattern of the decisions [on Bible-reading] began to change."[166] It was the first time that the "minority view found favor" and Bible-reading was declared to be "sectarian instruction."[167]

In his commentary on the decision in 1890, A. H. Wintersteen praised the Court for its jurisprudence in the decision as "dignified and careful" and was a "thorough review of both the legal principles involved and the historical aspects of the controversy."[168] Joseph Schaefer, however, one-time editor of the *Wisconsin Magazine of History*, analyzed one segment of Justice Lyon's opinion in which Lyon asserted that the Wisconsin constitution was framed with an eye to attracting immigrants to the state. Schaefer claimed that Lyon's interpretation of "sectarian" was historically different than that of the framers, who did not write the constitution so as to attract immigrants to the state. The decision, Schaefer concluded, was based on the exigencies of the day and reflected the currents of the times rather than the intention of the framers.[169]

Seven years later Schaefer returned to his thesis and said that the decision relied on "social history" and that the Supreme Court would have confirmed the Circuit Court decision had it followed historical evidence. The Bible would not have been included in the framers' definition of "Sectarian instruction" and that the meaning of that term historically in Wisconsin was not ambiguous as Lyon had said.[170]

Yet, given Lyon's definition of "sectarian," Schaefer's charge of "judge-made law," seems overdrawn. Justice Lyon determined that whatever it once was, Bible-reading was sectarian instruction in 1890. His definitions of sect and sectarian, stated in his opinion, when applied to the Wisconsin of 1890 made Bible-reading sectarian instruction and consequently a violation of the rights of conscience of at least one sect—the Catholics. For Catholics, copies of the Protestant Bible were on the Index of prohibited books. Further, Catholics were discouraged to read the Bible "indiscriminately." They were to follow the Church in its interpretations of the meaning of Scripture, since they believed the Church had been divinely commissioned by Jesus Christ to be the infallible teacher on faith and morals. Thus it is difficult to see how, for Catholics, the reading of the common Protestant version of the Scriptures could be defined as anything other than sectarian instruction. Whatever it had been, Bible-reading was now sectarian instruction. The case had the effect of separating "dogmatic Christianity and the law."[171] No longer would there be, at least in Wisconsin, partiality in law toward Protestantism. The *Albany Law Review* averred that the Court could not have come to any different conclusion and gave some parting advice to Protestant ministers: "The clergy may as well wake up to the idea that common schools are not religious seminaries."[172]

The *Wisconsin Journal of Education* opined that the elimination of Bible-reading from the schools was not a serious blow to education. It editorialized that: "The schools of Wisconsin have long been secularized. Only here and there has one clung to the New England tradition of opening each day's session with the reading of scripture and prayer. The change has come gradually and silently, and the action of the court simply legalizes it."[173]

Wisconsin's Superintendent of Schools, Jesse B. Thayer, felt the decision was "far-reaching in its application" because while it described reading the Bible as "sectarian instruction," yet in its "scope and spirit it has a direct and manifest application to other practices." Among these were Catechism lessons, religiously oriented text books, teachers in public schools wearing religious garb, the leasing of parochial school buildings by the public school district and requiring children to attend school where classes were taught by persons designated by religious bodies. From the yardstick of community relations, the use of the Bible in schools has sometimes had an adverse effect and "other means have been advised for the inculcation of reverence, virtue and all moral qualities."[174]

Available evidence indicated that the decision stood and was observed. According to federal sources, garnered from the reports of fifty-three city and county superintendents in Wisconsin in 1898, the decision of the Court in the Edgerton Bible case was being observed.[175]

Conclusion

The agreement that had been worked out by mainstream Protestantism on the place of religion in education, which featured the reading of the King James version of the Bible, was unacceptable to Catholics and some other citizens. As the nation's population grew more ethnically and religiously diverse, conflicts arose over what had been called "nonsectarian" instruction. Wisconsin, with its high percentage of immigrants, especially those of the Catholic faith, was a natural site for a court test of the constitutionality of such practices.

The Catholic Church had fought the ascendancy of Protestantism in the public schools of the nation, embodied especially by devotional Bible-reading, with little success for much of the nineteenth century. Viewed in this context, the Catholic "dissenters" from general educational practice undoubtedly won a victory. The decision may also be seen as a victory for the rights of individual conscience. As Wintersteen observed, not even the sacred symbol of the Bible, with all that it represented in the minds and hearts of many Wisconsinites, was deemed legally permissible when challenged by the rights of conscience of a religious minority group, the Catholic "dissenters."[176]

Notes

1. Benjamin Rush, "Plan for the Establishment of Public Schools" (1786), in *Essays on Education in the Early Republic*, ed. Frederick Rudolph, Cambridge, MA: Harvard University Press, 1965, 13.

2. Wayne J. Urban and Jennings L. Wagoner, Jr., *American Education: A History*, 2nd edition, New York: McGraw-Hill, 2000, 81.

3. R. Freeman Butts, *A History of Education in American Culture*, New York: Holt, Rinehart and Winston, 1953, 172.

4. Ibid.

5. Ray Allen Billington, *The Protestant Crusade 1800–1860: The Origins of American Nativism*, New York: Macmillan, 1938, 147.

6. William Kailer Dunn, *What Happened to Religious Education?* Baltimore, MD: The Johns Hopkins Press, 1958, 260.

7. Rush Welter, *Popular Education and Democratic Thought in America*, New York: Columbia University Press, 1962, 106.

8. Harold A. Buetow, *Of Singular Benefit: The Story of U.S. Catholic Education*, New York: Macmillan, 1970, 135; Warren A. Nord, *Religion & American Education: Rethinking a National Dilemma*, Chapel Hill: University of North Carolina Press, 1995, 73.

9. Horace Mann, "Twelfth Annual Report (1848)," in *The Republic and the School: Horace Mann on the Education of Free Men*, ed. Lawrence A. Cremin, New York: Teachers College Press, 1959, 102–6.

10. Milo M. Quaife, ed., *The Movement for Statehood, 1845–1846*, Madison, WI: Wisconsin Historical Society, 1918, 188.

11. Milo M. Quaife, ed., *The Convention of 1846*, Madison, WI: Wisconsin Historical Society, 1919, 538.

12. Ibid., 744; Milo M. Quaife, ed., *The Struggle over Ratification, 1846–1847*, Madison, WI: Wisconsin Historical Society, 1920, 95, 122–23.

13. Ibid., 421.

14. Milo M. Quaife, ed., *The Attainment of Statehood*, Madison, WI: State Historical Society of Wisconsin, 1928, 714.

15. Herbert M. Kliebard, ed., *Religion and Education in America: A Documentary History*, Scranton, PA: International Textbook Company, 1969, 112.

16. H. C. Whitford, "Early History of Education in Wisconsin," in *Reports and Collections of the State Historical Society of Wisconsin, V, Part III*, Madison, WI: Atwood and Rublee, 1869, 343.

17. *The Seventh Census of the United States: 1850*, Washington, DC: Robert Armstrong, Public Printer, 1853, 925.

18. *The Catholic Almanac for 1848*, Baltimore, MD: F. Lucas, Jr., n.d., 190.

19. *The Metropolitan Catholic Almanac and Laity's Directory for 1855*, Baltimore, MD: Lucas Brothers, n.d., 289–90.

20. Ibid., 290.

21. *The Revised Statutes of the State of Wisconsin, 1849*, Southport, WI: C. Latham Sholes, 1849, 404–5.

22. Ibid., 736.

23. Ibid., 541.

24. Ibid., 89.

25. Ibid., 195.

26. *Decisions in Appeals. Wisconsin Superintendents of Public Instruction, I*, The State Historical Society of Wisconsin, Madison, December 3, 1894, 94; August 28, 1851, 240.

27. Ibid., May 5, 1851, 187.

28. Ibid., July 1851, 226.

29. Ibid., 227.

30. Dwight L. Agnew, et al., eds., *Dictionary of Wisconsin Biography*, Madison, WI: The State Historical Society of Wisconsin, 1960, 306.

31. *Decisions in Appeals*, I. February 21, 1852, 287–88.

32. Ibid., November 15, 1853, 399.

33. *Annual Report of the State Superintendent of Public Instruction for the State of Wisconsin, 1853*, Madison, WI: David Atwood, 1854, 23.

34. *Decisions in Appeals, I*. February 4, 1854, 410.

35. Ibid., June 10, 1854, 451.

36. Ibid.

37. Agnew, et al., eds., *Dictionary of Wisconsin Biography*, 28.

38. *Annual Report of the State Superintendent of Public Instruction of the State of Wisconsin for the Year 1856*, Madison, WI: Calkins and Proudfit, 1857, 73.

39. *Annual Report of the State Superintendent of Public Instruction of the State of Wisconsin, for the Year 1857*, Madison, WI: Atwood and Rublee, 1858, 9.

40. Lyman C. Draper, "Moral and Religious Instruction in Public Schools," in the *Tenth Annual Report on the Condition and Improvement of the Common Schools and Educational Interests of the State of Wisconsin for the Year 1858*, Madison, WI: Atwood and Rublee, 1858, 242–43.

41. Ibid., 243.

42. Ibid., 244.

43. *Eleventh Annual Report on the Condition and Improvement of the Common Schools and Educational Interests of the State of Wisconsin for the Year 1859*, Madison, WI: James Ross, 1859, 34.

44. Rev. Charles Brooks, "The Best Method of Teaching Morals in Common Schools," *Wisconsin Journal of Education* 1 (August 1856): 161.

45. Rev. M. P. Kinney, "Religious Instruction in Common Schools—Method of Imparting It," *Wisconsin Journal of Education* 4 (September 1859): 71.

46. Josiah L. Pickard, "Experiences of a Wisconsin Educator," *Wisconsin Magazine of History* 7 (December 1923): 147.

47. *Fourteenth Annual Report of the Superintendent of Public Instruction of the State of Wisconsin for the Year 1862*, Madison, WI: W. C. Roberts, 1862, 81.

48. *Fifteenth Annual Report of the Superintendent of Public Instruction of the State of Wisconsin, for the Year Ending August 31st, 1863*, Madison, WI: William J. Park, 1863, 109.

49. *Decisions in Appeals, II*. February 18, 1860, 2.

50. *Tenth Annual Report on the Condition and Improvement of the Common Schools and Educational Interests of the State of Wisconsin for the Year 1858*, 246; *Twelfth Annual Report on the Condition and Improvement of the Common Schools and Educational Interests of the State of Wisconsin, for*

the Year 1860, 80; *Fifteenth Annual Report of the Superintendent of Public Instruction of the State of Wisconsin, for the Year Ending August 31, 1863*, 102.

51. "Religion in Schools," *Wisconsin Journal of Education* (NS) 1 (September 1864): 80.

52. "Mr. McMynn's Address," *Wisconsin Journal of Education* (NS) 1 (September 1864): 80.

53. Francis Wayland, *The Elements of Moral Science*, edited by Joseph L. Blau, Cambridge, MA; Harvard University Press, 1963, 129.

54. Ibid., 132.

55. *Annual Report of the Superintendent of Public Instruction of the State of Wisconsin for the Year Ending August 31, 1867*, Madison, WI: Atwood and Rublee, 1867, 53.

56. "Morals-Religion-The Bible," *Wisconsin Journal of Education* (NS) 1 (May 1865): 289–90.

57. *Ninth Census—Volume I. The Statistics of the Population of the United States, Compiled from the Original Returns of the Ninth Census, June 1, 1870*, Washington, DC: US Government Printing Office, 1872, 324–25, 336–40.

58. Ibid., 508–23.

59. *Sadlier's Catholic Directory, Almanac and Ordo, For the Year of Our Lord 1870*, New York: D. J. Sadlier and Co., 1870, 220, 196.

60. Agnew, et al., eds., *Dictionary of Wisconsin Biography*, 126.

61. "The Relation of the Church to the Common School," in the *Minutes of the Twenty-Fourth Session of the Wisconsin Annual Conference of the Methodist Episcopal Church 1870*, Milwaukee, WI: Index Printing Company, 1870, 29.

62. Ibid., 29–30.

63. Ibid., 30–31.

64. John R. Pradt, "Official Opinions," *Wisconsin Journal of Education* (NS) 2 (October 1873): 387.

65. Will Herberg, "Religion and Education in America," in *Religious Perspectives in American Culture, II*, eds. James A. Smith and A. Leland Jamison, *Religion in American Life*, Princeton, NJ: Princeton University Press, 1961, 29.

66. *Statistics of the Population of the United States at the Tenth Census (June 1, 1880)*, Washington, DC: US Government Printing Office, 1883, 446, 492–95.

67. "Moral Lessons," *Wisconsin Journal of Education* (NS) 11 (February 1881): 76.

68. *State of Wisconsin. In Assembly. 1878. I. Bill 91A*.

69. *In Assembly. Journal of Proceedings of the Thirty-First Annual Session of the Wisconsin Legislature, 1878*, Madison, WI: David Atwood, Printer and Stereotyper, 1878, 766.

70. *State of Wisconsin. In Senate. 1878. Bill 95B; In Senate. Journal of Proceedings of the Thirty-First Annual Session of the Wisconsin Legislature, 1878*, Madison, WI: David Atwood, Printer and Stereotyper, 1878, 328.

71. *Statistics of the Population of the United States at the Tenth Census (June 1, 1880)*, 456.

72. *Proceedings of the Common Council and Ordinances of the City of Milwaukee for the Year Ending April 17th, 1878*, published by Order of the Council, 1878, 250–51.

73. *The Laws of Wisconsin Passed at the Annual Session of the Legislature of 1880, together with Joint Resolutions and Memorials*, Madison, WI: David Atwood, State Printer, 1880, chapter 61, section 1, 58.

74. *The Laws of Wisconsin, Except City Charters and Their Amendments, Passed at the Biennial Session of the Legislature of 1883*, Madison, WI: Democrat Printing Co., State Printer, 1883, chapter 253, section 4, 202–3.

75. Alvin V. Johnson, *The Legal Status of Church-State Relationships in the United States*, Minneapolis, MN: The University of Minnesota Press, 1934, 39–40; A. H. Wintersteen, "Commentary," *American Law Review* 29 (May 1890): 321, 322.

76. Johnson, *The Legal Status of Church-State Relationships*, 41; Wintersteen, "Commentary," 323.

77. Wintersteen, "Commentary," 326.

78. Johnson, *The Legal Status of Church-State Relationships*, 52.

79. *The Laws of Wisconsin, Except City Charters and Their Amendments, Passed at the Biennial Session of the Legislature of 1883*, Madison, WI: Democrat Printing Co., State Printers, 1883, chapter 251, section 3, 202–3.

80. M. D. Ewell, "The Bible in Schools," *American Law Register* 24 (April 1885): 252, 255.

81. *Catholic Citizen*, February 13, 1886, 4.

82. Ibid., February 20, 1886, 4.

83. Ibid.

84. Ibid., February 27, 1886, 4.

85. *Wisconsin Tobacco Reporter*, November 12, 1886, 5.

86. *Catholic Citizen*, June 12, 1886, 4.

87. "Petition of Relators, State ex rel. Weiss and others, Appellants, vs. The District Board of School District No. Eight of the City of Edgerton, Wisconsin," *Wisconsin Reports*, 76 Wis. 177, 179–80, Chicago: Callaghan and Co., 1886.

88. "Return of the District Board," Ibid., 181–86.

89. Ibid., April 2, 1888, 5.

90. Ibid., July 13, 1888, 4.

91. *Catholic Citizen*, June 23, 1888, 3.

92. John R. Berryman, *History of the Bench and Bar of Wisconsin, II*, Chicago: H. G. Cooper, Jr., and Company, 1898, 483–84.

93. Judge John R. Bennett, *Opinion in the Case of Weiss et al. vs. the School Board of Edgerton*, Edgerton, WI: F. W. Coon, 1889, 56–67.

94. Ibid., 69–77.

95. *Catholic Citizen*, November 24, 1888, 1.

96. Ibid., 4.

97. Ibid., December 1, 1888, 4.

98. Ibid., March 9, 1889, 5.

99. Ibid., June 29, 1889, 4.

100. Ibid., August 17, 1889, 4.

101. Ibid., September 21, 1889, 4.

102. John D. Gregory, "Humphrey J. Desmond," *Southeastern Wisconsin: A History of Old Milwaukee County, III*, Chicago: The S. J. Clarke Publishing Company, 1932, 74; Agnew, et al., eds., *Dictionary of Wisconsin Biography*, 100.

103. *Counsel's Brief for the Appellant*, Humphrey J. Desmond, of Counsel for Appellant, Winans and Hyzer, Attorneys for Appellant. *State of Wisconsin. In Supreme Court*, Milwaukee, WI: Ed Bulfin, Printer, 1890, 11–29; Brief: "The Bible in Our Common Schools," Winans and Hyzer, Attorneys for Appellants, Madison, WI: State Historical Society of Wisconsin, 1890, 1–66; *Appellant's Brief: Bible Case*. J. H. M. Winans, Counsel for Appellants. Green Bay: Associate Print, 1890, 1–17. All are bound pamphlets in *Bible in the Public School* (Binder's Title), in the Library of the State Historical Society of Wisconsin, Madison.

104. *Respondent's Brief,* F. P. Towne and A. A. Jackson, Attorneys for Respondent. *Brief of A. A. Jackson. State of Wisconsin. In Supreme Court. The State of Wisconsin ex rel. Frederick Weiss, et al., Appellant, vs. The District Board of School District No. Eight of the City of Edgerton, Respondent.* Edgerton: F. W. Coon, 1890, 24. A bound pamphlet in the *Bible in the Public School* (Binder's Title), in the Library of the State Historical Society of Wisconsin, Madison.

105. Ibid., 29, 37.

106. Ibid., 47.

107. Ibid., 50.

108. Ibid., 42–43.

109. Ibid., 156.

110. Ibid., 171.

111. Ibid., 198.

112. John R. Berryman, *History of the Bench and Bar in Wisconsin, I,* 114; John B. Sanborn, "The Supreme Court of Wisconsin in the Eighties," *Wisconsin Magazine of History* 15 (September 1931): 18.

113. Berryman, *History of the Bench and Bar in Wisconsin, I,* 206–7; Sanborn, "The Supreme Court of Wisconsin in the Eighties," 18.

114. Berryman, *History of the Bench and Bar in Wisconsin, I,* 245; Sanborn, "The Supreme Court of Wisconsin in the Eighties," 8, 18; A. M. Thomson, *A Political History of Wisconsin.* Milwaukee, WI: E. C. Williams, 1900, 318–19.

115. Berryman, *History of the Bench and Bar in Wisconsin, I,* 214–15; Sanborn, "The Supreme Court of Wisconsin in the Eighties," 17.

116. Justice William Penn Lyon, *Opinion, Decision of the Supreme Court of the State of Wisconsin Relating to the Reading of the Bible in Public Schools,* Madison, WI: Democrat Printing Company, 1890, 12–22.

117. Justice John B. Cassoday, *Opinion, Decision of the Supreme Court of the State of Wisconsin, Relating to the Reading of the Bible in Public Schools,* Madison, WI: Democrat Printing Company, 1890, 23–32.

118. Justice Harlow S. Orton, *Opinion, Decision of the Supreme Court of the State of Wisconsin Relating to the Reading of the Bible in Public Schools,* Madison, WI: Democrat Printing Company, 1890, 32–35.

119. *Minutes of the Wisconsin Baptist Anniversaries 1890,* Janesville, WI: H. M. Antes, 1890, 29.

120. *Minutes of the Forty-First Annual Session of the Dane Baptist Association 1890,* Madison, WI: Tracy, Gibbs and Co., 1890, 9.

121. *Minutes of the Fiftieth Annual Meeting of the Congregational Convention of Wisconsin 1890,* Madison, WI: Tracy, Gibbs and Co., 1890, 45.

122. Ibid., 4.

123. J. J. Blaisdell, *The Wisconsin Bible Case. The Decision of the Supreme Court of Wisconsin.* A paper read before the Beloit Congregational Convention at Palmyra, Wisconsin, May 23, 1890, and accepted for substance, by that body as an expression of its views. It is published in pursuance of a vote of the Convention, Madison, WI: State Historical Society of Wisconsin, 1890, 28.

124. Ibid., 28–29.

125. Ibid., 35.

126. Ibid., 35–36.

127. Ibid., 36.
128. *Minutes of the General Assembly of the Presbyterian Church in the United States of America 1890*, New Series, 13, Philadelphia: MacCalla and Co., 1890, 104.
129. Ibid., 35–36.
130. *Minutes of the Synod of Wisconsin of the Presbyterian Church 1890*, Madison, WI: Tracy, Gibbs and Co., 1890, 13–14.
131. Ibid., 14.
132. Rev. W. A. McAtee, "The Bible in the Public Schools," in the *Minutes of the Synod of Wisconsin of the Presbyterian Church 1891*, Madison, WI: Tracy, Gibbs and Co., 1891, 15.
133. Ibid., 16.
134. Rev. W. A. McAtee, "Letter to the Editor," *Wisconsin State Journal*, April 2, 1890, 4.
135. Ibid.
136. Rev. W. A. McAtee, "Letter to the Editor," *Wisconsin State Journal*, April 5, 1890, 1.
137. Rev. W. A. McAtee, *Must the Bible Go?* Madison, WI: Tracy, Gibbs and Co., 1890, 14.
138. Ibid., 26, 27, 58.
139. Ibid., 72, 65–68.
140. *Minutes of the Wisconsin Annual Conference of the Methodist Episcopal Church, Forty-Fourth Session 1890.* John Schneider, Editor and Publisher, 1890, 62.
141. *Minutes of the Thirty-Sixth Annual Session of the West Wisconsin Conference of the Methodist Episcopal Church 1890*, Evansville, WI: R. M. Antes, 1890, 47.
142. Ibid., 50.
143. *Milwaukee Sentinel*, April 14, 1890, 12.
144. *The Bennett Law. Newspaper Clippings*, May 11, 1890. A scrapbook in the Library of the State Historical Society of Wisconsin, Madison.
145. *Minutes of the Forty-Fourth Annual Council of the Diocese of Milwaukee 1890.* (Protestant Episcopal), Milwaukee, WI: Burdick, Armitage and Allen, 1890); *Journal of the Sixteenth Annual Council of the Protestant Episcopal Church in the Diocese of Fond du Lac 1890.* Fond du Lac, WI: P. B. Haber, 1890.
146. *Milwaukee Sentinel*, March 23, 1890, 12.
147. Ibid. June 24, 1890, 4.
148. Ibid.
149. Ibid., June 30, 1890, 4.
150. Ibid.
151. Ibid.
152. *Hoffman's Catholic Directory and Clergy List Quarterly 1890*, Milwaukee, WI: Hoffman Bro's., 1890, 90, 266, 293.
153. *Wisconsin's Catholic Heritage, 1848–1948.* A Centennial Souvenir Booklet. With the Approval of the Ordinary, 26.
154. *Catholic Citizen*, March 22, 1890, 1.
155. Ibid., 4.
156. Ibid.
157. Ibid., April 16, 1890, 4.
158. Ibid., May 3, 1890, 4.
159. *Wisconsin Tobacco Reporter*, March 21, 1890, 4.
160. Ibid., 5.

161. Ibid., April 18, 1890, 4.

162. *New York Times*, March 20, 1890, 4.

163. Quaife, ed., *The Attainment of Statehood*, 931.

164. *The Blue Book of the State of Wisconsin. 1889*, compiled and published under direction of Ernest G. Timms, Secretary of State, 1889, 493–501; 577–85.

165. *Wisconsin Tobacco Reporter*, April 4, 1890, 4.

166. Robert R. Hamilton and Paul R. Nort, *The Law and Education, With Cases*, Brooklyn: The Foundation Press, Inc., 1959, 31.

167. Robert F. Coan, "Bible-Reading in the Public Schools," *The Albany Law Review* 22 (January 1958): 156, 167.

168. A. H. Wintersteen, "Commentary," 321.

169. Joseph Schaefer, "The Courts and History," *Wisconsin Magazine of History* 9 (March 1926): 350–52, 357.

170. Joseph Schaefer, "The Courts and History—Again," *Wisconsin Magazine of History* 16 (March 1933): 322, 326–27.

171. A. H. Wintersteen, "Christianity and the Common Law," *American Law Register* 29 (May 1890): 273, 285

172. "Current Topics," *The Albany Law Review* 42 (December 20, 1890): 489, 490.

173. *Wisconsin Journal of Education* XX (May 1890): 192.

174. *Biennial Report of the State Superintendent of the State of Wisconsin, for the Two Years Ending June 30, 1890*, Madison, WI: Democrat Printing Co., 1890, 43.

175. *Report of the Commissioner of Education for the Year 1897–1898, II*. Washington, DC: US Government Printing Office, 1899, 1555.

176. A. H. Wintersteen, "Commentary," 321, 329–30.

· 6 ·

PROTESTANT DISSENT
IN THE NINETEENTH CENTURY

Three Presbyterians

Historians have often pointed out that most Protestants supported the creation of common-school systems in the mid-1800s. They did so because they believed that the common school with its pan-Protestant character evidenced by, for example, Bible-reading would help maintain a Protestant Christian culture in the face of increasing religious pluralism spurred in large measure by the growing number of Roman Catholics. Protestant support for public education, however, was neither unanimous nor unequivocal. Some Protestants expressed reservations about the extent of the government's role in education and the gradual secularization of common schooling. Some Lutherans and Presbyterians created or attempted to create denominational schools as an alternative to public schooling. A few objected to the very idea of state involvement in education and asserted that the family was responsible for educating the young, while others embraced public schooling along with safeguards for parental liberty.

Varying degrees of dissent from the public school paradigm can be seen in the work of three Presbyterians. Charles Hodge, a Princeton Seminary professor and probably the most widely read theologian of his day; Robert L. Dabney, a son of the Old South and Union Seminary faculty member; and William M. Beckner, a Presbyterian layman and social reformer; each contributed significantly to debates about the nature and extent of public schooling in the nineteenth century. Moreover, the questions they raised and issues they confront-ed remain part and parcel of current discussions regarding parental choice in education, homeschooling, school-state separation, and other forms of educational dissent.

Charles Hodge: Ambivalent Dissenter

Born in Philadelphia in 1797 and reared in a strong Presbyterian community, Charles Hodge embraced the doctrines of Calvinism early in life. In addition to attending a local primary school, his widowed mother, Mary Hodge, and Ashbel Green, a well-known Presbyterian pastor, instructed Hodge in the doctrines of the Reformed faith. After attending an academy in Somerville, New Jersey, the future Presbyterian theologian continued his education at the College of New Jersey (Princeton College). Upon completing his studies in 1815, he enrolled in the newly created Presbyterian seminary at Princeton where he matured spiritually and intellectually under the tutelage and personal influence of Archibald Alexander and Samuel Miller, the first and second members of the seminary faculty, respectively. By the time Hodge graduated in 1819, Alexander was sufficiently impressed with the young scholar's academic progress and Christian growth that he offered him an appointment at the seminary. After a year of private study and preaching, he accepted a one-year appointment as an instructor in biblical languages. Hodge's teaching performance and scholarship earned him a permanent appointment as Professor of Oriental and Biblical Literature in 1822, thus commencing a calling at Princeton that ended with his death in 1878. In 1825, he founded the *Biblical Repertory and Princeton Review* (hereafter cited as *BRPR*), a journal that initially translated and reprinted European biblical scholarship.[1] With the exception of a leave of absence between 1826 and 1828, when Hodge studied in Europe in order to remedy what he considered shortcomings in his theological education, he served as editor of the journal until 1868. During his tenure, he transformed it into a widely respected theological journal that spoke to a wide variety of contemporary religious, cultural, and political issues from a traditional Calvinistic or Reformed perspective. Hodge himself published around 140 trenchant reviews, essays, and articles on diverse topics, including slavery, temperance, revivalism, Kant, Emerson, church-state issues, "Romanism" and American civil liberties, science, current debates within the Presbyterian Church and its General Assembly, popular education, and the role of religion in the common schools and public life.[2]

Of this impressive number and range of contributions to the *BRPR*, many of Hodge's lengthy essays were devoted to questions related to the educational responsibilities of parents, the church, and the state as well as the role of religion in education. Indeed, he penned at least a dozen major articles on education-related subjects, not to mention numerous shorter commentaries. In addition to his journal articles, he addressed educational issues in speeches and other publications. Though a strong supporter of Presbyterian parochial schools and the absolute necessity of religious instruction, not mere moral education, in any worthwhile education, Hodge often asserted that the state shared responsibility with parents and the church to ensure the proper education of all children. He conditioned his support for public education, however, on the inclusion of meaningful religious instruction, including the use of the Bible as a textbook. The Princeton scholar dissented vigorously from the position that the state could only offer secular instruction and that Protestant Christian doctrines of sin, redemption, and salvation had no place in the common schools. Indeed, he often argued that education without biblical religion was not "neutral" but in fact irreligious or atheistic and ultimately destructive of the individual and society.[3]

First Thoughts on Education

Charles Hodge expressed his initial thoughts on American educational matters in his "Introductory Lecture" given to seminary students upon his return from Europe in 1828, and published in the *BRPR* in 1829. After discussing differing church-state relationships in the United States and European countries, Hodge devoted the bulk of his commentary to topics on which he would write regularly and passionately for most of the rest of his public life—education and religion. Like Horace Mann, whose biography he would review several years after the common-school reformer's death in 1859, he was impressed with Prussia's effort to provide universal education. Of greater import, however, was the fact that "religion is as regularly and as systematically taught as any other subject." Such an example, he maintained, "demands attention of all friends of knowledge and religion." He recognized, however, that religious pluralism and restrictions on the role of the government in purely religious matters in the United States presented challenges to the provision of religious instruction in the emerging state-controlled schools. Hodge suggested that since denominations united to distribute Bibles and tracts, perhaps they could collectively develop textbooks that taught "historical facts and essential doctrines" of the Christian (meaning Protestant Christian) faith. If this approach proved unsatisfactory, he asserted that the Bible could be at least studied, not merely read, in the public schools.

Like most Protestants living in United States at that time, Hodge believed that the Bible was authoritative.[4] As historian Mark Noll has pointed out, however, he and his colleagues at Princeton, were distinguished "not so much by . . . allegiance to the Bible as by . . . insistence that the Bible be studied academically as well as devotionally, that it be treated as the norm for corporate action as well as a fount of personal inspiration."[5] Failure to adopt some plan to insure biblical literacy, Hodge claimed, would result "in a large portion of our population growing up in ignorance of the first principles of moral and religious truth." As far as he was concerned, the task was too great for parents and pastors alone. For its own safety and well-being, the state was obligated to teach religion. As Hodge often reiterated, "If public virtue be necessary to the existence of free institutions; if reason and experience teach that religious knowledge and culture are essential to virtue; to leave people destitute of this knowledge and culture, is to secure the destruction of our civil liberty." The young Princeton don concluded his lecture with another theme common to his writing on religion and education—localism. If religious instruction could not be introduced into all the schools in the country or even throughout a whole state, "we may at least endeavor to effect the object in our own immediate neighborhood."[6]

Hodge returned to several of these themes two years later in a review of William Sprague's *Lectures to Young People*. Lamenting the neglect of religious education of children on the part of parents and schools, he stressed the importance of teaching children the doctrines of sin and salvation and urged that adults encourage them to "treasure up" the "facts" of the Bible. Noting the difficulty of creating a universal school system in a country as diverse as the United States to accomplish this purpose, Hodge pondered the possibility either of each church having its own school or of different denominations cooperating to establish Christian schools in the same manner as they had worked to create the Sabbath school system. As would be the case throughout his life, Hodge seemed much more concerned about the end of education—knowledge of the Bible and its principal doctrines that would fit the child to carry out duties to God—than the means, whether accomplished by parents, the church, and/or the state.[7]

In 1833, Hodge commented for the first time on the developing common-school systems in various northern states. He noted, "the best interests of every civil community are intimately involved in the extensive establishment of common schools, and in the general dissemination of knowledge through all classes. . . ." If in addition to instruction in subjects necessary for discharging the normal duties of life, Hodge continued, "could be added a well digested and thorough arrangement for imparting, in due proportion, sound moral and religious instruction, there would be but little for us to desire in the matter of common schools." He speculated, however, that the establishment of a uniform common-school system might preclude "all extended plans for the religious instruction of children." If common schooling indeed developed in that direction, Hodge once again recommended that either churches or groups of churches create schools to provide all children "within their respective limits . . . the means and opportunity to acquire sound, wholesome instruction in morals, religion, and in all the branches of an elementary education." Specifically, he reminded his readers that the most important knowledge that a child could acquire was the "knowledge of God and of his son Jesus Christ, whom to know is life eternal." Hodge then pointed out that some states, like New Jersey, distributed public funds to school trustees in proportion to the number of children enrolled in the local district. As Archbishop John Hughes and other Roman Catholic leaders would argue almost ten years later and beyond, Hodge asserted that church schools were entitled to their share of public funds as well. Such funds would help poor parents defray tuition charges for an education they deemed appropriate for their children. Given that since the colonial period the line between public and private schooling was often blurred, that schools were viewed as public, regardless of control, if they served public purposes, and that public funds were often distributed to religious schools, Hodge's contention is not surprising. He apparently understood, however, that common-school reformers and their allies frequently asserted that only government-controlled schools had a claim on tax dollars for education. The Princeton professor concluded his essay with the observation that if the churches could not obtain a share of public funds, then they should proceed at their own expense for the benefit of their children.[8]

Throughout the remainder of the 1830s, Hodge commented frequently on education-related topics in the United States and abroad in the *BRPR*. Even when discussing developments in England or Scotland, he always reminded his readers of the importance of religious education in this country. In his words, "The Bible is the grand instrument of education."[9] He was also increasingly aware of two trends that generated heated debate regarding popular education in the United States in the mid-nineteenth century: the growing presence of the Roman Catholic Church and government assumption of the provision of elementary schooling. Hodge was neither hostile to state involvement in education nor as virulently anti-Catholic as many of his fellow Protestants. Nevertheless, he frequently expressed concern about "Romanism" and centralized control of schooling. Of the growing presence of the state and implications for religious instruction of the public, he remarked, "The matter of education is, in this country, becoming more and more nearly allied to the grand actions of governments; it would be dreadful indeed, if our worthy legislators were to go to work after a wrong fashion." Concerns related to these trends as well as fears regarding inadequate doctrinal training of the rising generation of Presbyterians led eventually to concrete proposals for a system of parochial schools.[10]

Tension between the Old School and New School Presbyterians, which led to schism in 1837 over the latter's embrace of a form of revivalism associated with Charles G. Finney and its presumed drift toward Arminianism, as well as the growing controversy over slavery and abolitionism, dominated the General Assembly meetings of the Old School wing in the latter part of the 1830s. The Assembly, however, did not ignore education issues. In 1839, it appointed a committee to "secure for children and young people of the church more full advantages of Christian education than they have hitherto enjoyed." The committee comprised the entire faculty of Princeton Seminary, including Hodge. The next year the committee recommended that each congregation establish at least one school for young children and that each Presbytery sponsor an academy in order to counter the neglect of religious education. In 1841, the General Assembly adopted the committee's proposal. According to Lewis Sherrill, the author of the definitive history of the Presbyterian parochial school system, the proposal then lay dormant for several years.[11]

The Common-School Dilemma

In the meanwhile, though, debates regarding religion in the public schools in New York City and Massachusetts sparked Hodge's attention and concern. In an 1841 issue of the *BRPR*, he penned an essay more than fifty pages long on swirling controversies in both places. Claiming that the most important question at hand was "upon what foundation shall education rest," he once again turned to the place of religion in the "process of popular education" and asserted that officials in both states deemed the teaching of Bible doctrines and associated religious instruction "sectarian" and intended to eliminate them from the public schools. Hodge argued that mere secular education was in effect "irreligious" education rather than "neutral" education. He also dissented firmly from Horace Mann's proposal to "introduce sublime truths of ethics and natural religion." Moral truth, Hodge claimed, "requires divine sanction." Mere Bible-reading was inadequate.[12]

Hodge noted, however, that proposals to remove religious instruction from the common schools ran counter to current practice in most places. In a departure from his earlier contention that citizens would not tolerate the complete elimination of religion from the common schools, he wondered if in the future such might be the case. He remarked presciently that the "purging" of religious instruction might follow increased state funding and centralized control by, in his words, an "aristocracy of educators." Indeed, he speculated that those working for a more "efficient organization" to improve the schools, could exercise power to eliminate practices that offended Catholic and Protestant alike. The result, he continued, might be that the "irreligious" would rise up and forbid the use of public monies for others' creeds and dogmas, save their own. That said, however, Hodge asserted that religious education of a Protestant Christian nature (free use of the Bible and essential doctrines, excluding denominational particulars) was necessary for the welfare of the republic and fully consistent with the wishes of the vast majority of citizens whose taxes supported the public schools. Sounding very much like President John Adams, the Princeton theologian opined, "Our country cannot maintain its present form of government . . . unless the general education of our children is accompanied with or built upon a religious education. . . . Our public schools must have a religious character—without it their utility is exceedingly questionable."[13]

Finally, Hodge considered three possible courses of action that might settle the controversy surrounding the "school question." First, he pointed out that secularists and Unitarians, like Mann and several other common-school reformers, might lead the schools toward eventual secularization. This, he feared, would subvert "evangelical morality" and work "a corresponding deficit in all social and civil relations of life." Nevertheless, he still believed that most Americans would not accept this option. Second, every Protestant religious group might decide to educate its own children. Hodge clearly recognized the legitimacy of this approach. He thought that parents of all religious persuasions desired religious instruction for their children "by some means or another." Even some "irreligious parents" would send their children to these schools, preferring "their children should at least be taught to fear God and obey his laws." Such schools should receive, as a matter of fairness and past practice, a share of tax dollars. Though critical of Roman Catholic theology and polity, Hodge, unlike many of his Protestant brethren, believed Catholics also had a legitimate claim on a share of state funds. Indeed, he noted that had they requested funds in New York between 1814 and 1824, instead of 1840, authorities could not have rejected their application.[14]

Despite his sympathy for this course, Hodge feared that many children would not receive a proper education, namely a religious education. He concluded: "We are inclined to therefore adopt the only remaining course suggested, namely to embrace in our public school system generally, the efficient, practical, intelligent constant inculcation of scriptural truth as received by the great body of Protestant Christendom in the United States, and that the patronage and countenance of Christian people in the respective districts, should not be extended to any schools from which religious instruction is excluded." Hodge explained that Protestant Christianity, without dogmatism or proselytism, should influence public schools because of its role in shaping American institutions and its majoritarian status. Here, he counseled his fellow Protestants to avoid the extremes of either urging instruction in specific doctrines, like the Trinity, or supporting removal of all meaningful religious instruction from the public schools. Instead, he recommended that all Protestants unite behind the doctrines of the Reformation, including inspiration of the Scriptures, justification through the atonement of Christ alone, and the resurrection of the just and unjust. Ninety-five percent of religious Protestants in the United States, Hodge declared, embraced these doctrines. After briefly criticizing Mann's proposals for moral education as long on "rhetorical flourish" but short on an understanding of fallen human nature and devoid of biblical sanction, he protested "current secularizing trends in New York and Massachusetts" and once more urged the "free and unrestricted use of the Bible for all lawful and public purposes in all public schools."[15]

He concluded his analysis with "an appeal to Christian men of all denominations and parties to renounce all connexion [sic] with any system of public instruction which does not fully and distinctly recognize the religion of Jesus Christ, revealed in the gospel as the groundwork of the whole scheme. . . . Unbelievers in his gospel, bigots, fanatics, and ultraists of any class may have their own schools on their plan." Hodge's support for public education was clearly conditional, and he was open to alternative schools for conscientious objectors. If public schooling became completely secular, however, Hodge was prepared to embrace a separate system of Presbyterian schools, with or without a share of the state school fund, for children of the church as well as the needy desirous of the kind of education he thought appropriate for the nation.[16]

Presbyterian Parochial Schools

Three years later in 1844, the General Assembly of the Presbyterian Church, U.S.A. (Old School) appointed a committee to "consider the expediency of establishing Presbyterian Parochial Schools." Two years later the committee submitted its report to the General Assembly. Noting that any education that did not include "instruction in the scriptures" was incomplete and that Presbyterians could not always depend on the common schools to carry out that task, the report commended local congregations that had founded schools and recommended "the whole subject of Parochial education to the serious attention of the church." The report sparked considerable debate between delegates who supported the creation of Presbyterian schools and delegates who urged support for the common schools. Despite objections of the proponents of public education, the Assembly adopted the committee's report and referred it to the Board of Education for further action.[17] Though Hodge was not a member of the committee, he expressed strong support for its findings and recommendations. In unusually sharp language that marked a distinct departure from his earlier reluctant embrace of common schooling, he asserted that the emerging state system of education was becoming increasingly "anti-Christian," that Presbyterians and believers pay for schools but have no right to teach their own beliefs, that secular education enforced by exclusion from public funds was "unjust," and that increasing centralization of control of the common schools was "tyrannical." Indeed, in direct reference to Horace Mann, he charged that common schools were under the influence of "a clique of Unitarian or infidel statesmen." In his mind, the solution was to follow the example of the "Romanists" and found schools as nurseries for the church, ministries, and the whole land. Hodge once again acknowledged that Catholics had a legitimate claim to a proportionate share of public funds set aside for education. If such funds were not available for Presbyterian schools, however, he urged the faithful to proceed. A good school that included the Bible and Catechism, the Princeton don concluded, would sustain itself and be able to provide tuition for needy students.[18]

At the next General Assembly in May 1847, the delegates debated the Board of Education report on denominational schooling. The thirty-two page document provided an extensive rationale for the creation of a parochial school system and recommended that the church create such a system.[19] Hodge shared his thoughts regarding the topic at hand in an invited sermon preached at an evening session of the Assembly entitled, "Public Religious Education Enforced in a Discussion of Different Plans." He once again asserted that all children needed religious education, by which he meant a thorough knowledge of the "facts and doctrines of the Bible," and pointed out that few persons seriously doubted that this was a "duty of the very highest necessity." On whom this duty was incumbent—parents, the church, or the state—was a matter of debate. Hodge claimed that no one denied that parents had the primary responsibility for the religious education of their children. Some parents, however, were either unwilling or unable to do their duty in a satisfactory manner. Given that religious education or the lack thereof, had social and civic consequences, what should be the role of the church and the state in supplementing or supplanting the role of the family? On this question, Hodge pointed out, the "minds of even wise and good men are very much divided." He then outlined five "plans" for the "respective rights and duties of the Church and of the State in reference to the subject of education."[20]

In the "Church and State Plan," Hodge maintained that both are equally involved. The state establishes schools, prescribes the course of instruction, and requires religious education, while the church selects religious texts and appoints instructors. Though common in many European countries with established church traditions, Hodge pointed out that religious pluralism and legal strictures put this plan out of the question in the United States. In the "Independent Plan of Church and State," the government establishes schools and provides competent teachers but leaves decisions regarding religious instruction to each local community or district. Though sympathetic to this model and its antecedents in New England, Hodge realized that increasing religious diversity would render this approach impracticable and might lead to banishing religion entirely from the public schools. Hodge was particularly wary of the third option, "The Compromise Plan." Through its schools, the state teaches religious doctrines on which all denominations agree. Sometimes called the "lowest common denominator approach," Hodge realized that this plan was in vogue in the United States and criticized it roundly. He averred that given the increasing religious diversity of the country, this approach led inevitably to the rejection of "positive doctrines" of the faith and to either very superficial views or "even infidelity itself."[21]

Hodge then maintained that the difficulties associated with the aforementioned plans had led many "public men" and some coreligionists to adopt

"The Secular Plan," which, in simple terms, confines the state to secular education and leaves religious instruction to parents and churches. Religious diversity, growing popular sentiment that the state should have nothing to do with religion, and sensitivity to religious liberty, Hodge admitted, attracted many Americans to this approach. He cautioned, however, that serious problems attended this plan. The Princeton theologian claimed that any system of education devoid of religious education would eventually become irreligious. "The most positively irreligious works," he asserted in terms that, outside of "infidel," sound very contemporary, "are those that proceed on the assumption that there is no God (no Supreme Being) to whom we sustain the relation of responsible creatures. All that the most ardent infidel need desire, in order to propagate infidelity through the community, would be that nothing be said about religion." To deny God's involvement in history and nature, he continued, would, in effect, result in a false and atheistic education. Furthermore, removing religious instruction from the common schools would deny many unchurched children knowledge essential to the well-being of society. While acknowledging the important role of the Sabbath school in the Christian nurture of children, Hodge opined that it was no match for a secular public school system "that assumes that they have no souls." Hodge concluded his critique of this plan with several familiar objections. He asserted that banning religion from the schools was contrary to the experience of most other countries, that it was unscriptural, and that it burdened the religious rights of Protestants and Catholics alike who pay taxes for an education they deem inappropriate for their children, yet often could not obtain a share of state education funds for their religious schools.[22]

Having determined that the first four plans were unsatisfactory, Hodge urged the delegates to support "The Church Plan." Departing somewhat from his earlier reluctant embrace of common schooling, he claimed, "There may be great doubt whether God ever intended to devolve upon the State the religious education of the young; but there can be no doubt that this duty rests upon the Church. . . . Her work is to teach." Hodge then chastised the Church for "enlisting the State as her agent." "Good people," he continued, "cannot consent to have religion banished from those institutions in which the mass of people learn almost all they ever know. We are, therefore, persuaded that the time is fast coming in which all denominations of Christians will address themselves in earnest to the establishment of schools, under their immediate control." As he had done in the past, Hodge commended the "Romanists" for discerning the need for parochial schools before his fellow Protestants. Each Presbyterian congregation, he urged, should establish a common school to instruct children, regardless of their economic circumstances, in "our doctrines and discipline, and be brought up to fear God and reverence the Church of their fathers." This approach, he believed, would also lessen the likelihood that as adults they would be "carried away by every wind of doctrine." Implementation of the plan would be difficult. Cost and a shortage of qualified teachers were significant obstacles, but Hodge was more concerned, and rightly so, about the inertia of the church. Great exertion would be required to overcome a tradition of expecting the state to play a significant role in the provision of religious education. Nevertheless, the establishment of Presbyterian schools was of eternal importance. Hodge concluded his sermon with a ringing endorsement of an alternative to the state system. He proclaimed that "the welfare of the Church and the salvation of men require that children should be thoroughly taught the facts and doctrines of the Bible, and that this instruction is not and cannot be adequately taught in public schools." Hodge then charged all pastors to establish "a truly Christian school . . . in which all children shall be taught to worship Christ, and to know 'the Scriptures, which are able to make them wise unto salvation.'"[23]

Hodge's sermon apparently had a powerful effect on the General Assembly. Even one of the staunchest opponents of the parochial school plan, J. H. Thornwell, a delegate from South Carolina and later president of South Carolina College who believed that the church's mission did not include providing secular education, acknowledged that the address gave "additional impulse to the cause." Hodge was certainly pleased when the Assembly approved the Board of Education's resolution that "immediate and strenuous exertions should be made, so far as practicable, by every congregation, to establish within its bounds one or more primary schools, under the care of the session of the church, in which, together with the usual branches of secular learning, the truths and duties of our holy religion shall be assiduously inculcated." The Assembly had committed itself to a system of Presbyterian schools. Hodge called this action a "subject of gratulation."[24]

Most Presbyterian congregations did not share Hodge's optimism regarding an alternative to government-sponsored education. Though 1848 and 1849 witnessed the creation of forty-seven and thirty-four new schools, respectively, their numbers tapered off over the next five years. In his 1850 and 1851 reports on the General Assembly, Hodge noted congregational apathy and occasional prejudice against denominational schools. Most Presbyterians either did not share Hodge's assessment of the state of public education and his enthusiasm for church schools or, like their representatives at the General

Assembly, focused their attention and energy on the increasingly emotional debates regarding slavery and abolitionism.[25]

By 1854, the number of new Presbyterian schools established dropped to twelve, and once again, Hodge addressed "The Education Question" in the pages of the *BRPR*. In a lengthy review essay, which Sherrill calls the "most mature expression of his thinking on this matter," the veteran Princeton theologian revisited and elaborated upon several themes from his previous commentaries. Once again, he reaffirmed his commitment to the education of the public and the shared responsibility of parents, the church, and the state. Despite his strong support for denominational schools and his criticism of the increasing secularization of public education, he still maintained that the state should play an important role in the religious education of the young, especially those children who were unchurched or whose parents were either negligent or incompetent. As he had in the past, he argued that the government had a duty to enhance the public good by means of religious education. Moreover, since the United States rested on a Protestant Christian foundation and most Americans were Protestant, Hodge believed religious instruction should reflect that foundation. He wrote:

> If the design of the State is the promotion of the public good; if religious education is necessary for the attainment of that object, and if such education cannot in a multitude of cases be secured otherwise than by State intervention, then we must either admit that the State is bound to provide for the religious education of its members, or assume the absurd position, that the State is not bound to answer the very end of its existence.

He feared, however, that many in the religious community and those in control of public education did not share his position and supported the removal of meaningful religious instruction from the common schools in an effort to placate certain groups, that is, "Papists, Infidels, and scheming politicians." Once again, Hodge opined that if the state eliminated religion from the public school system, then it would likely be "swept away" and the country would experience "fearful results." Education without religious instruction equated to irreligious education and such an education would eventually erode the social and civic order.[26]

Hodge believed that the common schools should and could teach the basic doctrines and beliefs on which all Protestants agreed, for example, the authority of the Scriptures and doctrines of the fall, sin, and salvation. Mere Bible-reading and instruction in the natural moral law would not suffice. He realized, however, that while the common schools should respond to what he called the "majority conscience," the "minority conscience" deserved protection. On this point, Hodge proposed several solutions to the problem of religious pluralism and common schooling. For Catholics as well as others who objected to the Protestant character of the public school system, Hodge recommended that they establish their own schools. In stark contrast to common-school reformers and most fellow Protestants, he stated that as a matter of fairness parents sending their children to these schools either be exempted from public school taxes or that their schools receive a share of the school fund. In essence, Hodge proposed the equivalent of tuition tax credits and vouchers. By this time, of course, a growing number of states were eliminating any form of education revenue sharing with nonpublic schools. Despite his strong reservations regarding the Roman Catholic Church and its theology, he asserted that its schools would contribute to the public good. Such an arrangement would be far better than, in his words, "the suicidal and futile attempt to banish from our Protestant institutions everything to which a Papist can object." For those families that did not have access to a private school, Hodge recommended what amounted to a released time option. If parents objected to the inculcation of the general facts and doctrines of the Bible, the Lord's prayer, and/or catechism, then their children should be exempted from such instruction or provided with alternative religious instruction of their parents' choosing. In sum, Hodge envisioned a common-school system that transmitted Protestant beliefs widely held in mid-nineteenth-century America and various mechanisms for accommodating dissenters, among whose number he would increasingly find himself.[27]

His hopes and proposals aside, Hodge appeared to be coming to the realization that increasing numbers of public schools would likely fall short of his expectations for religious training of the young, thus necessitating the creation of Christian schools, with or without state support. While not abandoning efforts to improve the state's schools, he argued that the church was obligated to provide a thoroughly Christian education for its own children. In his words, "It is the duty of the Church, while endeavoring to make the State education as good as possible, to provide at least for her own members a course of instruction more thoroughly according to her own views." As he had argued many times, this would involve regular, continuous, and thorough study of the Bible. Instruction in "general Christianity" was too superficial. But, Hodge pointed out, if the "State institutions are truly Christian, as we know is often the case, especially as it concerns common schools, it would be most unwise to set up rival institutions." Hodge's support of common schooling was, therefore, contingent on the inclusion of thorough Protestant Christian instruction. Absent such teaching, the church was morally obligated to establish its own schools.[28]

Despite his growing sense that public education would not meet his standard for religious education and his somewhat veiled frustration with Presbyterians' tepid response to the call to create schools, Hodge seemed pleased with the ongoing discussions regarding the roles of the state and the church in education. "We look back on the recent discussions on this whole subject with great satisfaction," he concluded on a hopeful note. "It has, on the one hand, led to a clearer view of the duty of the State in reference to the work of education, and to a deeper sense of the importance of Christians exerting themselves to give a truly religious character to the public schools; and, upon the other hand, it has served to produce a stronger conviction of the high part the Church is called to act in this matter, and of the importance of the Board of Education continuing and extending their efforts to establish schools, academies, and colleges."[29]

Despite Hodge's hopes for a "stronger conviction" regarding parochial schools, between 1855 and 1861 Presbyterian congregations founded only twenty-seven institutions. Though he continued to press for Christian schools, he was less confident of his vision for a Presbyterian system of education. Consequently, he devoted much more attention to the growing secularization of public education. He often warned his readers to watch out for the proper place of religion in the "great educational reform" of the era.[30] In an 1859 Jeremiad on the right to worship as a Protestant nation, Hodge assailed those who demanded the elimination of religion in general and the Bible in particular from the public schools. Directing his wrath at extreme individualists and Catholics, he objected vigorously to the removal of religion and the Bible from public education and predicted it would have dire consequences for American culture and education. With what some contemporary educational dissenters would consider remarkable prescience, Hodge declared

> For this great public school system is an all-moulding power upon the ideas themselves which are entertained of education, among all classes of society. The views of education which prevail in the public schools will soon come to prevail in the nation. Religious instruction and influence driven from these, soon cease to form any part of the idea of education in the community at large. . . . If the Bible is driven out of the public school, it can never maintain the position it has hitherto occupied.

Should this occur, he concluded, the country would eventually become an "infidel nation" and invite God's judgment.[31]

Demise of the Presbyterian Parochial School Plan

In the minds of many Americans, God's judgment fell on the country between 1861 and 1865, as men in blue and gray slaughtered each other at places such as Manassas, Cold Harbor, Shiloh, Antietam, Fredericksburg, and Gettysburg, and Hodge's beloved denomination split into northern and southern branches. During the Civil War years, Hodge said little about education, save for a few brief comments about the threat of "Romanism" and the necessity of Presbyterian schools. Churches founded only twelve schools during those years, and by 1865, the effort to create a system of schools was for all practical purposes over, except for a dozen or so missionary schools established between 1866 and 1870. Despite the persistent efforts of Hodge and his allies, Presbyterian congregations founded only around 265 schools between 1847 and 1870. Though the political turmoil leading up to the War Between the States and the conflict itself no doubt dampened efforts to create an alternative to "government education," a term Hodge used occasionally, most of his fellow Presbyterians willingly accepted the state's provision of free elementary education. Like most other Protestants, the vast majority of rank and file Presbyterians did not share either Hodge's somewhat gloomy assessment of the decline of religious education in the common schools or his passion for parochial schools. They seemed content to vest their energy in efforts to deny Catholics a share of public funds for education and to maintain Bible-reading and other symbols of Protestantism in the schools. Doctrines, creeds, and facts of the Bible seemed less and less important to American Protestants as the century progressed. As historian Timothy L. Smith has demonstrated, an ever declining number of American Protestants affirmed traditional Calvinistic doctrines in the years leading up to the Civil War. Revivalism with its emphasis on human will and emotion associated with the Second Great Awakening had superseded Reformed Christianity that had been dominant in seventeenth- and eighteenth-century America. Religious experience had trumped religious instruction in the minds of many Americans.[32]

Even the aging Princeton theologian seemed to realize that his hope for a Presbyterian school system would not likely come to fruition. After Appomattox, he said very little about an alternative to public education. Prior to stepping down as editor of the *BRPR* in 1868, he penned several essays on educational topics. Rather than harshly condemning the growing secularization of public education and touting parochial schools, he continued to emphasize the role of parents, the church, and the state in educating the young. Though still dissenting from the tendency to divorce religious from secular instruction in the common schools, Hodge tried to make the best of the situation. He noted that though state and local officials had often excluded direct religious instruction, "a large amount of religious influence" remained in the public schools. Teachers, he pointed out, were usually Christians and authorities had not completely removed the Bible from most schools. This is not to say he was pleased with the status quo. As had been the case in past commentaries, Hodge argued that education could never be "neutral" on matters of religion.[33] In a review of a biography of Horace Mann, written by his wife, for example, he was sharply critical of the reformer's beliefs in the goodness of human nature, social progress, and "natural religion," which Mann claimed was preeminent over the "revealed religion" of the Bible. Mann, Hodge asserted in language similar to that critics of "secular humanism" in the public schools often employ, attempted surreptitiously to promote these views through an increasingly centralized educational system in Massachusetts, while at the same time denouncing as fanatics and bigots orthodox Calvinists who openly advocated "the philosophy of Christ's gospel" in the common schools. Though he did not profess to know the extent of Mann's "revolution" to establish his Unitarian beliefs in the common schools of Massachusetts and beyond, Hodge urged ministers and ruling elders to pay close attention to common schools in their neighborhoods and attempt to secure religious and moral teachers as well as suitable books, including the Bible.[34]

After relinquishing the editorship of the BRPR in 1868 until his death in 1878, Hodge wrote little else new on the "school question." He focused more on theological matters and the debates swirling around "Darwinism." In 1869, however, the Princeton theologian responded to a letter regarding his views on education from a Rev. Morris Sutphen. He wrote to the New York pastor, "I am not aware that my views have undergone any change on the education question. I still believe that the Church is bound to see to it that all within her influence, especially her own children, have a religious education; to which end parish or church schools are indispensable." Such schools, he stated, "are entitled to a share of the school fund of the State, proportioned to the number of children they educate." Provision of such schools should be the duty of all denominations, Hodge continued, but with "such a heterogeneous and liberty-abusing population as we have in this country, church schools cannot reach the masses sufficiently, . . . therefore State schools are a necessity." Hodge concluded his professed "creed" with a previously unmentioned assertion most likely rooted in his distrust of the political intentions of the Roman Catholic Church.

He asserted that the right to vote be extended to only those educated in schools approved by the State. He did not elaborate on what he meant by "approved."[35]

Hodge's Legacy

Indeed, Charles Hodge's views on education did not change significantly over nearly fifty years of public life. He consistently championed Presbyterian parochial schools, yet realized that the government had a significant role to play in the education of children. He objected strenuously to the elimination of regular religious instruction from public education but came to grips with the fact that having Bible-reading and Christian teachers might be all that could be expected in the common schools. That said, however, Hodge remained adamant that education could never be "neutral" on matters of religion. When matters of conscience arose in the context of religious instruction, he argued for accommodations and options for dissenters rather than elimination of instruction approved by the Protestant majority. Moreover, unlike most of his fellow Protestants, Hodge consistently supported distribution of tax dollars to religious schools, even those operated by the Catholic Church, because such schools contributed to the education of the public.

Though Charles Hodge's carefully argued and balanced dissents regarding the secularization of education, centralization of control, and the public school system's exclusive claim on tax dollars for education and his arguments for shared educational responsibility engaged nineteenth-century readers, his work is largely overlooked in educational circles today. Even contemporary dissenters, such as school choice advocates, school-state separationists, and home-schoolers, seldom mention Charles Hodge. That is not the case, however, with another nineteenth-century Presbyterian theologian, Robert L. Dabney.

Robert Dabney: Radical Dissenter

Robert Lewis Dabney was born in Louisa County, Virginia in 1820. His parents, Charles and Elizabeth Dabney, had deep roots in Virginia and were related to or friends of many of Old Dominion's patriots and leaders, including Patrick Henry, Thomas Jefferson, and John Marshall. Young Dabney imbibed the class and racial attitudes common in the Old South on his parents' modest plantation, and his formal education was typical of that afforded to children of the small planter class, including "old field schools" and tutors. After attending

Hampden-Sidney College in 1836–1837, where a revival cemented his commitment to the Christian faith, Dabney taught school briefly before continuing his education at the University of Virginia, where he completed work for a master's degree and apparently acquired distaste for instructors from outside the South. In 1844, he entered Union Theological Seminary, a staunchly Old School Presbyterian institution then located at Hampden-Sidney. While at Union, Dabney embraced the same tenets of Calvinism held by Hodge and his Princeton colleagues, including the absolute authority of the Bible and God's sovereignty. Upon graduation in 1846, he accepted a call from Tinkling Spring Church located near Staunton, Virginia. During his pastorate, Dabney wrote articles on a variety of topics, including slavery and Roman Catholicism. His reputation for sharp, conservative social and religious commentary earned him an appointment to the Union faculty in 1853, where he served as a professor of church history and polity until 1859. From 1859 until 1883, he taught theology and served as co-pastor of the college church. He declined an appointment at Princeton Seminary in 1860, despite the fervent recruiting efforts of Charles Hodge, preferring to stay in the South. A loyal Virginian and an intellectual leader of the southern Presbyterians, Dabney served as an officer under Stonewall Jackson, his brother-in-law, during the Civil War and as Moderator of the Southern Presbyterian Church in 1870. In 1883, he left Union due to ill health and accepted an appointment at the University of Texas where he taught philosophy until 1894 and helped found Austin Theological Seminary. He died in 1898.[36]

Like Hodge, Dabney was a man of considerable intellectual depth and breadth who enjoyed the respect of friends and enemies alike and penned essays on a wide variety of topics, including race, capitalism, geology, unions, the southern cause, ethics, and education. Indeed, most scholars recognize him as the preeminent Southern Presbyterian theologian after the War Between the States. Though the Union professor wrote far less on education than his Princeton counterpart, his work currently enjoys a much wider audience. While Hodge addressed education throughout his public life, most of Dabney's work on education appeared between 1875 and 1880. Moreover, as Iain Murray has observed, "as with all uninspired men (in the biblical sense), he could not always distinguish exactly between his own inherited prejudices of upbringing and the unchanging revelation of Scripture," to whose authority he appealed in his assessment of the affairs of the day.[37] This is evident in some of his vehement objections to the establishment of a state school system in Virginia during Reconstruction, an era that Dabney found particularly odious, through the efforts of his longtime friend, William Henry Ruffner. Unlike Hodge, who argued that parents, the church, and the state shared responsibility for the education of the young, Dabney vigorously asserted that God had designated the family, not the church or the state, as the agency in charge of the education of children. Furthermore, he maintained, state-sponsored schooling would inevitably devolve into a thoroughly secularized, atheistic education. Revelatory of his Old South class and racial biases, Dabney also claimed that universal education would raise false hopes of equality and render freedmen unsuitable for menial labor, a station he believed Providence had ordained for them.[38]

Objection to the Virginia Public School System

The occasion of Dabney's first major dissent regarding state-sponsored schooling came as a result of Virginia's creation of a public school system headed by William Henry Ruffner, who took office in 1870 as the first Superintendent of Public Instruction. Ruffner, who had opposed slavery and supported the education of blacks before and after the Civil War, faced serious obstacles in his effort to establish a dual common-school system, including racism, economic devastation, hostility to "Yankee ideas," distrust of state authority, and elite opposition to popular education. Exacerbating the already difficult situation was the impending passage in 1874 and 1875 of a federal civil rights bill that contained a clause mandating "mixed schools." The threat of forced integration sparked a virtual declaration of war against Ruffner and the fledgling public school system.[39]

Critics like Professor Bennett Puryear of Richmond College proclaimed that the provision for public schools amounted to state paternalism and tended to "relax individual energy and debauch private morality." He asserted that the system violated the American principle that allowed each citizen to manage his own affairs without government interference. Despite the fact that the Bible would be read in the state's schools and common Christian ethics taught, Puryear maintained, "the public school is atheism or infidelity" in that it substituted state control for parental control of the child. The Baptist don condemned the system as a "negation of God's authority."[40]

Baptists were not the only detractors. Dabney, a former classmate of Ruffner's and fellow Presbyterian, soon joined the chorus of critics of the concept of public education. In the April 1876 issue of the *Southern Planter and Farmer*, the Union Seminary professor blasted the common-school system as a "quixotic project . . . the cunning cheat of Yankee statecraft." He condemned the "unrighteousness" of a system that "wrung by a grinding taxation from an oppressed people" enormous sums for use in the "pretended education of freed slaves." Expenditures for public education, he continued, were all the more deplorable at a time "when the state can neither pay its debt nor attend to its own legitimate interests." Evincing the prejudices of his culture, Dabney assert-ed that many intelligent white citizens were keeping their children at home to labor in the fields "to raise . . . taxes to give a pretended education to the brats of the black paupers" who "loaf and steal." As far as he was concerned, educa-tion could not alleviate the freedmen's low character and dependent nature and education for citizenship was a waste of time.[41]

Educated freedmen, Dabney opined, would develop "foolish and impossi-ble inspirations." They would become surly and disinterested in their true call-ing, manual labor. Miscegenation was an even greater danger. He argued that the real goal of the state school board was to bring about the "amalgamation" of the races and he urged the state government to thwart the plans of the rad-icals in Congress.[42]

Dabney was not merely opposed to educating blacks in Virginia under any circumstances. He rejected the very concept of state-sponsored schooling. His argument against public schooling rested on the assumption that the family was the primary unit of society. He maintained that parents were, or ought to be, the sole agents of the family. The state's duty was to protect the family, not to interfere with it, especially by usurping one of the family's principal functions, namely, the education of children. Basing his position on, among other things, an exegesis of Genesis and the Fifth Commandment, the Presbyterian theolo-gian asserted that God held parents alone responsible for their children's intel-lectual, moral, and spiritual training. Horace Mann's notion of a parental state was anathema to Dabney.[43]

Dabney had definite ideas about the nature of education for which parents were responsible. Sounding very much like Charles Hodge and stating an often repeated proposition, he asserted, "There can be no true education with-out moral culture and no moral culture without Christianity." True education, in other words, must be thoroughly Christian. "Natural theism" and Bible-reading, which reformers often touted as a means of keeping religion and moral education in the common schools, were not sufficient to accomplish this pur-pose. Moreover, since the state was secular, Dabney argued, "it is totally disqual-ified to conduct schools for all people." To proffer a "true education," would require the state school system to violate constitutional principles as well as the consciences of religious minorities. To exclude the religion of the Bible, on the other hand, would result in an atheistic education and tyrannical taxation of those who objected to it. Responding to the suggestion that dissenting parents should pay for a private school, Dabney wrote, "But he (the "fastidious parent") is taxed compulsorily to support this school which parental duty forbids him to use; so the system in this case amounts to an iniquitous penalty upon him for his faithfulness to his conscience." The state and the church, therefore, should recognize the parents as the primary agent of education and "should assume an ancillary instead of a dominating attitude. The state should only encourage individual and voluntary efforts and aid those whose poverty and misfortunes disable them from properly rearing their own children." In sum, the state should be the educational agency of last, rather than first resort.[44]

Dabney's Education Credo

Dabney's criticisms of the state school system and Ruffner, as well as the superintendent's counterarguments in the mid-1870s, appeared piecemeal in Virginia newspapers and popular periodicals. In 1879 and 1880, shortly after Hodge's death, Dabney published two lengthy essays on education in the nationally circulated BRPR. The first of these, his grand educational credo entitled "Secularized Education," offers complex, provocative, and at times prophetic answers to two foundational questions: "Who is the agent entitled to control education?" and "What is right education?" and circulates widely among leaders of contemporary dissenting movements.[45]

After a brief examination of current educational responsibility in Europe and the threats posed by both church and state control, Dabney turned his attention to the United States. In this country, he posited that if the state is the educator, then education must be "secularized totally." Departing from Hodge's position that state schools should teach the beliefs of the Protestant majority, Dabney enunciated what some modern scholars would label a "strict separationist" position. He wrote, "Since in theory our State is the *institute for realizing secular justice*. It has absolutely severed itself from all religions equally; it has pledged itself that no man's civil rights shall be modified or equality diminished by any religion or the lack of any; and has forbidden the establishment of any religion by law, and the imposition of any burden for a religious pretext on any." On this view, Dabney asserted that, as state agents, public school teachers should not teach religious beliefs and that school funds should not be used to teach certain religious beliefs "in preference to others." On the other hand, Dabney continued, some persons claim that though no religion can be established, the "State is not an atheistic institute, but must ground itself in the will of God, which is the standard of all rights" . . . and "ought to teach divine truths common to all." Whether "this be the just basis of a commonwealth or not," Dabney countered, "our *States do not avow it*." Moreover, agreeing on common beliefs or a particular version of the Bible would raise sectarian issues. In addition, Dabney maintained, "we do not believe . . . that the State can be atheistic, because it is an ethical institute, and the divine will is the only valid ethical rule. . . . But the State finds the theistic basis in natural theology."[46]

Dabney then reviewed four solutions often suggested on the "theory of State education" and a rebuttal to each. He rejected as simply "unjust" the proposal to force the religion of the majority on the minority. Likewise, Dabney deemed unsatisfactory the plan to distribute shares of the school fund to "endow" each denomination's schools. He claimed that in many areas many denominations did not have enough members to sustain a school. Furthermore, the seminary professor opined that the state had no right to assert in effect the "co-ordinate and equal value of opposing creeds" (in this case Catholicism and Protestantism) because the government has no right to "indicate of either of the creeds that it is or is not, true and valuable." Dabney also thought that because some citizens paid more taxes than others did, it was likely that some taxpayers would in effect subsidize instruction in religious beliefs they found abhorrent. Finally, he expressed concern about the potential negative impact of educating children in hostile religious camps.[47]

Dabney also questioned the proposal to offer religious instruction in the first hour of the school day and excusing children of dissenting parents. Once again, Dabney raised an establishment objection that foreshadowed many of the US Supreme Court's post-World War II decisions regarding state-sponsorship of religious activities in public schools. "This amounts to the State's establishing a religion and using the people's money to teach it," he wrote, "but *permitting dissent* without any other penalty than the taxation for a religious object which the taxpayer condemns." Such an approach, he pointed out, smacked of the English practice under William and Mary that exempted dissenters from penalties for failing to attend Anglican worship, while still exacting a tax to support the established church. "But," he informed his readers, "the thing Americans claim is *liberty* and not *toleration*. . . . They deny the State's right to select a religion, as the true and useful one, for anybody, willing or unwilling."[48]

As far as Dabney was concerned, the only option available was to "secularize the State's teaching absolutely, limiting it to matters merely secular and leaving parents or the Church to supplement it with such religious teaching as they may please, or none." Whether this approach was either possible or admissible, Dabney averred, "is really the vital question." In order to address it, he claimed, agreement had to be reached as to the meaning of education. Like Hodge, Dabney believed that true education required moral culture and moral culture could not exist apart from Christianity. Pointing out that all earlier civilizations understood that true education ultimately rested upon a religious foundation, he asserted that the American state school system could not claim to educate without some basis in religion. Thus, he argued, Americans were attempting something novel, namely, education without religion. He doubted that such an education would produce desirable results. "Every line of true knowledge," he stated, "must find its completeness in its convergency to God, even as every beam of daylight leads the eye to the sun. If religion be excluded from our study, every process of thought will be arrested before it reaches its proper goal." Merely teaching religious facts without either affirming or denying Christian truths would not do. A studied avoidance of truth claims, Dabney declared, was "in effect hostile" to Christianity. Neutrality, in other words, was not possible. Moreover, attempts to teach morality without a foundation in the Scriptures would prove futile. "There is but one ground of moral obligation, the will of God," Dabney proclaimed, "and among the people of this country, he who does not find the disclosure of that will in the Scriptures, most often finds it nowhere." He pointed out, however, that teachers in state schools could not "inculcate this Bible." Pagan morality would result. In sum, Dabney believed that moral culture rooted in the Christian religion was the primary purpose of a true education. Learning skills, such as reading, was mere training. Like Locke, he thought that learning in the languages and sciences without concern for virtue leads inevitably to the creation of a dangerous person. Yet, he maintained, the American situation prohibited the state from teaching the truths of Scripture that constituted the foundation of morality.[49]

So who should be responsible for the education of Christian citizens? Dabney rejected the proposal that the state train the intellect and the Christian parent and church educate the conscience on, among other grounds, that the conscience was inextricably intertwined with the intellect and thus inseparable. Furthermore, he asked, why should the Christian parent want the state to interfere with educating the young? Why should a Christian parent believe that Sunday teaching would be as effective as the teaching of the state school? "In a word," Dabney responded in remarkably modern terms, "to the successful pupil under an efficient teacher, *the school is his world*. Make that godless and his life is made godless."[50]

Regarding the role of the church in education, Dabney claimed that it could not compete with the state. "In fact," he continued, "the Church does not and cannot repair the mischief which her more powerful, rich, and ubiquitous rival, the secularized State, is doing in thus giving, under the guise of a non-Christian, an anti-Christian training." Furthermore, the Union professor stated that the school tax obstructed "parental and philanthropic effort." Yet, Dabney informed his readers, "nearly all public men and divines declare that the State schools are the glory of America, that they are a finality, and in no event to be surrendered." Their embrace of public education, he thought, was rooted in their belief that the cooperative educational effort that united church and state in colonial America could work in the nineteenth century. Given the cultural landscape and legal framework of the United States, however, secularization of the public education was logically inevitable. With remarkable prescience, he warned Christian supporters of common schooling that they should prepare themselves for the eventual removal of "all prayer, catechisms, and bibles."[51]

Therefore, what should be done in commonwealths "whose civil governments have absolutely secularized themselves and made the union of the secular and spiritual powers illegal and impossible?" Dabney recommended going back to a "first principle" broached at the beginning of the essay, namely, that education is properly a "domestic and parental function," not a civic or ecclesiastical responsibility. He offered several propositions in support of his position. First, he claimed that God had ordained the family, the antecedent of both the church and the state, by the union of a man and woman to produce a "godly seed." Parental authority over children and their education, therefore, was prior to that of the church and the state. Moreover, Dabney pointed out in words seemingly chosen to counter messianic claims that common-school advocates often advanced, God "has provided for parents social and moral influences so unique, so extensive, that no other earthly power, or all others together, can substitute them in fashioning the child's character." This "unique power" was guarded by the strongest of affections. "Until the magistrate can feel a love, and be nerved by it to a self-denying care and toil, equal to that of a father and a mother," he reasoned, "he can show no pretext for assuming any parental function." Furthermore, parents rightly resent any intrusion of any authority between their conscience and convictions and the soul of their child. According to Dabney, "If the father conscientiously believes that his own creed is true and righteous and obligatory before God, then he must regard the intrusion of any other power between him and his minor child, to cause the rejection of that creed, as usurpation. . . . If thus usurpation is made by the visible church it is felt to be in the direction of popery; if by the magistrate, in the direction of despotism."[52]

To those who maintained that since parents occasionally formed a child "amiss," there ought to be a superior authority to intervene, Dabney countered since supreme authority had to be placed somewhere, "God has indicated that, on the whole, no place is so safe for it as the hands of the parent, who has the supreme love for the child and the superior opportunity." He acknowledged that parents occasionally neglected their children, but so did the government. "In an imperfect state of society," Dabney reasoned in language similar to that of today's educational dissenters, "the instances of parental abuse of the educational function will be partial and individual. In the case of an unjust or Godless State, the evil would be universal and sweeping. Doubtless God has deposited the duty in the safest place."[53]

Dabney concluded his essay with an assault on the belief that the state had the right to educate in order to perpetuate itself and a plea for recognition of parental authority in education. Echoing Jefferson at his best, he suggested that "American republicans" never held that people have a right to subvert the moral order ordained by God and nature. They did grant, however, that the people had the right to change the civil order and its institutions. Thus, he reasoned, civil authority was not entitled to "shape a people to suit itself; the opposite is true, the people should shape the civil authority." Preaching and teaching (thus shaping or educating a people) were not appropriate functions of the state any more than administering secular justice was the prerogative of the church.[54]

"Let us suppose then," Dabney continued, "that both State and Church recognize the parent as the educating power; that they assume towards him an ancillary instead of a dominating attitude; that the State shall encourage individual and voluntary efforts by holding the impartial shield of legal protection over all property devoted to education; that it shall encourage all private efforts; and that it shall aid those whose poverty and misfortune disable them from properly rearing their own children." Such an approach, he claimed, would solve all the problems touching on religion in public schools because parents, not the state, would create schools. In words that once again sound very familiar, the Presbyterian scholar wrote that then "our educational system might present less mechanical symmetry, but it would be more flexible, more practical, and more useful."[55]

A year later, in 1880, Dabney's "Popular Education as a Safeguard for

Popular Suffrage" appeared in the *BRPR*. This essay reviewed educational arrangements in Europe and revisited several themes addressed in "Secularized Education," especially the value of true education in a free society. During his discussion of the relationship of education to government, Dabney returned to a concern he had voiced during his debate with Ruffner. He noted that the primary problem of free government was "How to trust to fallible men enough power to govern, and yet prevent its perversion." "The theory we discuss," he continued, "proposes popular education as the check." Yet, he argued, control of the state system of education resided in the hands of those it was designed to check. "The very selfishness in them which makes them dangerous," Dabney maintained speaking of government officials, "will be just as certain to prompt them to pervert the proposed check as to pervert any other public power." He worried that with the power concentrated in the state school system those in control would be tempted to use the schools as "*propaganda* for the rulers' partisan opinions instead of useful knowledge and virtue." Like many contemporary critics of public schooling on the political left and right, Dabney thought that a powerful state system of education was a potential threat to competition among parties and viewpoints, which he deemed a necessary condition for free government. Moreover, if public education ever became compulsory, the threat would be even greater. Better to leave education in the hands of parents, he believed, than in the hands of a parental and powerful state or a potentially dogmatic church.[56]

Dabney's Legacy

Dabney's provocative essays in the *BRPR* drew no formal responses. His dissenting views regarding the role of the state and the family in education, the eventual complete secularization of public education, centralized control of schools, and the nature of true education placed him at odds with most public school advocates and patrons. Moreover, most of his fellow Presbyterians, save for fellow unreconstructed Southerners, paid scant attention to his objections to the general direction of American culture and education. In the words of A. H. Freundt, Dabney was "at war with most of the developments of the latter half of the century and inflexible in resisting change," and his influence did not extend beyond the South. In 1883, he left Union for the University of Texas where he taught until 1894, when ill health and disagreements with university officials led to his dismissal. During his final years of life, the defender of the Old South and advocate of limited government seemed to realize that he was out of step with the times and had lost his audience. Thomas Cary Johnson, his biographer and colleague, wrote that Dabney "felt that he was in isolation . . . and had come to be looked upon as extreme." As noted above, however, Dabney's books and essays, particularly "Secularized Education," now enjoy a wider readership than was the case during his lifetime, especially among home-schoolers and advocates of separating school and state. He has gained a new audience.[57]

William M. Beckner: Protector of Dissenters

Unlike his fellow Presbyterians Charles Hodge and Robert L. Dabney, William M. Beckner was neither a well-known seminary professor nor a frequent crit-ic of state-sponsored education. Historians, however, count him among the most visible advocates of public schooling in late nineteenth-century Kentucky. Like Dabney, however, he worried about the possibility that his state might some day require all children to attend public schools. Recognizing that not all parents in good conscience could send their children to the state's schools, Beckner crafted a clause in the Bill of Rights of the Kentucky Constitution of 1890 that denied the state the power to coerce public school attendance. He thus dissented from the often-unstated belief held by many educators and cit-izens that all children should be in a common school and anticipated the action taken by Oregon in 1922, when it adopted legislation mandating that nearly all children attend state schools. The Supreme Court of the United States declared Oregon's compulsory public school attendance law unconsti-tutional in the famous *Pierce* decision of 1925, thirty-five years after the adop-tion of Beckner's unique contribution to American law that protected educational dissenters in Kentucky.[58]

William Morgan Beckner was born in 1841 in Nicholas County, Kentucky, to Jacob Locke Beckner, a merchant who held slaves and died leaving his fam-ily in dire economic straits, and Nancy Lancaster Beckner, who, perhaps due to her Quaker ancestry, opposed slavery. He attended neighborhood schools before enrolling at the Rand and Richeson Academy in Maysville in 1856. His collegiate studies at Centre College were cut short after five months due to a lack of funds. Beckner then tutored, taught school, and read law. Though he disliked slavery, his Jeffersonian states' rights sentiment led him to join John Hunt Morgan's Confederate raiders. His military career was short lived, how-ever, as his loyalist mother sent an attorney to Tennessee to persuade him to return to Kentucky where he apparently "sat out" the remainder of the war.[59]

In 1865, Beckner settled in Winchester, where he oversaw a local academy and opened his law practice. He soon became the first editor of the *Clark County Democrat* (later the *Winchester Democrat*), a position from which he advocated local improvements, Democratic Party politics of a progressive stripe, and the cause of popular education. In addition to his law practice and editorial responsibilities, Beckner assumed judicial duties after his election as county judge in 1870. Before the age of thirty, then, he had firmly established himself as a public figure. He was well-positioned to become one of the state's most zealous and visible crusaders for common-school reform over the next two decades.[60] Indeed, having followed Beckner's efforts on behalf of education for at least ten years, Henry Watterson, influential editor of the *Louisville Courier-Journal*, and a "New Departure Democrat," wrote of Beckner in 1890, "no man in Kentucky is a greater friend to education, probably, than Judge Beckner."[61]

Delegate to the Constitutional Convention

That year Beckner arrived at the Kentucky Constitutional Convention in Frankfort with a reputation as one of the state's most vocal and articulate advocates of public education. He would live up to his reputation during the 226-day convention. Indeed, twelve pages of the index to convention debates and proceedings of the convention were devoted to referencing Beckner's comments, resolutions, and speeches, most of which dealt with matters related to education.[62]

The delegate from Clark County signaled two of his major concerns during the second week of the convention. He then offered a resolution indicative of his longstanding commitment to adequate funding for public education and equitable resources for black and white schools. He recommended the "General Assembly shall have power, and it shall be its duty, to provide . . . for an adequate and efficient system of popular education and . . . in distributing the common school fund, no distinction shall be made on account of race or color."[63] Two days later, Beckner proposed an addition to the Bill of Rights that reflected his commitment to freedom of conscience in matters of education. He recommended adding to the section forbidding coercion in religious worship the words, "Or send his child or children to any school to which he may be conscientiously opposed." Both resolutions were referred to the Committee on Education to which Beckner had been appointed.[64]

Though it was initially sent to the Committee on Education, Beckner's freedom-of-conscience amendment was called up for debate during the lengthy discussion of the Bill of Rights, during which the deeply devout Presbyterian urged convention delegates to take time out to travel to Louisville to see a pre-sentation of scenes from Lew Wallace's *Ben Hur*. Referring to the Roman Catholic Church in October 25 remarks, he explained why the amendment was necessary. "As is well known," he asserted, "there is a large element of a great religious organization, to which many persons in Kentucky belong, opposed to the American system of public schools." He declared his opposition to propos-als for compulsory education in the new constitution and expressed concern about what a future legislature might do. "We do not know what may arise in the future in the zeal of those who come after us; and they may attempt to com-pel persons who are conscientiously opposed to the public schools to send their children to them, fixing pains and penalties for refusal." Claiming that his amendment would prevent this possibility, Beckner hoped that the convention would become known as having been "inspired by the love of liberty and absolute freedom of conscience of all men. . . . Conscience is God's province."[65]

Beckner's commitment to freedom of conscience, perhaps instilled by his Quaker mother, was probably stimulated by conflicts occurring in other states as well as the knowledge that Catholic/Protestant conflict was part of Kentucky's past, for example, the "Bloody Monday" riots that convulsed Louisville in 1855; recent Catholic editorials that portrayed Luther, Calvin, and Wesley as fools; and ongoing Protestant attacks on the "vampire" Roman Church.[66] A well-read newspaper man, Beckner was almost certainly aware of measures like the Edwards Law enacted by the Illinois legislature in 1889, which mandated that all children between the ages of seven and fourteen attend public school for sixteen weeks a year, eight of which were to be con-secutive.[67] Since the 1870s, Louisville's *Catholic Advocate* (published as the *Central Catholic Advocate* in the 1880s) had regularly carried accounts of Protestant/Catholic school wars, news of legislative proposals regarding religion and education, and editorials criticizing, among other things, public schools as either "Protestant" or "Godless."[68] Immediately prior to the convention, the *Catholic Advocate* ran several scathing condemnations of the Edwards Law and proposals for similar laws elsewhere. It expressed alarm that other states were trampling on the rights of Catholics, Lutherans, and Methodists, and urged the delegates to the convention to protect freedom of conscience in education. "Should an evil hour arrive," the *Advocate* opined, "it would be well to have safeguards established in our new constitution which will secure against such possibilities the dearest right of every citizen to educate his children in the faith which he believes best for their eternal welfare, whether he be Methodist, Baptist, Episcopalian, Jew, or Catholic."[69]

The Beckner Amendment

Beckner's amendment to provide such a safeguard for dissenters sparked, in his own words, a "lively fight" that spanned several days and spawned several alternatives to his proposal, none of which was adopted by the convention. Robert Rodes, a loquacious delegate from Warren County, cast aspersions on Plato's view, in *The Republic*, of the relationship of the state to the child. He also called on his fellow members to shun Beckner's idea and embrace a libertarian position on compulsory school attendance. Rodes warned the delegates about government paternalism and urged them to proclaim, "no man should be compelled to send his children to school, or attend a church, or anywhere else, against his conscientious convictions." John L. Phelps, on the other hand, expressed concern about educationally neglected children and proposed constitutional language to the Beckner amendment that would mandate attendance at "some other school tolerated by law."[70]

Beckner disagreed with both delegates. His amendment, the Clark countian asserted, would not interfere with compulsory education. He maintained that his language would allow exemption from school attendance altogether, if the courts determined that a parent's objection was "conscientious."[71]

Immediately after defeating the Phelps mandatory-attendance proposal, the Committee of the Whole adopted Beckner's clause as an amendment to the report of the Committee on Preamble and Bill of Rights.[72] Beckner was pleased that a potential threat to the common schools had been alleviated and freedom of conscience recognized. He wrote to his Clark County constituents that his amendment would relieve the public schools of "a fierce opposition which has dreaded the coming of the time when those who do not want to do so might be forced to accept the provision made by the state for the education of all." Freedom of conscience, Beckner continued, is "God's province and we have no right to invade it on any pretext whatever."[73]

Beckner's victory was short lived. On October 31, 1890, during the presentation of the Committee of the Whole report to the convention, a substitute religious freedom section was adopted that omitted the Beckner amendment. This sparked a debate between advocates of the Beckner clause and those who favored former Governor J. Proctor Knott's language: "no man shall be compelled to send his child to any school." Beckner opposed the Knott amendment because it precluded the legislature from ever passing any compulsory education law. He again claimed that his amendment protected those who objected to public schools but did not prohibit the legislature from requiring parents to send their children to some school. Asked again if a person objecting to attendance at any school was protected, Beckner once again seemed to allow for such an objection if the courts deemed it "conscientious." Knott's proposed language, he asserted, would tie the hands of future legislatures—a tendency among the delegates to which Beckner often objected.[74]

Knott replied that he did not have any children, but if he did and "any power in this Commonwealth was authorized to take them from the bosom of my family, to compel their attendance upon any school, I would leave the State." In language similar to that of today's "family values" debates, he urged the adoption of his amendment, which, he said, would "withhold from the Legislature, or any other power on earth, the right of invading the sanctity of a household; of severing . . . the ties of parent and child." He concluded his remarks, however, professing that it was a "matter of indifference . . . whether the gentleman's (Beckner's) language is adopted or not."[75]

Indeed, neither the Beckner nor the Knott amendment was adopted by the Committee of the Whole.[76] Yet, defeat of both amendments did not close the question of parental rights and compulsory education. When the report of the Committee of the Whole came before the convention, on November 10, 1890, the Beckner clause was submitted as an amendment to the religious freedom section of the Bill of Rights. Once again, Beckner urged the delegates to adopt his amendment. He asserted that while he was as ardent a friend of public schools as any person in Kentucky and that the welfare and prosperity of the state depended on good schools, he could not support compulsory education at that moment. He pleaded with the delegates, however, not to prematurely dispose of the option. Although he reiterated that his proposed language would permit the legislature to require attendance at some school, the educational reformer failed to address the issue of conscientious objection to school attendance in general.[77]

Knott and several other delegates still challenged Beckner on the questions of mandating attendance and potential threats to the integrity of the home and family. The delegate from Clark County simply acknowledged that such issues would be good to debate in a legislative body. He then asserted he was not proposing anything in favor of compulsory education. If, Beckner continued, "representatives of the people decide that neglected or overworked children ought to be sent to school to make them intelligent, good citizens and keep them from becoming paupers, then the future ought to decide that for itself."[78]

After several more exchanges, the convention disposed of Knott's proposal and on November 10, 1890, gave final approval to the Beckner amendment.[79] Beckner viewed this as a compromise with those who wished to forbid compulsory education altogether. Obviously pleased with this protection of parental and religious rights from potential abuse by future compulsory attendance legislation, Beckner told his readers with only thinly veiled pride, "I was beaten twice but by sticking to it finally won with votes to spare."[80]

Beckner's Legacy

Beckner, the staunch defender of public education and southern Presbyterian, nevertheless held a deep commitment to protecting the rights of Roman Catholics and others who dissented from the common-school paradigm. He likely feared that the Kentucky legislature might in the future follow Illinois' example, as did Oregon in a more draconian fashion in 1922.[81] Perhaps the Beckner amendment served as a deterrent, for Kentucky never passed a Bluegrass version of the infamous compulsion. The state did attempt, however, to prosecute "unapproved" Christian schools and parents who sent their children to them as a matter of conscience. In an ironic twist that even the thoughtful Beckner could not have anticipated, the Kentucky Supreme Court drew upon his unique amendment for the first time not to protect the rights of Roman Catholics during the xenophobic years bracketing 1900, but for another objective. In 1979, the state's high court used the amendment to protect the rights of parents and schools that shared his evangelical Protestant faith.[82]

In the midst of the protracted debate on the Bill of Rights, Beckner informed his constituents that the Committee on Education had taken little action. He explained that he hesitated to push educational reform beyond the limits of public opinion or usurp the future prerogatives of the legislature. Beckner also wanted to confer on the state legislature the power to provide for an "adequate and efficient" system of education for all children but not compulsory schooling. Beyond that, he opined, it was not safe to do much with education in the constitution.[83]

By the time the convention adjourned in March 1891, Beckner had accomplished his two major constitutional objectives: protection of educational dissenters and provision for an "efficient" system of public education. He left the assembly with his reputation as Kentucky's most visible and vocal advocate for the cause of popular education soundly reinforced. He continued to speak out on educational issues for the remainder of his life. For example, Beckner advocated federal land grants for the older states of the Union during a brief stint as a member of the US House of Representatives, 1894–1895, and criticized the so-called Day Law of 1904, which attempted to eliminate integrated education at Berea College. Nevertheless, his work at Frankfort was clearly the highlight of his educational crusade, the "leading passion" of his life.[84] There Beckner worked tirelessly to embody in the constitution principles of freedom of conscience, equality of educational opportunity, and racial justice as he understood them.

Like many reformers and dissenters, Beckner did not live long enough to witness the profound impact of his considerable efforts. He died in 1910, almost seven decades removed from the Kentucky Supreme Court's *Rudasill* decision, which protected the parents' right to send their children to an "unapproved" school, and *Rose* decision, which forced the state to restructure its method of school finance in order to provide for an "efficient" system. Both decisions, of course, drew heavily upon Beckner's constitutional language.[85]

Conclusion

The arguments and work of Hodge, Dabney, and Beckner provide considerable food for thought about questions regarding the educational roles of the family, the church, and the state; the nature of "true" education; and, of course, how to justly accommodate parents who, as a matter of conscience, dissent from the state's concept of what kind of education is appropriate for their children. Unlike most of their fellow Protestants, these three Presbyterians recognized the legitimacy of Catholics' and others' complaints about public schools that taught propositions of knowledge and dispositions of belief and value that were alien to their faith commitments. They understood, in different ways to be sure, that confessional pluralism was a stubborn fact of nineteenth-century American life and that one system could not accommodate the educational preferences of all families. Their insights remain powerful a century later, not only for contemporary dissenters but for the wider public as well.

Notes

1.   The *Biblical Repertory and Princeton Review* (hereafter BRPR) appeared under several titles during Hodge's editorship. BRPR is the most common title.

2. For biographical information on Hodge, see John W. Stewart, "Charles Hodge," in *Dictionary of the Presbyterian & Reformed Tradition*, eds. D. G. Hart and Mark A. Noll, Downers Grove, IL: InterVarsity Press, 1999, 122–23; and Mark A. Noll, ed., *Charles Hodge: The Way of Life*, New York: Paulist Press, 1987, 1–44.

3. For recent discussions of Hodge's and Dabney's beliefs regarding education, see Clark D. Stull, "Education at Home and at School: The Views of Horace Bushnell, Charles Hodge, and Robert Dabney" (Ph.D. diss., Westminster Theological Seminary, 2005); and Jerry Robbins, "R. L. Dabney, Old Princeton, and Fundamentalism" (Ph.D. diss., Florida State University, 1991).

4. Charles Hodge, "Introductory Lecture," *BRPR* 1 (1829): 78–86.

5. Noll, *Charles Hodge*, 21.

6. Hodge, "Introductory Lecture," 86–88.

7. Charles Hodge, "Review of Sprague's Lectures to Young People," *BRPR* 3 (July 1831): 295–304. See also Charles Hodge, "Babington on Education," *BRPR* 4 (January 1832): 84–87. Hodge expresses concern about the "mechanical" reading of the Bible.

8. Charles Hodge, "Common Schools," *BRPR* 5 (April 1833): 217–29. For thoughtful discussions of common-school reform in mid-nineteenth-century America, see Charles L. Glenn, *The Myth of the Common School*, Amherst: University of Massachusetts Press, 1988; and Carl F. Kaestle, *Pillars of the Republic: Common Schools in American Society, 1780–1860*, New York: Hill & Wang, 1983.

9. Charles Hodge, "Necessity of Popular Education as a National Object," *BRPR* 7 (January 1835): 55.

10. Ibid., 56. For a classic analysis of anti-Catholicism during antebellum period, see Ray Allen Billington, *The Protestant Crusade, 1800–1860*, New York: The Macmillan Company, 1938.

11. Lewis Joseph Sherrill, *Presbyterian Parochial Schools, 1846–1870*, New Haven: Yale University Press, 1932, 7–8.

12. Charles Hodge, "Untitled Article," *BRPR* 13 (July 1841): 322–24.

13. Ibid., 329–41.

14. Ibid., 345–54. For a discussion of the conflict in New York City regarding the Public School Society and the Catholic request for removal of offensive material and for a share of tax dollars for their schools, see Carl F. Kaestle, *The Evolution of an Urban School System: New York City, 1750–1850*, Cambridge, MA: Harvard University Press, 1973, 148–58; and Diane Ravitch, *The Great School Wars: New York City, 1805–1973*, New York: Basic Books, 1974, 27–76. For a discussion of how the state of New York dealt with the question of religious exercises in the public schools in the latter part of the nineteenth century without major "school wars," see Benjamin Justice, *The War That Wasn't: Religious Conflict and Compromise in the Common Schools of New York State, 1865–1900*, Albany: State University of New York Press, 2005.

15. Hodge, "Untitled Article," 355–67.

16. Ibid., 367–68. Sounding like some contemporary critics of state-funded vouchers, Hodge worried about possible strings attached to government grants to church schools. He even called such "patronage" a potential "curse."

17. Sherrill, *Presbyterian Parochial Schools*, 20–24.

18. Charles Hodge, "General Assembly: Parochial Schools," *BRPR* 18 (July 1846): 437–41.

19. Sherrill, *Presbyterian Parochial Schools*, 24–27.
20. Charles Hodge, "Public Religious Education Enforced in a Discussion of Different Plans," in *Home, The School, and The Church; or the Presbyterian Education Repository*, ed. C. Van Rensselaer, Philadelphia: William S. Martien, 1850, 95–98.
21. Hodge, "Public Religious Education," 98–100.
22. Ibid., 100–104.
23. Ibid., 104–7. Hodge's statement about "every wind of doctrine" reflected his concern with the emphasis on unchecked religious experience and a drift toward Arminianism that he associated with mid-nineteenth-century revivalism. See Noll, *Charles Hodge*, 20–21, 41.
24. Sherrill, *Presbyterian Parochial Schools*, 27; and Charles Hodge, "General Assembly: Parochial Schools," *BRPR* 19 (July 1847): 425.
25. Sherrill, *Presbyterian Parochial Schools*, 48–49, 56–64; Charles Hodge, "General Assembly: Parochial Schools," *BRPR* 22 (July 1850): 457; and Charles Hodge, "General Assembly: Parochial Schools," *BRPR* 23 (July 1851): 542–43.
26. Charles Hodge, "The Education Question," *BRPR* 26 (July 1854): 504–19.
27. Ibid., 520–29. For discussions of the changing patterns of state support of nonpublic schooling in the mid-1800s, see James C. Carper, "The Changing Landscape of US Education," *Kappa Delta Pi Record* 37 (Spring 2001): 106–8; and Robert J. Gabel, "Public Funds for Church and Private Schools" (Ph.D. diss., The Catholic University of America, 1937).
28. Hodge, "The Education Question," 530–40.
29. Ibid., 544.
30. Charles Hodge, "Popular Education," *BRPR* 29 (October 1857): 635.
31. Charles Hodge, "A Nation's Right to Worship God," *BRPR* 31 (October 1859): 682–84.
32. Sherrill, *Presbyterian Parochial Schools*, 48–63; Noll, *Charles Hodge*, 19–20; and Timothy L. Smith, *Revivalism & Social Reform: American Protestantism on the Eve of the Civil War*, Baltimore: The Johns Hopkins University Press, 1980, 22–33.
33. Charles Hodge, "Common Schools," *BRPR* 38 (January 1866): 31–32.
34. Charles Hodge, "Review of the Life of Horace Mann," *BRPR* 38 (January 1866): 76–89; and Charles Hodge, "General Assembly," *BRPR* 39 (July 1867): 471–72. Mann had as strong an aversion to Calvinism as he did to Roman Catholicism. He believed that a "Calvinist education" was an "unspeakable calamity." He despised doctrines of sin, the fall, divine sovereignty, and judgment, which he believed restricted human progress. See Glenn, *Myth of the Common School*, 82–83, 131–32, 158–73, 219–21.
35. Archibald Alexander Hodge, *The Life of Charles Hodge*, New York: Charles Scribner's Sons, 1880, 410.
36. For biographical information on Dabney, see A. H. Freundt, "Robert Lewis Dabney," *Dictionary of the Presbyterian & Reformed Tradition*, 76–77; and Robbins, "R. L. Dabney, Old Princeton, and Fundamentalism," 15–39.
37. Iain Murray, ed., *Discussions of R. L. Dabney*, vol. 3, Edinburgh, Scotland: The Banner of Truth Trust, 1981, vi.
38. Stull, "Education at Home and at School," 143–75.
39. For an account of the conflict between Ruffner and Dabney, see Thomas C. Hunt and Jennings L. Wagoner, Jr., "Race, Religion, and Redemption: William Henry Ruffner and the Moral Foundations of Education in Virginia," *American Presbyterians* 66 (Spring 1988): 1–9.

40. Ibid., 3–4.

41. Robert Lewis Dabney, "The Negro and the Common Schools," *The Southern Planter and Farmer* 37 (April 1876): 251–54.

42. Ibid., 257–58.

43. Hunt and Wagoner, "Race, Religion, and Redemption," 5.

44. Murray, *Discussions of R. L. Dabney*, 238–44, 257–58, 260–61, 266–70.

45. Hunt and Wagoner, "Race, Religion, and Redemption," 5–9; and Robert L. Dabney, "Secularized Education," *BRPR* 55 (September 1879): 377–400.

46. Dabney, "Secularized Education," 378–80. Unlike many nineteenth-century Protestant leaders, Dabney did not speak of the United States as a "Christian nation." The outcome and aftermath of the Civil War as well as his distrust of concentration of power in either the church or the state likely influenced his position.

47. Ibid., 380–81.

48. Ibid.

49. Ibid., 381–89.

50. Ibid., 391–93.

51. Ibid., 393–94.

52. Ibid., 396–97.

53. Ibid., 398.

54. Ibid., 399.

55. Ibid., 399–400.

56. Robert L. Dabney, "Popular Education as a Safeguard for Popular Suffrage," *BRPR* 56 (September 1880): 186–206.

57. Freundt, "Robert Lewis Dabney," 76–77; Stull, "Education at Home and at School," 174; and Thomas Cary Johnson, *The Life and Letters of R. L. Dabney*, Edinburgh, Scotland: Banner of Truth Trust, 1977, 410.

58. James C. Carper, "William Morgan Beckner: The Horace Mann of Kentucky," *Register of the Kentucky Historical Society* 96 (Winter 1998): 29–60.

59. H. Levin, ed., *The Lawyers and Lawmakers of Kentucky*, Chicago: The Lewis Publishing Company, 1897, 657–58; E. Polk Johnson, *A History of Kentucky and Kentuckians*, Chicago: The Lewis Publishing Company, 1912, 3:1419–22; and Lucien Beckner to Berry B. Brooks, November 15, 1955, *Lucien Beckner Papers*, Museum of History and Science, Louisville, Kentucky.

60. Ibid.

61. *Louisville Courier-Journal*, October 19, 1890. According to Harrison and Klotter, new departure democrats were "so named because they sought to break away from old issues and forge a new Kentucky. . . . Supporting a state and federal role in government and the economy that harkened back to the philosophy of the old Whig party, they advocated a vision that included support for industrialization, education, and, to a much more limited extent, some black rights." Lowell H. Harrison and James C. Klotter, *A New History of Kentucky*, Lexington, KY: University of Kentucky Press, 1997, 242–43.

62. *Official Report of the Proceedings and Debates in the Convention to Change the Constitution of the State of Kentucky*, 4 vols. Frankfort, Kentucky, 1890–1891, 4:6086–97. For an account of the context of the convention, see Rhea A. Taylor, "Conflicts in Kentucky as Shown by the Constitutional Convention of 1890–1891" (Ph.D. diss., University of Chicago, 1948).

63. *Official Report of the Proceedings and Debates*, 1:130.

64. Ibid., 1:162.

65. Ibid., 1:846–47.

66. Harrison and Klotter, *A New History of Kentucky*, 123; *Louisville Central Catholic Advocate*, January 3, 1884; and "Several Mainstreet Merchants" to Governor Buckner, July 17, 1891, Simon Bolivar Buckner Correspondence, Kentucky Department for Libraries and Archives, Frankfort, Kentucky.

67. John Diefenthaler, "Lutheran Schools in America," in *Religious Schooling in America*, ed. James C. Carper and Thomas C. Hunt, Birmingham, AL: Religious Education Press, 1984, 48.

68. *Louisville Catholic Advocate*, July 15, 1875; February 3, 1876; March 24, 1881; March 20, 1884; and November 11, 1886.

69. Ibid., April 17; June 12; and August 21, 1890.

70. *Official Report of the Proceedings and Debates*, 1:847–48.

71. Ibid., 1:849.

72. Ibid.

73. *Winchester Democrat*, October 29, 1890.

74. *Official Report of the Proceedings and Debates*, 1:1032–35.

75. Ibid., 1:1035.

76. Ibid., 1:1035–36.

77. Ibid., 1:1134–38.

78. Ibid., 1:1138–41.

79. Ibid., 1:1145.

80. *Winchester Democrat*, November 19, 1890.

81. The debate over the Beckner amendment occurred thirty-five years before the United States Supreme Court in *Pierce v. Society of Sisters* (1925) ruled that the state could not mandate public school attendance to the exclusion of private schools. For a discussion of the Oregon law that *Pierce* addressed, see William G. Ross, *Forging New Freedoms: Nativism, Education, and the Constitution, 1917–1927*, Lincoln, NE: University of Nebraska Press, 1994; and David B. Tyack, "The Perils of Pluralism: The Background of the Pierce Case," *American Historical Review* 74 (October 1968): 74–98; and Lloyd P. Jorgenson, *The State and the Non-Public School, 1825–1925*, Columbia, MO: University of Missouri Press, 1987.

82. *Kentucky State Board for Elementary and Secondary Education v. Rudasill*, 589 S. W. 2d 877–84 (Ky. 1979). See also William B. Ball, "Family Freedom in Education," *Human Life Review* 6 (Summer 1980): 62–69; Lyndon G. Furst and Charles J. Russo, *The Legal Aspects of Nonpublic Schools: A Casebook*, Berrien Springs, MI: Andrews University, 1993, 109–20; E. Vance Randall, *Private Schools & Public Power: A Case for Pluralism*, New York: Teachers College, Columbia University, 1994, 50–115; and H. C. Hudgins, Jr. and Richard S. Vacca, *Law and Education: Contemporary Issues and Court Decisions*, Charlottesville, VA: Michie Law Publishers, 1995, 153–66.

83. *Winchester Democrat*, October 15 and 29, 1890. For a discussion of Beckner's efforts to ensure provision for an "efficient" system, see Carper, "William Morgan Beckner," 52–59.

84. Levin, *Lawyers and Lawmakers of Kentucky*, 659–60; "William M. Beckner to W. G. Frost, March 30, 1904," *William G. Frost Papers*, Special Collections and Archives of Berea College, Berea, Kentucky.

85. In 1979, the state's high court in *Kentucky State Board for Elementary and Secondary Education v. Rudasill* ruled that the state's attempts to regulate fundamentalist Christian schools' teacher qualifications, textbooks, and curriculum and to prosecute parents who sent their children to "unapproved" schools that refused as a matter of conscience to abide by such regulations violated a principle embodied in the Bill of Rights of the Kentucky Constitution. The court based its decision on a clause in Section 5, which has no counterpart in any other state or federal constitutional document. It states "nor shall any man be compelled to send his child to any school to which he may be conscientiously opposed." In *Rudasill* the court recognized parental rights in education and, in effect, liberated private schools from broad, programmatic state regulation. Ten years later, in *Rose v. The Council for Better Education Inc.*, the Kentucky Supreme Court concurred with Circuit Court Judge Ray Corns' ruling that the state's method of public school finance was unconstitutional. Furthermore, it declared that the inequities in Kentucky's public education system were of such a magnitude as to render the entire system in violation of Section 183 of the state constitution, which mandates that "The General Assembly shall, by appropriate legislation, provide for an efficient system of common schools throughout the State." The court then ordered the legislature to "recreate" and "reestablish" the state's public school system. Kentucky's widely publicized and still controversial Educational Reform Act of 1990 (popularly known as KERA) was the result of the court's sweeping mandate. See Carper, "William Morgan Beckner," 29–30, 59.

· 7 ·

THE CHRISTIAN DAY
SCHOOL MOVEMENT

New Protestant Dissenters

Protestant-sponsored weekday schooling is not new to American education. Prior to the advent of state common-school systems in the middle decades of the nineteenth century, the rich religious diversity that characterized overwhelmingly Protestant colonial and early national America was manifested in an equally rich diversity of Protestant schools. Throughout this period, the Lutherans, Friends, Moravians, Baptists, German and Dutch Reformed, Presbyterians, Methodists, and Anglicans established elementary schools and academies for their children and charity schools for children of the poor.[1] Even most of the so-called town schools of colonial New England and the quasi-public district schools and charity schools of the early 1800s were de facto Protestant schools.[2]

The 1830s, 1840s, and 1850s, however, marked an era of intense debate and reform focusing on issues of control, finance, and curriculum that led to a major alteration of schooling arrangements in the United States. By the 1850s in the North and the 1870s in the South, states had established the general framework for a free, tax-supported, state-regulated, common-school system. Student enrollment shifted to the free "common schools"; the earlier practice of distributing tax dollars and land to schools under private or religious control for the accomplishment of public purposes was sharply curtailed, and nonpublic schools, Protestant and Catholic alike, were increasingly viewed as un-American and divisive.[3] During this period several Protestant denominations, such as the Methodist and Episcopal, considered creating alternative school systems, and in the case of the latter, a number of dioceses, mostly in the South, encouraged establishment of schools. In the 1840s and 1850s, the Old School Presbyterians attempted to establish a system of schools to transmit orthodox beliefs. Although this Presbyterian body founded around 260 schools, a lack of enthusiasm and schism bred by intersectional strife ended the experiment. Individual churches continued to maintain schools, but with the exception of the Lutheran Church—Missouri Synod, major Protestant denominations and most of their members accepted government provision of elementary schooling, though not without occasional expressions of concern regarding secularization of the public schools. They embraced them because nineteenth-century "common" schools were, for the most part, general Protestant schools and thought to be a principal means to creating a moral, disciplined, and unified Protestant citizenry. Furthermore, as Roman Catholics asked for tax dollars to support their schools and complained about offensive practices in the common schools, such as Bible-reading without comment, most Protestants set aside their denominational differences and united behind the purportedly "nonsectarian" common school.[4]

Indeed, as David Tyack, Timothy Smith, James Carper, Lloyd Jorgenson, and other historians have demonstrated, Protestant leaders were often in the vanguard of the common-school movement as a means of fashioning a Christian, by which they meant Protestant, America. In the words of Robert T. Handy, a noted church historian, elementary schools did not need to be under the control of particular denominations because "their role was to prepare young Americans for participation in the broadly Christian civilization toward which all evangelicals were working."[5] While the common school, by means of Bible-reading, prayers, hymns, Protestant teachers, and the ubiquitous McGuffey readers, inculcated the mutually reinforcing dispositions and beliefs of nondenominational Protestantism, republicanism, and capitalism, many Protestant leaders expected the Sunday school to stress the particular tenets of the various denominations. This educational arrangement of "parallel institutions" satisfied most Protestants in the last half of the nineteenth century. As William B. Kennedy, an authority on Protestant education, has argued, "By 1860 there had emerged a general consensus in American Protestantism that the combination of public and Sunday school teaching would largely take care of the needed religious teaching of the young. In that pattern the public school was primary; the Sunday school was adjunct to it, providing specific religious teaching it could not include."[6] Protestant-sponsored weekday schools were not necessary. Indeed, by 1900, around 15,500,000, or nearly ninety-two percent of the approximately 16,850,000 elementary and secondary students, attended public institutions, while only around 1,350,000 students, or about eight percent, attended private institutions. Eight hundred fifty-four thousand, or sixty-three percent of these students were enrolled in the burgeoning Catholic schools, while most of the remaining 496,000 souls were scattered among Lutheran, Christian Reformed, Baptist, Presbyterian, Methodist, Episcopal, Congregational, and secular private schools.[7]

Contemporary Christian Day School Movement

Much has changed since the formulation of the "parallel institutions" strategy. Evangelical Protestantism no longer shapes American culture and the public schools as it did in the 1800s. The early twentieth century witnessed its gradual decline as the dominant culture-shaping force and the growing influence of secularism, particularly among social elites.[8] Pointing out the disruptive effect on American Protestantism of, among other things, higher criticism of the Bible, Darwinism, growing cultural and religious pluralism, and the fundamentalist-modernist controversy that fractured many Protestant denominations, James Davison Hunter has asserted, with only slight exaggeration, that "in the course of roughly thirty-five years (ca. 1895–1930), Protestantism had been moved from cultural domination to cognitive marginality and political impotence. The worldview of modernity had gained ascendancy in American culture."[9] In his wide-ranging work, *Religion in American Public Life*, A. James Reichley echoed Hunter's assessment and maintained that since the 1950s this value-belief system—which posits an evolutionary view of the cosmos, touts naturalistic science and reason as the keys to human progress and knowledge, denies the relevance of deity to human affairs, and assumes that moral values can be derived from human experience—has been dominant within the intellectual community. This "secular humanistic" worldview, in his opinion, has exerted considerable influence on the entertainment industry, the media, and parts of the educational enterprise.[10]

In a similar vein, noted church-state scholar Leo Pfeffer was probably correct when he claimed in 1977 "secular humanism is a cultural force which, in many respects, is stronger in the United States than any of the major religious groups or any alliance among them."[11] On the other hand, the public outcry following the 1962 and 1963 Supreme Court decisions declaring state-sponsored prayer and devotional Bible-reading in tax-supported schools unconstitutional, the resurgence of evangelicalism amidst the cultural and political crises of the 1960s and 1970s, and the political activism of conservative Protestants since the 1970s at the national, state, and local levels suggest that a significant minority of the general public is very uncomfortable with a quasi-official secular worldview and a public square that is devoid of symbols of America's Christian heritage.[12]

Contributing Factors

Profoundly dissatisfied with what they perceive to be the secularistic—not neutral—belief system embodied in the public school curriculum, unsatisfactory behavioral and academic standards, and the centralized control of public education, a growing number of conservative Protestants have tried to regain control of their children's education that they believe has been usurped by, among others, secular elites, the courts, teacher unions, and "educrats." Since the 1960s, they have utilized several strategies. Many evangelical and fundamentalist Protestants have sought to incorporate theistic symbols and perspectives in the public schools through, for example, urging consideration of creationism or intelligent design in science classes, posting Ten Commandments plaques, holding voluntary religious activities on high school campuses, and advocating history texts that recognize the influence of Christianity on the development of the United States and sex education curriculum that stresses abstinence.[13] Others have either protested the use of curricular materials that they believe advance secularism, e.g., certain home economics and literature texts, or sought to have their children exempted from exposure to the offending materials or their complete removal from the school curriculum. Widely publicized textbook controversies in Kanawha County, West Virginia; Mobile, Alabama; and Hawkins County, Tennessee in the 1970s and 1980s are cases in point.[14] Still other conservative Protestants have forsaken their historic commitment to public schools and either looked to the private sector to provide an education congruent with their beliefs or opted for home-based education.[15]

Since the mid-1960s, a growing number fundamentalist and evangelical Protestants and their churches, few of which are affiliated with "mainline" denominations, such as the United Methodist Church or Presbyterian Church in the United States, have been establishing and patronizing alternatives to public education that are usually referred to as Christian day schools or fundamentalist academies (so-called in order to distinguish them from schools sponsored by Christian denominations, for example, the Lutheran Church-Missouri Synod). Between 1920 and 1960, independent fundamentalist churches and conservative parachurch organizations founded as many as 150 of these institutions. The vast majority of conservative Protestants, however, remained wedded to public schooling during this period. In the aftermath of intradenominational battles between fundamentalists and modernists and the Scopes "Monkey Trial" in 1925, fundamentalist leaders concentrated on developing their own radio stations, colleges, Bible schools, camps, missionary societies, and publishing houses. Their withdrawal from American culture, however, did not lead to the creation of significant numbers of separate elementary and secondary schools. Liberal and conservative Protestants alike considered the public school "theirs."[16] By the mid-1960s, however, growing disenchantment with the ongoing secularization of public education, deepening concern about trends in American culture related to drugs, sex, and disorder; a resurgent evangelical faith; and, in some cases, fears related to desegregation sparked the phenomenal increase in the number of Christian day schools.[17]

Growth Pattern

Assessing the growth of these modern-day dissenting academies was initially difficult. Some Christian schools were of such a separatist persuasion that they refused to report enrollment data to state and federal education agencies. For similar reasons, others chose not to affiliate with any of the national associations of Christian schools, a primary source of statistics on these institutions. Nevertheless, most scholars now estimate that between 8,000 and 12,000 of these schools have been founded since the mid-1960s. Current enrollment is probably between 1.2 and 1.4 million students (K–12) or nearly twenty percent of all private school students.[18] Some of these schools have closed their doors. Institutions founded with more enthusiasm than resources and leadership have had short lives. Estimating the number of schools that have closed since the 1960s is as difficult as determining the exact number of schools that have been established. Many are simply invisible and pass from the educational landscape unnoticed. In the mid-1990s, however, the Association of Christian Schools International (ACSI) estimated that about 1,100 schools had closed since the mid-1960s.[19]

The most concrete evidence of the growth of the independent Christian school movement is readily apparent in the membership figures of the two major associations that provide, among other things, legal and legislative services, administrator and teacher support, curriculum, certification and accreditation, and early childhood services to their member schools. The Western Association of Christian Schools, which in 1978 merged with two smaller organizations—the National Christian School Education Association and the Ohio Association of Christian Schools—to form ACSI, claimed a membership in 1967 of 102 schools (K–12) with an enrollment of 14, 659. By 1973, the figures were 308 and 39, 360, respectively. In 1983, ACSI figures were approximately 1,900 and 270,000; in 1989, 2,347 and 340,626; in 1993; 2,801 and 463,868; in 2000, 3,849 and 707,928; and in 2005, 3,957 and 746,681. The American Association of Christian Schools (AACS), a rival organization of a more fundamentalist nature, was founded in 1972 with eighty schools enrolling 16,000 students. By 1983, the association claimed a membership of more than 1,100 schools and 160,00 students, and in 1991, 1,200 and 187,000. In 2004, AACS reported around 1,050 schools with approximately 175,000 students (part of the recent decline is likely due to the withdrawal of a state organization and its schools in the early 1990s). Despite the fact that some of these schools appeared long before they affiliated with either ACSI or AACS, these figures testify to the vigor of the Christian day school movement since the 1960s.[20]

Though the growth of evangelical Christian schools has outpaced that of other types of schools in the private sector since the 1970s, their expansion has apparently slowed since the early 2000s. Aside from the increasing cost of competing with the government sector and a soft economy, anecdotal evidence suggests that an increasing number of parents are opting for homeschooling in lieu of private schooling. While the number of Christian day schools and their enrollments is unlikely to increase as fast as it did in the last three decades of the twentieth century, the Christian school movement remains one of the more dynamic segments of the American educational enterprise and represents the first widespread and lasting institutional dissent from the public school paradigm since the establishment of large numbers of Roman Catholic schools during the latter part of the nineteenth century. Furthermore, along with the explosive growth of homeschooling since the mid-1980s, which, though becoming more diverse demographically, is still dominated by evangelical Protestants, this movement marks a significant erosion of conservative Protestants' once nearly universal loyalty to public education.[21]

Diversity of Christian Day Schools

Scholars have shown considerable interest in these schools since the early 1980s. They have examined, among other things, the relationship of the aforementioned growth pattern to the evangelical revival and concomitant alienation from American culture and its educational institutions, charges of racial discrimination against these schools, clashes with state officials regarding the legitimacy of state licensing and teacher certification requirements, the quality of Christian day schools compared to their public counterparts, curriculum formats, parent and student characteristics, and various features of these schools.

Researchers have discovered that although all Christian day schools profess the centrality of Jesus Christ and the authority of the Bible in their educational endeavors, they are quite different in many respects. For example, though most of these schools are attached to a local church (ACSI reports that about eighty-five percent of its schools fall into this category) a significant minority, often the largest and/or most prestigious, are governed by a local school society or foundation. Facilities range from poorly equipped church basements to modern multibuilding campuses. While a majority are elementary schools, an increasing number are offering prekindergarten and secondary education as well. Programs of study vary considerably from standardized, though narrow, to the most comprehensive available anywhere. Enrollments also vary from school to school from fewer than ten students to over 2,000. In general, these schools are smaller and more intimate than their state-controlled counterparts. The average enrollment is currently between 150 and 200.[22]

Educational environments also differ among these institutions. Some Christian school classrooms are reminiscent of those of the public schools of the 1950s, while others resemble Skinnerian learning labs where students work independently through a series of curriculum packets without benefit of a teacher in a conventional sense (the Accelerated Christian Education program or ACE). Many schools use Christian curricula published by Bob Jones University Press, A Beka, or ACSI, while others use secular materials and expect instructors to provide Christian perspectives. Some schools mix healthy doses of patriotism with religious instruction. Others shun this practice. Some have very relaxed codes of conduct. Others require uniforms and forbid physical contact between boys and girls during school-related activities.[23]

Several excellent studies testify to the diversity of institutional climates manifest in Christian day schools. For example, Alan Peshkin's pioneering study of a fundamentalist Christian high school in central Illinois described the attitudes and behavior of parents, students, teachers, administrators, and pastors who shaped the institution. He concluded that the school well served the educational needs of a fundamentalist Christian community, particularly its emphasis on salvation, social separation, and missions but expressed concern about the separatist, authority-oriented nature of the school that he opined discouraged exploration of America's cultural riches and tolerance of differences. Susan Rose compared and contrasted the climate of a fundamentalist Baptist school and that of a school sponsored by a charismatic Christian fellowship. While the former school stressed strict rules, routinization, drill, and individual work, the latter emphasized creativity, flexibility, and group work. In a similar vein, Peter Lewis examined the ethos of a free school and that of a Christian school. He found that though both embodied a strong dissent from public school culture, the former valued creativity and freedom, while the latter stressed discipline, basics, and religious instruction. After studying a variety of Christian schools affiliated with fundamentalist, charismatic, and mainline evangelical fellowships, Melinda Wagner claimed that the schools had to some extent compromised with American culture and were not as separatist as their rhetoric often suggests. Likewise, David Sikkink identified and described a variety of Christian day schools, including an example of a growing number of classical Christian schools whose distinctive features often include rigorous instruction in a trivium of grammar, dialectic, and rhetoric (often with a base in Latin). In sum, although all Christian day schools are committed to transmitting a Christian worldview, this commitment is embodied in institutions that are remarkably diverse in structure, program, and climate.[24]

Black Christian Academies

Increasing minority enrollment and the growing number of what Christian school advocates frequently call Black Christian Academies are also contributing to diversity within the Christian school movement. Although often viewed as stalwart supporters of public education—the arena in which many early civil rights battles were fought and won—Americans of African descent have often resorted to private or quasi-public schools when public education was either unavailable or inadequate. For example, after the American Civil War they established schools in places like Camden, South Carolina, that educated hundreds of freedmen and in the early twentieth century contributed significant amounts of time, materials, and money to construction of Rosenwald schools throughout the South.[25]

Since the 1980s, black enrollment in private schools has increased steadily. By the late 1990s, approximately six percent of black elementary and secondary school students enrolled in nonpublic schools. Though a majority of these students were in Catholic schools (minorities accounted for about twenty-seven percent of enrollment in these institutions in 2006), some of the recent increase is evident in the Christian day school sector. Although often unfairly stereotyped as "white flight academies," particularly in the South, these institutions do enroll minority students and their number, though still comparatively small, has grown in recent years.[26] Christian day schools are, to some extent, interracial and about ten percent of their current enrollment is African-American.[27]

Of greater significance to both the Christian day school movement and urban public education is the rapid growth of Black Christian Academies, most of which are located in metropolitan areas. Americans of African descent initiate, sustain, and govern these schools, which usually are not dependent upon organizations outside the black community. Such schools, however, do identify themselves with the contemporary evangelical school movement. Indeed, many are members of the Association of Christian Schools International (ACSI). Most black Christian schools stress racial heritage, discipline, and academic achievement as well as a Christian worldview.[28]

Although the creation of Afrocentric schools has sparked some interest in the scholarly community, only a handful of researchers have paid close attention to the growth and ethos of black Christian schools. This oversight is, at least in part, due to their "invisibility." Like the predominantly white evangelical schools founded in the 1960s and 1970s, their black counterparts have been springing up out of the public eye since the early 1980s. They are often unknown to government agencies, public school districts, religious associations, and other usual sources of school statistics. Only the most intrepid of researchers is likely even to locate many of these institutions.[29]

Using newspaper articles, obscure school directories, word of mouth, and extensive fieldwork, Jack Layman, a veteran student of independent Christian schools, documented at least 200 black Christian schools located in cities throughout the United States by the early 1990s. He found, for example, over a dozen each in Atlanta, Philadelphia, and Washington, DC; eight in Baltimore; six in Jackson, Mississippi; and over thirty in greater Los Angeles. During the 1990s, this segment at the Christian school movement continued to expand. In Philadelphia, for example, these schools now number better than fifty. As was the case with the schools founded in the 1960s and 1970s, diversity characterizes the newer black Christian schools. According to Layman, "many are in their first or second year, while others are veterans; some have modest facilities while others have built new plants or renovated former public schools; some have hundreds of students and others fewer than fifty. Locations range from New York City to Pawley's Island, South Carolina, from inner city 'ghettos' to exclusive suburbs."[30] Whatever their characteristics, these institutions, which Layman dubbed "Black Flight Academies," embody a significant dissent from a longstanding faith in public education among African-Americans. In this sense, they are "soul mates" of their still predominantly white Christian day schools.

Snapshot of a Christian Day School

Though different in many ways, Christian day schools have much in common. Teachers attempt with varying degrees of success to provide a biblical perspective on their subjects; budgets are usually tight and teachers are often paid significantly less than their public school counterparts are; control is local; independence is zealously guarded, academic achievement is valued; prayer is frequent, and missions work receives considerable attention. These educational institutions also experience problems faced by public and other private schools, for example, a teacher struggling for control in the classroom and disengaged students.

All these challenges and characteristics were apparent during a daylong visit to the Ben Lippen (a Scottish phrase for mountain of trust) High School (BLS) in Columbia, South Carolina in November 1999. Founded in 1940 in Asheville, North Carolina as a boarding school that primarily served the sons of missionaries, Ben Lippen relocated to Columbia in 1988 as a coeducational, college-preparatory school for boarding and day students affiliated with Columbia Bible College and Seminary (now Columbia International University). Since then, school officials have added a middle school and three satellite elementary schools. Approximately 800 students from all over the world are enrolled at this mainstream evangelical, nondenominational Christian institution, about 340 of whom are in the high school.

At 7:30 AM, faculty members meet for their regular Friday prayer session. They share concerns about students who are struggling spiritually, emotionally, academically, and physically. In addition to these students, participants offer prayer for Christian teachers in public schools and several families in the community. The session closes with group prayer as individual faculty members call out the names of each student in the sophomore class.

Doors at BLS open at 8:00 AM, and after fifteen minutes of socializing, green- and tan-clad middle and high school students head for class. John Smith's first period Courtship, Marriage, and Family class is one of the more popular at the school. Effervescent, affable, and student-centered, Smith initially asks each student to predict the score in the Saturday football game between his alma mater, Georgia, and the University of South Carolina. Joshing abounds. From his perch on a stool, he shares bits of church humor and biblical advice and then prays for a sick class member before quizzing the students on a memory verse. As he is about to start his lecture, perhaps conversation would be a better term, on the New Testament book of Philippians, a student arrives very late and tries to sneak to his seat. Smith cries out "no Nigerians allowed." The class howls, as does an athletic international student (now playing in the National Football League). Compared to most public and private schools in South Carolina, Ben Lippen's student body is quite diverse. Approximately twenty percent of the students are internationals or Americans of African descent. Racial and ethnic harmony seems to be the rule at BLS, and Smith's comment and the responses to it confirm that widely held perception.

Smith's comments on love, joy, and peace as he guides students through Philippians reveal another characteristic of Ben Lippen. While academic knowledge is certainly important (the median SAT score for the class of 2000 was over 1,100), so are relationships. Throughout his discussion of the Christian life, he stresses the need to depend on the Holy Spirit (a vertical relationship) as a necessary condition for joyous service to and fellowship with others (horizontal relationship).

A steady stream of talkative but orderly students then heads for second period Geometry class. After prayer for five or six students and thanks for God's providence at Ben Lippen, Bill Heath, a Johns Hopkins and Columbia Seminary graduate, returns quizzes and, against a backdrop of the Ten Commandments in Reader's Digest format and several pieces of Escher art on the front and side walls, quietly reviews each item. Heath answers questions in a low-key fashion. He devotes the last half of the period to the development of if-then statements and truth tables. Like all BLS faculty members, Heath integrates the Bible and his academic discipline. For example, he points out that Scripture includes many if-then statements, most of which have to do with God's blessing. He asks students to mine the Bible for fifty examples.

Mike Edwards' World Cultures class is next on many juniors' schedules. This is the no nonsense world of one of Ben Lippen's systematic thinkers. The culture of the classroom is reminiscent of an early nineteenth-century academy. Armed with a long pointer in one hand and, paradoxically, a laser pen in the other, maestro Edwards conducts his regular opening exercises where he calls a student to the front of the room, introduces him or her, and then fires a random geography question: What is the capital of the Solomon Islands? Answer: Honiara—for five extra credit points. After the student returns to her seat, he reads the entry on the Solomons from *Operation World*, considered by some evangelicals the best current reference work on world missions. As is the case at many Christian day schools, Ben Lippen emphasizes missionary activities. Indeed, about twenty percent of the high school students will leave later in the day for a weekend Student Missionary Fellowship retreat. Edwards devotes the remainder of the time to showing the students how to analyze the sources and biases of information about current events.

The last class of the morning is Religions and Cults, one of several Bible courses from which students must choose one each year, taught by the cerebral Daniel Jansen. After prayer and a Bible memory quiz, he spends most of the period discussing the central principles of Confucianism. Students seem very interested in Confucian ethics, particularly the Silver Rule that is similar to the Golden Rule. Jansen concludes the class with speculation regarding Shang Ti or Supreme Ancestor and a possible link to the God of the Bible.

In the lunchroom, Dr. Morris Dawson, the headmaster of Ben Lippen, greets several students before sitting down with several school officials and friends of the school. Though the cafeteria brims with students, civility prevails and raised voices are not necessary for conversation. Dawson talks about a disgruntled former employee who apparently had a problem accepting duly constituted authority and ponders how the school should handle this problem. He speculates that the devil would like to use this incident to disrupt the progress of the school. The ease with which he speaks of a spiritual dimension to what most would consider a mere personnel issue is remarkable. Seeing matters through the lens of Christian faith sets this school apart from many private, not to mention, public schools where the implicit worldview is naturalistic.

As some first year high school students head for a science class, they pass older students gathering their gear for the missions trip. They seem enthusiastic about the weekend retreat in North Carolina. Ninth graders in the class, however, seem bored and restless. A first year teacher struggles to keep her charges quiet while explaining the agenda for the period. No prayer time or Bible graces this class, just a struggle for survival! Once lab begins, however, the students settle down.

During the last hour of the day, a veteran faculty member talks with several senior faculty members about the new instructor's struggles to manage the classroom and address evolution/creation/intelligent design issues. He points out that though Friday afternoon may be a factor, he is aware of some of his colleague's difficulties. Several faculty members agree to assist the new member of the BLS family. Faculty and administration alike, he notes, make a concerted effort to maintain a tightly knit community of teachers, parents, and students based on a commitment to helping the family and the church raise children who are disciples of Christ and his Kingdom.[31]

Conclusion

Though Ben Lippen is not a typical evangelical Christian school in that it was established in 1940 as a boarding school for missionary children and is now operated under the aegis of Columbia International University as opposed to a local church, it does share much in common with church-affiliated institutions that have been founded since the 1960s and will likely face some of the same difficulties that other Christ-centered, dissenting institutions will face in the early twenty-first century. In the 1970s, when Christian schools were multiplying at a rate of better than one per day, leaders focused on seemingly routine problems such as how to get started, adequate facilities, and methods of discipline. More critical matters, such as articulating a positive philosophy of Christian school education, and combating legal and legislative efforts to impose state accreditation and teacher licensing requirements on these schools, also consumed immense amount of time, energy, and resources.[32]

As the Christian school movement has matured, many of those issues have been at least partially resolved. Weaker schools have closed, while others have developed better administrative processes and educational programs. Christian schools know why they exist and are able, perhaps more clearly than any other segment of formal education in the United States, to articulate their philosophy of education. Furthermore, their right to exist free of intimate state control has been largely settled in most states. Legal and legislative concerns are shifting to issues such as employment policies, state and federal involvement in childcare and, most recently, the acceptability of courses informed by Christian perspectives by state universities.[33]

The most pressing concerns now facing Christian day school leaders are those of financial stability and spiritual vitality. In the heady early days, starting a school involved an enthusiastic crusade marked by volunteered time and money, but now the more mundane realities of student and teacher recruitment and annual budgets press upon these dissenting institutions. As school programs broaden and as expenditures for public education escalate, particularly for teacher salaries, Christian schools are facing more costly expectations. They are responding by establishing development offices and looking for ways to ensure their long-term viability. Nevertheless, many schools live close to the edge of financial difficulty.

Although movement leaders give considerable attention to financial matters, they express greater concern over the spiritual vitality of Christian schools. In the early years of the movement, advocates were confident that Christian schools would contribute to a robust revival of Christian life in the United States, as an army of young people benefited from the combined nurturing of home, church, and Christian school. Indeed, some went as far as to claim that Christian schools were the hope of the increasingly "godless" American republic. Evidence of this revival, particularly in regard to teenage lifestyles, is scanty. Some observers argue that Christian education per se is no more a panacea for America's real and perceived ills than public schooling, and that Christian schools are just as likely to reflect as to determine the spiritual levels of their constituency.

Though their growth rate has apparently slowed in the new millennium and time and experience have tempered earlier messianic expectations, Christian day schools still make up the most robust segment of the private school sector. While enrollments in other religious schools have either stagnated or declined, these schools continue to grow, and they are clearly a fixed feature of the educational landscape. Whether this segment of the increasingly pluralistic American educational enterprise will continue to expand remains to be seen. Financial difficulties are, of course, a constant threat to many of these schools and especially their patrons who in effect must pay twice—taxes and tuition—for the right to choose the kind of education they deem appropriate for their children. Of greater importance for the long-term health of Christian day schools, however, is maintaining the dissenting spirit and alternative vision of education that provided the impetus for their creation.[34] As one wise man once commented, "Where there is no vision, the people perish."[35] That is true for dissenting educational institutions as well as dissenting communities of faith.

Notes

1. Francis X. Curran, *The Churches and the Schools: American Protestantism and Popular Elementary Education*, Chicago: Loyola University Press, 1954, 1–14; and Mark A. Noll, *A History of Christianity in the United States and Canada*, Grand Rapids, MI: W. B. Eerdmans, 1992, 7–8.

2. Lawrence A. Cremin, *American Education: The Colonial Experience, 1607–1783*, New York: Harper & Row, 1970, 31–57, 167–95; and Carl F. Kaestle, *Pillars of the Republic: Common Schools and American Society, 1780–1860*, New York: Hill and Wang, 1983, 13–61.

3. James C. Carper, "The Changing Landscape of U. S. Education," *Kappa Delta Pi Record* 37 (Spring 2001): 108–9.

4. Louis J. Sherrill, *Presbyterian Parochial Schools, 1846–1870*, New Haven: Yale University Press, 1932; Kaestle, *Pillars of the Republic*, 75–103; and James C. Carper and Thomas C. Hunt, eds., *Religious Schooling in America*, Birmingham, AL: Religious Education Press, 1984.

5. David Tyack, "The Kingdom of God and the Common School," *Harvard Education Review* 36 (Fall 1966): 447–69; Timothy L. Smith, "Protestant Schooling and American Nationality," *Journal of American History* 53 (March 1967): 679–95; James C. Carper, "A Common Faith for the Common School?: Religion and Education in Kansas 1861–1900," *Mid-America* 60 (October 1978): 147–61; Lloyd M. Jorgenson, *The State and the Nonpublic School, 1825–1925*, Columbia, MO: University of Missouri Press, 1987; and Robert T. Handy, *A Christian America: Protestant Hopes and Historical Realities*, New York: Oxford University Press, 1971, 102.

6. William B. Kennedy, *The Shaping of Protestant Education*, New York: Association Press, 1966, 27.

7. James C. Carper, "Protestant School Systems," in *Encyclopedia of Education*, 2nd ed., New York: Macmillan, 2003, 1942.

8. James C. Carper, "The Christian Day School Movement, 1960–1980," *Educational Forum* 47 (Winter 1983): 135–37.

9. James D. Hunter, *American Evangelicalism: Conservative Religion and the Quandary of Modernity*, New Brunswick, NJ: Rutgers University Press, 1983, 37.

10. A. James Reichley, *Religion in American Public Life*, Washington, DC: Brookings Institution, 1985, 47. See also Richard J. Neuhaus, *The Naked Public Square: Religion and Democracy in America*, Grand Rapids, MI: William B. Eerdmans, 1984.

11. Leo Pfeffer, "The Triumph of Secular Humanism," *Journal of Church and State* 19 (Spring 1977): 211.

12. James C. Carper and William J. Weston, "Conservative Protestants in the New School Wars," *History of Education Quarterly* 30 (Spring 1990): 79–81; James D. Hunter, *Culture Wars: The Struggle to Define America*, New York: Basic Books, 1991; Stephen L. Carter, *The Culture of Disbelief: How American Law and Politics Trivialize Religious Devotion*, New York: Basic Books, 1993; and Richard A. Baer, Jr. and James C. Carper, "'To the Advantage of Infidelity,' or How Not to Deal with Religion in America's Public Schools," *Educational Policy* 14 (November 2000): 600–21.

13.   Warren A. Nord, *Religion & American Education: Rethinking a National Dilemma*, Chapel Hill: University of North Carolina Press, 1995; William Martin, *With God on Our Side: The Rise of the Religious Right in America*, New York: Broadway Books, 1996; James W. Fraser, *Between Church and State: Religion and Public Education in a Multicultural America*, New York: St. Martin's Press, 1999; and Casey Luskin, "Alternative Viewpoints about Biological Origins as Taught in Public Schools," *Journal of Church and State* 47 (Summer 2005): 583–617. Modern evangelicalism, which emerged from fundamentalism after World War II, shares many beliefs with its progenitor, which was born of the early twentieth-century battles within Protestantism over, among other things, higher criticism of the Bible and Darwinism. Evangelicals and fundamentalists alike embrace classical Protestant doctrines such as the divinity of Christ, his atoning sacrifice on the cross for the sins of the world, and his bodily resurrection; stress the necessity of a conversion experience or "new birth"; believe in the authority of the Scriptures; and emphasize missionary work and evangelism. Fundamentalists are generally distinguished by their embrace of dispensational theology with its emphasis on the premillennial return of Christ and rapture of true believers from the world, biblical literalism, and varying degrees of separation from American culture and its "worldly" practices as well as religious organizations that cooperate with "liberal" churches. They also tend to belong to independent as opposed to denominational churches.

14.   George Hillocks, Jr., "Books and Bombs: Ideological Conflict and the Schools," *School Review* 86 (August 1978): 632–54; Charles L. Glenn, "Religion, Textbooks, and the Common Schools," *Public Interest* 88 (Summer 1987): 28–47; and Stephen Bates, *Battleground: One Mother's Crusade, the Religious Right, and the Struggle for Control of Our Classrooms*, New York: Poseidon Press, 1993.

15.   James C. Carper, "Pluralism to Establishment to Dissent: The Religious and Educational Context of Home Schooling," *Peabody Journal of Education* 75 (2000): 8–19.

16.   Carper and Hunt, *Religious Schooling*, 111–12. For a thoughtful discussion of the impact of the Scopes trial on Protestant fundamentalism, see Edward J. Larson, *Summer for the Gods: The Scopes Trial and America's Continuing Debate over Science and Religion*, New York: Basic Books, 1997. Larson asserts that concern about teaching Darwinian evolution in the public schools has contributed to the growth of "creation-affirming" Christian schools and homeschooling.

17.   Detailed discussion of the cultural context and characteristics of the Christian day school movement between 1960 and 1980 may be found in Carper, "Christian Day School Movement," 139–43; and William J. Reese, "Soldiers of Christ in the Army of God: The Christian School Movement in America," *Educational Theory* 35 (Spring 1985): 175–94. In "The Forces Behind the Christian Day School Movement," *Christian School Comment*, 1977, 1, Paul A. Kienel, former Executive Director of the Association of Christian Schools International, summed up what he believed to be the primary metaphysical/epistemological divide between Christian schooling and public education: "Christian schools are Christian institutions where Jesus Christ and the Bible are central in the school curriculum and in the lives of the teachers and administrators. This distinction removes us from direct competition with public schools. Although we often compare ourselves academically, we are educational institutions operating on separate philosophical tracks. Ours is Christ-centered education, presented in the Christian context. Theirs is man-centered edu-

cation presented within the context of the supremacy of man as opposed to the supremacy of God. Their position is known as secular humanism."

18. US Department of Education, National Center for Education Statistics, *Characteristics of Private Schools in the United States: Results from the 2001–2002 Private School Universe Survey*, Washington, DC: US Government Printing Office, 2004, 10. See also US Department of Education, National Center for Education Statistics, *The Condition of Education 2005*, Washington, DC: US Government Printing Office, 2005, 31, 106.

19. *Association of Christian Schools International, ACSI Directory*, Whittier, CA: ACSI, 2001.

20. James C. Carper, "Independent Christian Day Schools: The Maturing of a Movement," *Catholic Education: A Journal of Inquiry and Practice* 5 (June 2002): 502. Current enrollment data is available on ACSI and AACS websites. See also US Department of Education, *Characteristics of Private Schools*, 27.

21. Carper, "Pluralism to Establishment to Dissent," 16–17.

22. Carper, "Independent Christian Day Schools," 506.

23. Paul F. Parsons, *Inside America's Christian Schools*, Macon, GA: Mercer University Press, 1987.

24. Alan Peshkin, *God's Choice: The Total World of a Fundamentalist Christian School*, Chicago: University of Chicago Press, 1986; Susan D. Rose, *Keeping Them Out of the Hands of Satan: Evangelical Schooling in America*, New York: Routledge, Chapman and Hall, 1988; Peter S. Lewis, "Private Education and the Subcultures of Dissent: Alternative/Free Schools (1965–1975) and Christian Fundamentalist Schools (1965–1990)" (Ph.D. diss., Stanford University, 1991); Melinda B. Wagner, *God's Schools: Choice and Compromise in American Society*, New Brunswick, NJ: Rutgers University Press, 1990; and David Sikkink, "Speaking in Many Tongues," *Education Matters* 1 (Summer 2001): 36–45. See also Nancy T. Ammerman, *Bible Believers: Fundamentalists in the Modern World*, New Brunswick, NJ: Rutgers University Press, 1987.

25. James D. Anderson, *The Education of Blacks in South, 1860–1935*, Chapel Hill, NC: University of North Carolina Press, 1988, 7–8, 152–83.

26. David Nevin and Robert E. Bills, *The Schools That Fear Built*, Washington, DC: Acropolis Books, 1976; Virginia D. Nordin and William L. Turner, "More Than Segregation Academies: The Growing Protestant Fundamentalist Schools," *Phi Delta Kappan* 61 (February 1980): 391–94; Peter Skerry, "Christian Schools Versus the I.R.S.," *The Public Interest* 61 (1980): 18–41; and James C. Carper and Jack Layman, "Black-Flight Academies: The New Christian Day Schools," *Educational Forum* 61 (Winter 1997): 114–21.

27. Parsons, *Inside America's Christian Schools*, 113–26; and US Department of Education, *Condition of Education 2005*, 107.

28. Carper and Layman, "Black-Flight Academies," 114–15.

29. Ibid., 16.

30. Jack Layman, "Black Flight: The Rise of Black Christian Schools" (Ph.D. diss., University of South Carolina, 1992), 6.

31. Names of the Ben Lippen faculty members have been changed to protect their privacy.

32. James C. Carper and Neal E. Devins, "The State and the Christian Day School," in *Religion and the State: Essays in Honor of Leo Pfeffer*, ed. James E. Wood, Jr., Waco, TX: Baylor University Press, 1985, 211–32.

33. Sean Cavanagh, "Suit Claims Anti-Religious Bias in Calif. System," *Education Week*, September 7, 2005, 14–15.
34. US Department of Education, *Condition of Education 2005*, 31; and Carper, "Changing Landscape," 106–10.
35. Prov. 29:18, King James Version.

· 8 ·

THE STATE AND THE NEW
PROTESTANT DISSENTERS

The *Whisner* Decision

The proliferation of Christian day schools in the 1970s and 1980s and their explicit repudiation of public education sparked a number of clashes with government authorities regarding whether and to what extent the state should regulate these dissenting institutions. Unlike Catholic, Jewish, and other Protestant schools, which had by that time generally embraced most forms of state accreditation, many new Christian schools, particularly those of a more fundamentalist persuasion, and their patrons asserted that to comply with certain state-prescribed "minimum standards" and teacher licensing procedures would violate their religious convictions. They maintained that the Free Exercise Clause of the First Amendment exempted them from submitting to regulations that they deemed objectionable on religious grounds. Furthermore, Christian school officials argued, state regulations violated the Ninth and Fourteenth Amendment right of parents to direct their children' education and upbringing and the First Amendment's prohibition of government efforts to "establish" religion. Their schools, they concluded, should not comply with expansive state procedures that would govern the content and practice of Christian education.[1]

State authorities, on the other hand, asserted their right to impose "reasonable" regulations on religious schools in order to ensure that each child would receive an adequate education. These officials contended that extant regulations were both necessary and unobtrusive. As far as they were concerned, schools that did not conform to these regulations were not schools and that parents sending their children to them were not in compliance with compulsory attendance statutes. Furthermore, government officials claimed, nonconforming institutions could be prohibited from continued operation.[2]

During the 1970s and 1980s, these conflicting assertions of state interest and First Amendment rights bred significant litigation in at least a dozen states. Court decisions on the Christian day school issue frequently provoked strong responses from both government officials and Christian educators. Among the most widely publicized confrontations were those involving schools in Nebraska, Kentucky, Maine, Michigan, and Ohio. It was in the Ohio case, however, that a dissenting school would raise many questions common to all such conflicts regarding the legitimacy of state efforts to force newly established Christian schools into conformity with the established public school paradigm.[3]

The Roots of *Whisner*

As had been the case with many other fundamentalist and evangelical Protestants in the late 1960s and early 1970s, dissatisfaction with increasingly secular public schooling and a "growing conviction" that the church should reclaim its responsibility for educating its children spurred Levi W. Whisner, pastor of the nondenominational God's Tabernacle Church located near Bradford, Ohio, in rural Darke County, and several members of his congregation to consider the possibility of starting a school in 1971.[4] After two years of prayer and discussion, Tabernacle Christian School opened its doors to twenty-five students on September 4,1973. Little did Whisner, who served as the principal, and the parents who sent their children to the school in the basement of God's Tabernacle Church know that within a month they would be involved in a conflict with the state regarding school accreditation requirements and the right of free exercise of religion that would culminate nearly three years later in an Ohio Supreme Court decision of profound importance to Christian day schools in Ohio and elsewhere.[5]

Just prior to opening Tabernacle Christian School, Whisner obtained a copy of *Minimum Standards for Ohio Elementary Schools, Revised 1970*. Issued by the Ohio Department of Education, the document outlined, among other things, the minimum curriculum, organization, facility, and personnel standards or requirements with which all public and private schools had to comply in order to be chartered or accredited by the state. Of critical importance was the stipulation that chartering required compliance with *all* of the minimum standards.[6] After reading the 149-page bulletin, Whisner and the governing board of the school concluded that as a matter of religious principle they could not conform to all of the standards and, therefore, decided not to initiate the prescribed procedures for obtaining a charter.[7]

The consequences of that decision became evident in early October 1973. As a result of a routine attendance check, city and county school officials discovered that thirteen children were enrolled in Tabernacle Christian School, which was not state approved or chartered. Informed of this situation, the county probation officer sent the following letter to the children and a similar one to their parents:

> I have had the fact brought to my attention that you are failing to attend a school which conforms to the minimum standards prescribed by the State Board of Education, as required by law.
>
> I am required to warn you pursuant to section 3321.19 of the Ohio Revised Code, that attendance of all children of compulsory school age is expected every day the school is in session. You are required to attend school forthwith and to continue to attend a school which conforms to the minimum standards prescribed by the State Board of Education.
>
> If you fail to attend school, as required by law, I am required to make complaint against your parent or guardian for failing to cause you to attend, or if he shows that you do not obey his requirement, against you in the Juvenile Court.[8]

At the same time the county superintendent's office advised Whisner to discuss the charter problem with the Ohio Department of Education. Although the parties arranged a meeting for October 5, Whisner later informed the department that due to a prior commitment he could not keep the appointment. Two months passed before another contact occurred.[9]

Based on the continued attendance of children at the unchartered school and no evidence of negotiations with the Ohio Department of Education, the county prosecutor's office took the matter to the Darke County Grand Jury. On November 30, 1973, fifteen parents, including Whisner, were indicted for failure to send their children to school. At their arraignment on December 10, they entered pleas of not guilty.[10]

Commentary immediately following the arraignment suggested that the parties involved approached the matter from different perspectives, a tendency that was to have important ramifications as the case developed. To the county prosecutor and local school officials, the issue was conformity to

state-mandated minimum standards. In the words of the assistant county prosecutor: "We're not concerned with their religion, we're just interested in seeing that the parents send their children to an accredited school."[11] To Whisner,
codefendants, and a growing number of sympathizers in Ohio and elsewhere,
the crux of the matter was free exercise of religion and parental liberty. As
Whisner asserted, the issue was "the freedom of the Christian church and parents to be able to guide their children the way they think they ought to, under
God."[12] Thus, while state officials tended to view the issue as merely a violation of state law, Whisner and his followers spoke frequently of the "battle" to
secure the right of the church to educate its children without undue state
regulation.

To fight this "battle," the defendants retained the services of the
redoubtable William Bentley Ball, an expert in church-state questions, who
recently had successfully defended the First Amendment rights of the Amish
in the well-known *Wisconsin v. Yoder* case. Upon arriving in January 1974, Ball
pointed out that the local situation was "not yet a case" and expressed hope that
a solution could be worked out with state officials. He noted, however, "if it got
to the courts . . . there would certainly be a question of religious liberty.
Religious liberty, parental freedom, and the rights of children were involved in
the Amish case and they could be involved here, too."[13]

Hoping to reach a compromise with the Ohio Department of Education,
on January 22,1974, Ball, Whisner, a member of the Tabernacle Christian
School Board, and several pastors met with John E. Brown, Director of
Elementary and Secondary Education. Ball attempted to convince him to give
the group permission to operate the school, but Brown insisted that all standards had to be met prior to actual operation of the school. According to
Brown, "The meeting was very congenial, but I don't think it changed anything."[14] Whisner, however, thought that the conference was fruitful. After consulting with members of the school board and leaders of the Accelerated
Christian Education organization, developers and suppliers of the individualized, Bible-centered curriculum used at Tabernacle Christian School and a
growing number of similar institutions, he decided to seek a compromise. On
January 28, he wrote Brown and proposed: "Upon receiving a favorable response
to this letter, we will submit to the Department of Education, on or before April
1, 1974, a plan showing the total school organization and program. Such a plan
will contain information and commitments on our part corresponding to those
contained in your publication 'Minimum Standards for Ohio Elementary
Schools,' as far as is consistent with our religious beliefs."[15]

The Ohio Department of Education did not respond and legal proceedings continued. At a pretrial hearing on February 11, authorities decided that the defendants would be tried collectively, a jury trial was waived, and the trial date was set for May 7, 1974 in the Court of Common Pleas of Darke County, Ohio.

The Trial Court

The trial of Whisner and his codefendants commenced as scheduled in a packed courtroom in the Darke County Courthouse in Greenville, Ohio. The trial court proceedings revealed again that to the state the primary issue was noncompliance with state law while the defendants believed that free exercise of religion was at the heart of the matter.

Lee Fry, the prosecuting attorney, produced only two witnesses. Surprisingly, neither offered a strong defense of the state's compelling interest in mandating compliance with all of the minimum standards. Though the prosecutor called the county probation officer to testify that the defendants had been warned by letter that they were in violation of state compulsory school attendance laws, the state's key witness was John E. Brown of the Ohio Department of Education. After discussing the statutory authority granted the department to establish minimum standards, he described the steps necessary to obtain a charter and claimed that Whisner and Tabernacle Christian School had not initiated the process.[16] Brown concluded his testimony with the assertion that while it was difficult for church schools to obtain a charter, many had done so.[17]

In his opening remarks, Ball outlined the religious liberty claim of the defendants. He maintained that the accused parents were "committed by their consciences to enroll their children in a Christian Bible-oriented school" and had a constitutional right to send their children to such a school as long as it met reasonable minimal requirements. Tabernacle Christian School, he contended, met those requirements. Ball then asserted that the state had no compelling interest in enforcing all of the minimum standards, a practice which he felt burdened unduly the defendants' free exercise of religion.[18]

In his cross-examination of Brown, Ball established three points of significance. First, the Department of Education did not respond to Whisner's letter of January 28, 1974. Second, although a school might be chartered without meeting all minimum standards, total compliance would be expected eventually. Third, if the statement of a school's philosophy of education, a mandated standard, ran counter to other minimum standards and made it impossible to fully embrace them, the department would not approve the school.[19] In other words, despite the requirement that "implementation of instructional and operational programs shall be in accordance with the philosophy and objectives set forth in the statement," conformity to the state minimum standards, regardless of the school's philosophy, would be required for accreditation.[20]

After cross-examining Brown, Ball called Levi Whisner, who spent nearly three hours on the witness stand defining the religious convictions associated with God's Tabernacle Church and Tabernacle Christian School and outlining religious and educational objections to several of the 500-plus minimum standards. Ball and Fry probed his religious beliefs, which he maintained imbued both the church and the school. The former attempted to establish the scope and sincerity of those convictions while the latter tried to demonstrate that Whisner's beliefs were vague and not reflective of an established religious creed.

Whisner testified that though the church did not have a lengthy formal doctrinal statement, he and those who attended the church and governed the school subscribed to a "Bible-oriented religion . . . a historical religion that dates back to the New Testament." He stated that it was a religion that involved being "born again" through faith in Christ, accepting the Bible as the sole rule of faith and practice, seeking guidance by the Holy Spirit, and separation from sin and worldliness.[21] Such beliefs, Whisner claimed, led him and others to found Tabernacle Christian School. The centrality of those convictions was evident when he was asked specifically why the school was established. He replied:

> I have three brief answers. . . . One is, I feel as a pastor, and as a spiritual leader, when God speaks we have to do something and God spoke to Isaiah, and Isaiah had to move. God spoke to us, and we felt we had to do something.
>
> Secondly, we wanted to give our children a good spiritual and moral foundation. A Bible foundation to guide their lives and to prepare them for the hideous things that are surely facing this generation.
>
> And thirdly, we could not find in this general area a school that afforded us what we felt that our children must have and basics that should be instilled in our children.[22]

Speaking for Tabernacle Christian School, Whisner then outlined objections to the minimum standards. The first standard to which he objected was "A charter shall be granted after an inspection which determines that all standards have been met." To comply with all standards and receive a charter, Whisner argued, meant accepting state control and a state philosophy of education in lieu of a Christian philosophy. Quoting the Bible to the effect that "we are not to be conformed to this world," he maintained:

If we go by all the standards the state would be running the school and we want it to be God's school. There are some areas that I am sure the state are going to call it God's school, or we want it belong to Him, we feel God ought to have the controls. And we are trying desperately to keep our hands off, and let [sic] His hands on.[23]

Besides objecting to the chartering process, Whisner took exception to the minimum standard which required that based on a five-hour school day, or one of greater duration, four-fifths of the day had to be devoted to "language arts, mathematics, social studies, science, health, citizenship, related directed study and self-help" and one-fifth to "directed physical education, music, art, special activities and applied arts." He testified that while Tabernacle Christian School offered nearly all subjects mentioned in the standard, such precise time allocation left little or no room for Bible-training, scripture memory, and spiritual counsel sessions. This, he argued, "put God's program in a vise" and severely restricted the ability of the school to carry out its primary mission.[24]

The principal of the school also voiced religious objections to two standards that dealt with school-community relations. Asserting the importance of separation, he claimed that the standard requiring all school activities to conform to the policies adopted by the local school board gave public authorities the power to control the entire operation of Tabernacle Christian School. A related standard that mandated "cooperation and interaction between the school and the community" also disturbed Whisner. Maintaining that a Christian school could not seek direction from the community, he asserted, "I think God has to give this direction. For the Bible said, 'The Lord is my light and my salvation.'"[25]

After criticizing a standard that prohibited parental access to certain student records, Whisner concluded his comments regarding the minimum standards contending that three of them reflected a philosophy of secular humanism.[26] Although he believed "humanism" was sprinkled throughout the minimum standards, he objected specifically to three which, among other things, urged consensus thinking, stressed the need for social controls in organized group life, and referred to changing moral standards and values. Such "humanistic" doctrines, he posited, left God out and were antithetical to the school's emphasis on prayerful decision-making, separation, and moral absolutes.[27]

After the unchallenged testimony of a pastor who described his diligent but fruitless efforts to secure state approval of his school, the defense called two expert witnesses, Ralph O'Neal West and Donald A. Erickson. West, Director of Evaluation for the Commission on Independent Secondary Schools of the

New England Association of Schools and Colleges, commented on, among other things, the lack of clarity in the procedures for obtaining a charter and the extent to which standards regarding philosophy and objectives and school community relations placed nonpublic schools under direct public control. Mandating private school compliance to each of the minimum standards, he concluded in by and large unchallenged testimony, was not a matter of compelling state interest.[28]

Erickson, professor of educational administration and director of the Mid-West Administration Center at the University of Chicago, asserted that the state must regulate education, but, he continued: "I am also firmly convinced that the state can fulfill all its fundamental responsibilities in education without prescribing how people must be educated; where they must be educated; what kind of buildings they must be educated in; what must be in the program, and what must be the nature of the individual who instructs them."[29] Yet this was exactly the character of Minimum Standards for Ohio Elementary Schools, Revised 1970, and, according to the professor, constituted his fundamental objection to it.

In precise, persuasive, and uncontradicted testimony, Erickson elaborated on his disapproval of the basic nature of the minimum standards document. He raised four specific objections. First, he argued that requiring all schools to comply with all the minimum standards went "a long way . . . toward obliterating any distinction between public and private education." This, he asserted, constituted an infringement on freedom. Second, though the state required a non-tax-supported school to formulate its own philosophy of education and construct programs in accordance with it, he pointed out that the state then proceeded to mandate compliance with its educational program "founded upon a particular philosophy." This would, in effect, he contended, "take away from the school the right to run its philosophy" and impose the state's "secular humanism philosophy." Third, Erickson posited that the minimum standards document inhibited "departures from conventionality" and contained many requirements, particularly in the areas of school and class size, curriculum content, and certification, for which there was no basis in fact. Fourth, he stated that Ohio's minimum standards "are about the weakest way I know of to try to accomplish what they are designed to accomplish . . . this is not . . . an effective way to separate between the poor schools and the good schools." Erickson finished his testimony claiming: "I don't think the state has any compelling interest at all in requiring schools to live up to the minimum standards in this book as a whole."[30]

After concluding his defense by calling a teacher at Tabernacle Christian School to testify as to its educational quality as evidenced by excellent student progress, two parents of children at the school to explain why public education was not compatible with their religious beliefs, and a student, Whisner's daughter, to express satisfaction with the school, Ball moved for acquittal.[31] "We are not attacking the compulsory attendance law on its face," he explained. "Our complaint goes to the application of that statute through the so-called minimum standards. A religious liberty claim has been raised."[32] Ball then listed violations that resulted from the application of the compulsory attendance law to the defendants:

> First, a violation by the state of the right of the defendants and their children to the free exercise of religion as guaranteed by the First Amendment to the Constitution of the United States and of Article I, Section 7, of the Constitution of the state of Ohio.
>
> Second, a violation by the state of rights in education as guaranteed by the First and Fourteenth Amendments to the Constitution of the United States and Article 1, Sections, 1, 7, and 11 of the Constitution of Ohio, including the right to the expression, transmission and reception of ideas in their most basic form.
>
> Third, a violation by the state of rights of parents in the nurture and education of their children as guaranteed by the Ninth and Fourteenth Amendments to the Constitution of the United States.
>
> Fourth, a denial by the state of due process of law to the owners of Tabernacle Christian School by unreasonably penalizing attendance thereat, in violation of Due Process Clause of the Fourteenth Amendment to the Constitution of the United States and Article 1, Section 19, of the Constitution of the state of Ohio.[33]

On August 15, 1974, the trial court rendered its opinion that the defendants were guilty as charged. Noting that an appeal was certain, Judge Howard Eley departed from normal criminal trial procedure and explained briefly the basis for the verdict.

After making a sweeping assertion of the state's power to promulgate minimum standards and enforce compulsory school attendance laws, the trial court judge turned to the defendants' religious claims.[34] He dismissed their religious "objections to and position in regard to the minimum standards" as an afterthought. "In other words," he continued, "they did not specifically exist prior to the indictments and constitute the results of a hasty effort thereafter to prepare a defense thereto."[35]

Having disposed of the defendants' religious convictions in two paragraphs, Eley examined several specific objections to the minimum standards. Because he assigned little significance to the defendants' beliefs, the judge felt that their complaints had "no basis in logic." Failing to grasp the essence of Whisner's testimony, he averred that Tabernacle Christian School could meet all standards and still be "God's school." Among other objections that he criticized, Eley also disagreed with the defendants' contention that rigid time allocation for certain subjects interfered with the religious mission of the school.[36]

The expert witnesses did not impress the judge, either. West and Erickson, he thought, were "hard pressed for specific objections and some that they referred to could only be termed as 'grasping at straws.'" After examining several minor points of their testimony, he concluded: "Shorn of all rhetoric the basic thrust of the defense appears to be that there should be two sets of standards one for tax-supported schools and another of lesser requirements for church or private schools. Surely to do so would be to deny the children attending these schools of lesser requirements of the right to equal educational opportunities."[37] Despite uncontradicted testimony that, based on Stanford Achievement Test scores, children at Tabernacle Christian School had made better than average educational progress, Eley implied that children at the unchartered school were not enjoying "equal educational opportunities." Here he seemed to assume that different standards, lesser requirements, and inferior education were one and the same.

Reaction to Eley's decision that Whisner and his codefendants had failed to sustain a defense and were, therefore, guilty of violating state law was subdued. Members of God's Tabernacle Church continued work on a new school building, which they hoped would be ready to accommodate the anticipated sixty enrollees for the 1974–1975 school year. None of the members seemed concerned about the likelihood of facing a second charge. Reflecting the feelings of the group, Whisner's wife proclaimed, "We're trusting the Lord to work it out, just like He did back in the Bible days."[38]

On August 30, 1974, Judge Eley fined each defendant the maximum amount of $20.00. The parents were also required to post a bond of $100.00 to guarantee their children's attendance at a state-approved school. He then suspended execution of the sentences pending appeal, thus permitting them to return their children to Tabernacle Christian School.[39]

The defendants appealed their convictions that fall to the Court of Appeals for Darke County. On June 13, 1975, the appellate court affirmed their convictions. Justice Joseph Kerns, writing for the court, asserted that the "critical issue in the appeal is whether the beliefs and practices of the appellants are entitled to constitutional protection from the standards prescribed for all schools by the state of Ohio."[40] Like the trial court, the appellate court attached little significance to the defendants' religious convictions and thus effectively eviscerated their case. Whisner's testimony, Kerns stated, "however well meant, is inadequate to justify on religious grounds a complete departure from the minimum standards of the State Department of Education." In fact, he continued in a judicially questionable assessment, "his testimony reflects the subjective attitudes of the members of his congregation, and his reasoning is based essentially upon a subjective interpretation of biblical language."[41]

Kerns then asserted that the state was not required to defend every minimum standard and that its case was complete when it demonstrated that the defendants failed to initiate the chartering process.[42] In conclusion, he wrote: "The motives of the appellants cannot be challenged. They like many others, may be fed up with executive insistence upon bureaucratic paternalism, legislative insistence upon excess regulatory baggage, and judicial insistence upon prayer-less schools, but the constitutional protection afforded by the Free Exercise Clause must rest upon a stronger foundation than portrayed by the record in this case."[43]

Appeal to the Supreme Court of Ohio

Whisner and his codefendants appealed immediately to the Supreme Court of Ohio. On October 10, 1975, the state's high court agreed to hear the case. From that point until the supreme court rendered its verdict the following summer, Whisner's "battle" with the state received attention, and in some cases support, from many and diverse sources. Most major state newspapers carried articles on Tabernacle Christian School, Levi Whisner, and the legal proceedings. The case also received some national attention. Utilizing the David and Goliath metaphor, syndicated columnists Russell Kirk and the perspicacious observer of the courts, James Jackson Kilpatrick, advocated Whisner's cause and chided the state for attempting to suppress religious liberty.[44]

Even Governor James A. Rhodes became involved, thus adding a political dimension to the issue. On December 8, 1975, approximately 8,000 Bible-carrying, hymn-singing supporters of Christian schools rallied at the state capitol to protest school accreditation practices. Ohio's chief executive, whose children purportedly attended church-related schools, addressed the throng. Rhodes praised Christian education and proclaimed, "I fully support the right of every citizen of Ohio to send their children to church-sponsored schools." He also criticized the state school bureaucracy for imposing too many restrictions on small church schools, urged the group to continue their "fight" in the courts, and pledged his efforts to resolve the differences between the state and the Christian schools.[45]

Within a week, Rhodes met with representatives of Christian Schools of Ohio, the organization which sponsored the rally, and Martin W. Essex, Ohio's Superintendent of Public Instruction, to discuss the charter issue. Though no solution was reached, one misunderstanding was cleared up. Essex explained that, contrary to many Christian school leaders' opinions, local officials, not the Ohio Department of Education, initiated legal proceedings against Tabernacle Christian School and similar institutions elsewhere in the state. He also stated that he would consider a proposal to exempt Christian schools from the minimum standards.[46]

The next instance of state interest in Whisner's case came in January 1976, when the Superintendent of Public Instruction filed a "friend of the court" brief urging the Ohio Supreme Court to affirm the decision of the appellate court. Recognizing the essentials of a religious liberty claim, the brief asserted that the defendants had failed to demonstrate that "the beliefs and practices disclosed by the evidence are entitled to constitutional protection under the Free Exercise Clause." Furthermore, the brief argued, even if the defendants could have made a "claim for relief" under the Free Exercise Clause, the state's reasonable and legitimate interest in insuring an adequate education for its citizens would outweigh minor infringements on their religious practices.[47]

Viewing the case as one that raised "serious issues about the rights of individuals to rear their children in faiths of their choice, the American Civil Liberties Union of Ohio Foundation also filed an amicus brief. Though not usually inclined to support fundamentalist Protestant groups in religion-related First Amendment issues, the ACLU backed Whisner and favored reversal of the appellate court's decision. The brief noted that the appellate court erred in judging the veracity rather than the sincerity of the defendants' beliefs. Maintaining that their statements and willingness to face criminal charges proved that the defendants' convictions were "truly held," the brief argued that they possessed First, Ninth, and Fourteenth Amendment rights to "direct the religious upbringing of their children." While granting that the state had a "reasonable right to impose regulations for the control of basic education," the brief continued the free exercise argument by asserting that the state had no compelling interest in requiring total compliance with the minimum standards "when such compliance is inimical to sincere religious beliefs and substantial compliance is available as a less restrictive alternative." The brief concluded that since the state demanded total compliance with the minimum standards and provided no means of accommodating the defendants' sincere religious convictions with state interests, the appellate court should be reversed.[48]

Suggestive of the widespread interest in the case among fundamentalist pastors throughout Ohio was the brief filed by over 125 ministers. Like the ACLU brief, it claimed that the lower courts had misinterpreted the defendants' religious beliefs and ignored the fact that the state had not even attempted to prove a "compelling interest" in total compliance with the minimum standards. The brief also urged the high court to recognize that Tabernacle Christian School was in "substantial compliance" with the standards and that its students were, as indicated by standardized test scores, receiving an education equivalent to instruction given to pupils in public schools. Concluding its lengthy argument for reversal, the brief offered a unique proposition of law. In light of the exemption from compulsory attendance laws given the Amish on the basis of their religious beliefs, it submitted that "the favored position granted to the Older Order Amish in *Yoder* contrasted with the Appellants' convictions . . . , constitutes a violation of the Establishment Clause of the First Amendment. The violation arises because of the obvious unequal treatment afforded (by an arm of the government) the Old Order Amish, under substantially identical laws."[49]

The *Whisner* Decision

On July 28, 1976, the Supreme Court of Ohio rendered its verdict thus ending, at least temporarily, nearly three years of conflict between the religious beliefs of several parents, as embodied in Tabernacle Christian School, and the state's school accreditation procedures. Writing for the court, Justice Frank Celebrezze commenced his lengthy and thorough explanation of the reversal of the Court of Appeals for Darke County by noting:

> This cause presents sensitive issues of paramount importance involving the power of the state to impose extensive regulations upon the structure and government of non-public education, and, conversely, upon the right of these appellants to freely exercise their professed religious beliefs in the context of providing an education to their children. Because both the Court of Appeals and the Court of Common Pleas fundamentally misconstrued the principles of law applicable to resolution of the instant cause, and because the issues presented herein are apparently questions of first impression in Ohio, a thorough examination of the relevant decisional law, as expressed by the Supreme Court of the United States, and of the applicable constitutional and statutory provision, both federal and state, is required.[50]

He then emphasized that the appellants neither attacked facially the state's compulsory education laws nor denied that the state had a right to promulgate and enforce *reasonable* regulations with respect to nonpublic schools. They did, however, contend that the "application of Ohio's compulsory attendance laws as to them, through the medium of the Minimum Standards for Ohio Elementary Schools," infringed upon their right of free exercise of religion.[51]

Turning to the appellants' religious beliefs, Celebrezze criticized the lower courts for "failing to accord the requisite judicial deference to the veracity of those beliefs." After reviewing Whisner's testimony and alluding to the fact that the appellants were willing to risk criminal prosecution for the sake of their convictions, he concluded that, based on the guidelines enunciated in *United States v. Ballard* and *United States v. Seeger*, their religious beliefs were "truly held."[52]

Noting that in order to sustain a free exercise case, one not only had to demonstrate sincere religious convictions, but also "show the coercive effect of the enactment as it operates against him in the practice of his religion," Justice Celebrezze reviewed Whisner's objections to several of the minimum standards. At this critical juncture, he observed astutely that while the language of the particular standards to which the appellants objected was "facially neutral," according to *Wisconsin v. Yoder*, "[a] regulation neutral on its face may, in its application, nonetheless offend the constitutional requirement for governmental neutrality . . . [because] it unduly burdens the free exercise of religion."[53] After pointing out that one of the minimum standards required compliance with all such standards, Celebrezze discussed the free exercise implications of standards requiring precise allocation of instructional time, conformity of all school activities to policies of the local school board, and school-community cooperation. Agreeing with the thrust of Whisner's testimony and Ball's assertions,[54] he determined that the appellants had "sustained their burden of establishing that the 'minimum standards' infringe upon the right guaranteed them by the First Amendment to the Constitution of the United States, and by Section 7, Article 1 of the Ohio Constitution, to the free exercise of religion."[55]

Celebrezze also agreed with Ball's argument that the minimum standards as applied would violate the appellants' Ninth and Fourteenth Amendment rights to direct the education of their children. Indicating that the lower courts had ignored this highly significant issue, he wrote: "In our view, these standards are so pervasive and all-encompassing that total compliance with each and every standard by a nonpublic school would effectively eradicate the distinction between public and nonpublic education, and thereby deprive these appel-

lants of their traditional interest as parents to direct the upbringing and education of their children."[56] The courts, he continued, had long recognized that
the right of parents to guide or determine the character of the education of their
children "is indeed a 'fundamental right' guaranteed by the due process clause
of the Fourteenth Amendment." That right, he concluded, citing Erickson's
expert testimony, "has been denied by application of the state's minimum standards as to them [appellants]."[57]

After reiterating that the application of the minimum standards violated
the appellants' rights in two different ways, Celebrezze turned to the question
of whether those standards could yet be sustained by the state. Here he pointed out that, in order to override the free exercise claim, it was incumbent upon
the state to demonstrate a "compelling interest" in mandating total compliance
to the minimum standards on the part of a nonpublic religious school. Based
on expert testimony and the fact that the state did not even attempt to "justify its interest in enforcing the minimum standards as applied to a nonpublic religious school," he maintained that the state had not established a "compelling
interest."[58]

Justice Celebrezze then reversed the Court of Appeals for Darke County,
discharged the defendants, and, most significantly, implied that many of the
state's provisions for chartering and regulating nonpublic religious schools
were unconstitutional. In effect, faith-based schools in Ohio were at liberty to
operate without a charter or regard to the state's minimum standards should they
desire to do so.[59]

Although the court was unanimous in its judgment, two of the six participating justices dissented from the syllabus and the majority opinion. Since the
state legislature never intended that the minimum standards be applied to private schools in the same fashion as to public institutions, they argued that the
majority should not have raised and considered constitutional issues. Rejecting
both the state's and the appellants' strict interpretation of the law requiring
attendance at a school meeting minimum standards, they believed that the convictions should have been reversed on the grounds that Whisner and his codefendants were not adequately informed of their rights and responsibilities
under that "impermissibly vague" statute which was never meant to be interpreted so strictly in the matter of standards as to curb religious freedom.[60]

Reaction to the sweeping *Whisner* decision was varied. Pointing to the possible impact of political pressure on the Ohio Supreme Court, Prosecutor Fry
was "shocked" by the outcome but offered no assessment as to its impact.
Although Superintendent Essex attempted to downplay the significance of the

decision, he warned that it might facilitate "white flight" from busing and "could subject our youngsters to the right of ignorance which has not been before considered an appropriate right." He also surmised that the decision might necessitate a separate set of standards for religious schools.[61]

Whisner, on the other hand, was elated and thought the outcome was very significant. He proclaimed: "This gives a great note of encouragement to Christians who want to have their children raised in a good Christian atmosphere. Praise the Lord." Assessing the impact of the decision, Whisner asserted that it would boost the Christian school movement, unite Christians of different theological persuasions in future "battles," curtail the power of the state education bureaucracy in Ohio and other states to regulate Christian schools, and promote a new appreciation of religious liberty and parental rights.[62]

Ball was also pleased with the Ohio Supreme Court's determination that the minimum standards overstepped "the boundary of reasonable regulation as applied to a non-public religious school." "It was a superb decision," he stated, "a real vindication of religious liberty . . . a strong recognition of parental rights . . . a strong recognition of the right to operate a private school without being drowned in governmental control." In essence, he declared, "it tells the state it may regulate in a reasonable way, but it may not regulate the philosophies of schools."[63]

Conclusion

Though it has not received widespread attention in either scholarly or professional journals, *Whisner* is significant for a number of reasons. First, as Whisner and Ball observed, the decision affirmed strongly parental and free exercise of religion rights pertaining to education and was extremely critical of the state's apparent assumption that its compelling interest was self-evident. Second, recognizing the primacy of those rights and scrutinizing the purported relationship between regulation and outcome, it assumed that when religious and parental liberty conflicts with state interest in regulating education the state is obliged to employ the least restrictive or burdensome means to satisfy its interest. This resulted in a circumscription of the state's authority to promulgate and enforce detailed rules or standards applicable to religious schools. As one commentator has suggested: "It appears that the court was approaching a theory that once it is demonstrated that the individual is being compelled to act contrary to his or her conscience, a strong presumption that the state can accomplish its objectives in another manner is imposed. If the court was in fact adopting this view, the free exercise clause is assured of becoming a much more potent instrument for resistance to future state regulation of religious schools."[64] *Whisner*, therefore, provided some clarification of the concept of "reasonable" regulation, that "vast area of ambiguity . . . between the incidental regulation of private schooling and the intimate and detailed regulation which constitutes the elimination of private schooling."[65] Third, although *Whisner* did not invent constitutional law, it created a precedent for religious and civil liberties that served as a reference point in similar litigation involving dissenting Christian day schools in, among other states, Kentucky, North Carolina, North Dakota, Nebraska, Michigan, and Maine.[66] Finally, leaders of the Christian school movement used the decision as a rallying point for their cause. As Americans of African descent have looked to the *Brown* case as a landmark in their struggle to gain constitutional rights in education and access to the mainstream of American society, proponents of the burgeoning Christian school movement in the 1970s and 1980s often viewed *Whisner* as a key victory in their "battle" to achieve liberty from the public school paradigm and, indirectly, a measure of separation from the mainstream of American society.

Since the decision in 1976, Christian day schools in most states have achieved a large measure of freedom from intrusive government regulation and have fended off threats of closure by means of litigation, legislation, and/or negotiation. Indeed, these dissenting institutions, which transmit propositions of knowledge and dispositions of belief, value, and appreciation that differ significantly from those taught in public schools, are now a permanent fixture on the educational landscape of the United States. Some of the schools involved in early conflicts with state authorities have, ironically, closed their doors, not as a result of state action, but due to, among other things, financial woes, the growing number of conservative Christian parents choosing to homeschool their children, population shifts, and an aging generation of leaders and concomitant withering of the spirit that sustained the creation and defense of these dissenting institutions. Levi Whisner's beloved Tabernacle Christian School is a case in point. It closed its doors in 2005. Though he hopes the school will reopen, Whisner, now in his early 80s, and "retired," believes that even if that does not occur, "God's School" and the controversy surrounding it played an important role in the crusade to free Christian schools from undue government interference in Ohio and throughout the nation.[67]

Notes

1. James C. Carper and Neal E. Devins, "The State and the Christian Day School," in *Religion and the State: Essays in Honor of Leo Pfeffer*, ed. James E. Wood, Jr., Waco, TX: Baylor University Press, 1985, 211–12.
2. Ibid.
3. Ibid., 215.
4. Interview with Levi W. Whisner, God's Tabernacle Church, Bradford, Ohio, May 12, 1980.
5. *State v. Whisner*, 47 Ohio St. 2d 181, 351 N.E. 2d 750 (1976).
6. Ohio Department of Education, *Minimum Standards for Ohio Elementary Schools, Revised 1970*, 6.
7. Interview with Levi W. Whisner, May 12, 1980.
8. Transcript of Testimony, *State v. Whisner*, 241.
9. Ibid., 66–67.
10. *Greenville* [OH] *Advocate*, December 11, 1973, 1.
11. Ibid., December 17, 1973, 1.
12. *Richmond* [IN] *Palladium-Item*, January 3, 1974, 1.
13. *Dayton Journal Herald*, January 22, 1974, 21.
14. *Greenville Advocate*, January 23, 1974, 1; and *Dayton Journal Herald*, January 23, 1974, 1.
15. Transcript of Testimony, *State v. Whisner*, 245.
16. "A new non-tax supported school may not begin operation unless the following conditions are met: (1) Prior approval of a plan submitted for the total school organization and program shall have been granted by the Superintendent of Public Instruction; (2) An enrollment of fifteen pupils in the first grade level of organization shall be minimum for the initial year of operation; (3) There shall be an annual increase in enrollment until the minimum requirements of Section (D) have been met; (4) In self-contained classroom situations, which are not designated as nongraded or multi-age groups, no more than two grade levels shall be combined; (5) The governing body of the school shall be responsible for initiating an application for approval; and (6) A charter shall be granted after an inspection which determines that all standards have been met" (*Minimum Standards for Ohio Elementary Schools, Revised 1970*, 6).
17. Transcript of Testimony, *State v. Whisner*, 11–13, 18–23.
18. *Dayton Journal Herald*, May 8, 1974, 1.
19. Transcript of Testimony, *State v. Whisner*, 25–36.
20. *Minimum Standards for Ohio Elementary Schools, Revised 1970*, 4–5.
21. Transcript of Testimony, *State v. Whisner*, 55–60, 103–13. God's Tabernacle Church is an independent, nondenominational, fundamentalist fellowship with no formal membership requirements. It stresses membership in the universal church rather than the local church and is composed of persons from Methodist, Baptist, Lutheran, Brethren, and Nazarene backgrounds. Though not strictly Arminian, the church's beliefs are similar to those of the Wesleyan Methodists and the Free Will Baptists. Separation is emphasized but not to the extent practiced by the Amish. Modesty in dress and demeanor is required. Television, alcohol, tobacco, gambling, vulgar language, and other "worldly" practices are forbidden.
22. Ibid., 62–63.

23. Ibid., 71, 76–77; and Interview with Levi W. Whisner, May 12, 1980.

24. Transcript of Testimony, *State v. Whisner*, 77–78, 126–29.

25. Ibid., 78–80.

26. Although the increasingly controverted issue of secular humanism in public education was not discussed in detail in this case, Alan Grover analyzed *Minimum Standards for Ohio Elementary Schools, Revised 1970* and concluded that the document reflects the philosophy of secular humanism. See Alan N. Grover, *Ohio's Trojan Horse*, Greenville, SC: Bob Jones University Press, 1977. See also Wendell R. Bird, "Freedom from Establishment and Unneutrality in Public School Instruction and Religious School Regulation," *Harvard Journal of Law and Public Policy* 2 (June 1979): 125–205; and John W. Whitehead and John Conlan, "The Establishment of the Religion of Secular Humanism and Its First Amendment Implications," *Texas Tech Law Review* 10 (Winter 1978): 1–66.

27. Transcript of Testimony, *State v. Whisner*, 83–88, 94–96.

28. Ibid., 61–66, 175–86.

29. Ibid., 191–92.

30. Ibid., 192–201.

31. Ibid., 204–39.

32. *Dayton Journal Herald*, May 9,1974, 15.

33. 47 Ohio St. 2d 192–93, 351 N.E. 2d 757–58.

34. At least four major cases recognize the primacy of parents' authority to direct their children's education and circumscribe the state's power in educational matters touching on religious convictions. *Meyer v. Nebraska*, 262 U.S. 390, 43 S.Ct. 625, 67 L.Ed. 1042 (1923); *Pierce v. Society of Sisters*, 268 U.S. 510, 45 S.Ct. 571, 69 L.Ed. 1070 (1925); *Farrington v. Tokushige*, 273 U.S. 284, 47 S.Ct. 406, 71 L.Ed. 646 (1927); and *Wisconsin v. Yoder*, 406 U.S. 205, 92 S.Ct. 1526, 32 L.Ed. 2d 15 (1972).

35. *Arcanum* [OH] *Early Bird*, August 19, 1974, 24.

36. Ibid.

37. Ibid.

38. *Dayton Daily News*, August 18,1974, 1.

39. 47 Ohio St. 2d 194 351 N.E. 2d 758–59.

40. Ibid., 195, 351 N.E. 2d 759.

41. Ibid. The critical issue is not the validity of religious beliefs but whether they are "truly held." *United States v. Seeger*, 380 U.S. 162, 85 S.Ct. 850, 13 L.Ed. 2d 733 (1965).

42. The defendants attacked the blanket *application* of the minimum standards to their school.

43. 47 Ohio St. 2d 196, 351 N.E. 2d 760.

44. Russell Kirk, "Darkness in Darke County," *National Review*, April 16, 1976, 398; and James J. Kilpatrick, "Preacher Fights Ohio School Law," *Boston Globe*, October 20, 1975, 27.

45. *Dayton Daily News*, December 9, 1975, 21.

46. *Columbus Dispatch*, December 11, 1975, C–1. After the meeting Essex remained puzzled about the issue raised by Whisner and other pastors who objected to accreditation. Since the state had chartered several hundred schools operated by religious groups, he saw no reason why state approval was a problem for fundamentalist schools. He did not perceive either the sense of alienation from American society and concomitant feelings of powerlessness or the reawakened religious consciousness and obligation to educate that motivated a

growing number of conservative Christians like Whisner. (Interview with Martin W. Essex, former Ohio Superintendent of Public Instruction, Columbus, Ohio, May 16, 1980.)

47. This brief made much of two aspects of religious freedom: the freedom to believe which is absolute and the freedom to act which may be circumscribed in the best interests of the society or community. While this concept can be faulted, for, after all, the key word is *exercise*, which implies action, it does provide a basis for balancing state interests and religious practices. Brief on the Merits of the Ohio Superintendent of Public Instruction as Amicus Curiae, *State v. Whisner*, 47 Ohio St. 2d 181 (1976), 7–20 passim.

48. Brief on the Merits of the American Civil Liberties Union of Ohio Foundation as Amicus Curiae, *State v. Whisner*, 47 Ohio St. 2d 181 (1976), 1–11 passim.

49. Brief on the Merits of the Ohio Ministers as Amici Curiae, *State v. Whisner*, 47 Ohio St. 2d 181 (1976), 2–28 passim. Whisner received financial as well as moral and legal support. Many conservative Protestant groups and individuals throughout the country helped defray the approximately $30,000 in costs associated with the case. (Interview with Levi W. Whisner, May 12, 1980.) On the other hand, many members of Whisner's congregation and leaders of some Christian schools in Ohio expressed strong reservations about the case. According to Whisner, they accused him of "stirring up trouble." Some later apologized. (Interview with Levi W. Whisner, Centerburg, Ohio, August 24, 2005.)

50. 47 Ohio St. 2d 197, 351 N.E. 2d 760.

51. Ibid., 197–98, 351 N.E. 2d 760–61.

52. Ibid., 199–200, 351 N.E. 2d 761–62.

53. Ibid., 204, 351 N.E. 2d 764.

54. See text accompanying notes 23–28 supra; and Brief of Defendants-Appellants, *State v. Whisner*, 2–7, 22–29.

55. 47 Ohio St 2d 205–11, 351 N.E. 2d 764–68. The court did not discuss objections to standards related to the teaching of social studies, citizenship, and health which the appellants believed espoused a philosophy of "secular humanism." It skirted the potential state establishment of religion issue by maintaining that those standards appeared in an interpretive section which was not technically part of the minimum standards. See notes 28–29 supra; and accompanying text.

56. Brief of Defendants-Appellants, *State v. Whisner*, 34–38; and 47 Ohio St. 2d 211–12, 351 N.E. 2d 768.

57. Ibid., 214–16, 351 N.E. 2d 769–70. See note 36 supra; and text accompanying notes 29–30 supra.

58. 47 Ohio St. 2d 217–18, 351 N.E. 2d 771. From the beginning of the legal proceedings, the state downplayed the religious aspect of the case and treated the matter as primarily a violation of a self-justifying state law. See Brief of Plaintiff-Appellee, *State v. Whisner*, 8–26 passim; and notes 11–12 supra and accompanying text.

59. 47 Ohio St. 2d 218–19, 351 N.E. 2d 771–72. See Robert Saltsman, "State v. Whisner: State Minimum Educational Standards and Non-Public Religious Schools," *Ohio Northern University Law Review* 4 (July 1977): 714–15, 717. After *Whisner*, churches and associations founded many Christian schools without state approval. Several established institutions returned their charters to the Ohio Department of Education. (Interview with Levi W. Whisner, May 12, 1980.)

60. 47 Ohio St. 2d 219–23, 351 N.E. 2d 772–75.

61. *Greenville Advocate*, July 29, 1976, 1; and *Cleveland Plain Dealer*, July 29, 1976, 14-A. Though race, regrettably, has been a motivation for establishing some church-related schools, the vast majority of Christian schools founded in the 1970s and 1980s, including Tabernacle Christian School, were not "segregation academies." See David Nevin and Robert E. Bills, *The Schools That Fear Built*, Washington, DC: Acropolis Books, 1976; Virginia Davis Nordin and William Lloyd Turner, "More than Segregation Academies: The Growing Protestant Fundamentalist Schools," *Phi Delta Kappan* 61 (February 1980): 391–94; Peter Skerry, "Christian Schools versus the I.R.S.," *Public Interest* 61 (Fall 1980): 28–31; and James C. Carper and Jack Layman, "Black-Flight Academies: The New Christian Day Schools," *Educational Forum* 61 (Winter 1997): 114–16.

62. *Cleveland Plain Dealer*. July 29, 1976, 14-A; *Greenville Advocate*, July 29, 1976, 1; and Interview with Levi W. Whisner, May 12, 1980.

63. *Arcanum Early Bird*, August 3, 1976, 1; and *Cleveland Plain Dealer*, July 29, 1976, 14-A.

64. Richard C. Daley, "Public Regulation of Private Religious Schools," *Ohio State Law Journal* 37 (Fall 1976): 923.

65. Stephen Arons, "The Separation of School and State: *Pierce* Reconsidered," *Harvard Educational Review* 46 (February 1976): 103.

66. For a discussion of issues raised in these cases, see Carper and Devins, "The State and the Christian Day Schools," 211–32.

67. Interview with Levi Whisner, August 24, 2005.

· 9 ·

HOMESCHOOLING *REDIVIVUS*

Accommodating the Anabaptists
of American Education

Though estimates of the number of children currently taught by their parents in a home setting vary widely from as few as 1.9 to as many as 2.4 million in 2006, no one doubts that their number has grown rapidly since the mid-1970s when between 10,000 and 20,000 children were educated at home.[1] Homeschooling is not, however, a new approach to educating the young in this country. It was commonplace in religiously pluralistic colonial America but virtually disappeared with the establishment and expansion of common-school systems in the nineteenth and early twentieth centuries. Home-based education, however, has experienced a renaissance since the 1970s. Though initially led and dominated by parents who embraced the progressive, child-centered pedagogy espoused by critics of institutional education such as John Holt, Paul Goodman, and Ivan Illich, conservative Protestants, deeply troubled by the de facto secularism and inflexibility of mass of public education and desirous of a reinvigorated family structure, accounted for most of the explosive growth as well as the leadership of the homeschooling "movement" in the 1980s and 1990s, and the concomitant clashes with state officials regarding the right of parents to teach their own children. In the new millennium, however, parents with increasingly diverse of educational philosophies/confessions/ worldviews, including Jews, Catholics, Muslims, and assorted secularists, have joined the ranks of the "Anabaptists" of American education whose legal right to homeschool is now recognized in all fifty states.[2]

Early Homeschooling

Prior to the central, transforming event in American educational history—the creation of state common-school systems in the middle decades of the nineteenth century—the rich religious diversity that characterized overwhelmingly Protestant colonial and early national America (Roman Catholics numbered only about 35,000 in 1789) was matched by an equally rich diversity of educational arrangements. With few exceptions—namely, when they were unable or unwilling to direct their children's upbringing—parents fashioned an education that was consonant with their religious beliefs.[3]

For the better part of the seventeenth and eighteenth centuries, the family was the primary unit of social organization and the most important educational agency. Writing in the late 1600s, Puritan divine Cotton Mather asserted, "families are the nurseries of all societies, and the first combinations of mankind."[4] In their recent work on the history of the family, historian Steven Mintz and anthropologist Susan Kellogg echo Mather's observation:

> Three centuries ago the American family was the fundamental economic, educational, political, social and religious unit of society. The family, not the isolated individual, was the unit of which church and state were made. The household was not only the locus of production, it was also the institution primarily responsible for the education of children, the transfer of craft skills, and the care of the elderly and the infirm.[5]

Colonists were, then, in Lawrence Cremin's words, "heir to the Renaissance traditions stressing the centrality of the household as the primary agency of human association and education."[6]

Parents, particularly fathers, bore the primary responsibility for teaching their children (and often those from other families who had been apprenticed or "fostered out") Christian doctrine, vocational skills, and how to read. That responsibility was not always carried out equally or effectively. According to historian Jan Lewis: "The effectiveness of home schooling varied depending particularly upon region and gender; literacy was much higher in the North than the South, and for males than females."[7] Though a growing number of seventeenth- and eighteenth-century white parents sent their children to school for short periods of time—especially in the northern colonies—much education still took place in the household. Indeed, a majority of colonial children probably acquired their rudimentary literacy skills at home rather than at school.[8]

Toward the end of the colonial era, the family began to lose its position as American society's most important economic and social unit. The slow shift of family functions, including education, to nonfamilial institutions occurred initially in the settled areas of the eastern seaboard. "By the middle of the eighteenth century," according to Mintz and Kellogg, "a variety of specialized institutions had begun to absorb traditional familial responsibilities. To reduce the cost of caring for widows, orphans, the destitute, and the mentally ill, cities began to erect almshouses instead of having such cared for in their own homes or homes of others. Free schools and common pay schools educated a growing number of the sons of artisans and skilled laborers. Workshops increasingly replaced individual households as centers of production."[9] Although parents increasingly looked to schools to carry out what had once been primarily a family function, the colonial approach to education continued virtually unchanged throughout the late 1700s and early 1800s. Despite proposals for more systematic, state-influenced schooling offered by luminaries such as Thomas Jefferson and Benjamin Rush, the unsystematic, discontinuous, and unregulated colonial mode of schooling suited to the Protestant pluralism of the period persisted well into the nineteenth century. Whether sponsored by a church or not, the vast majority of schools at this time embodied some variation of Protestant Christianity, and parents decided if and when their children would attend them.[10]

The Nineteenth-Century Educational Landscape

The middle decades of the nineteenth century marked a period of intense educational debate and reform that led to major changes in educational beliefs and practices in the United States; namely, the genesis of the modem concept and practice of public schooling. Distressed by the social and cultural tensions wrought by mid-nineteenth-century urbanization, industrialization, and immigration (which included a large number of Roman Catholics from Ireland) and energized by what Carl Kaestle has called the values of republicanism, Protestantism, and capitalism, educational reformers touted the messianic power of tax-supported, government-controlled schooling. Common schools, they believed, would mold a moral, disciplined, and unified population prepared to participate in American political, economic, and social life.[11] Some reformers went so far as to view the common school as a substitute for the family. Horace Mann, for example, often referred to the state and its schools as "parental." Private schools, on the other hand, were often cast as undemocratic, divisive, and inimical to the public interest.[12]

By 1900, about ninety percent of children ages five to fourteen attended public schools, while the supposedly "undemocratic" private schools accounted for less than ten percent. Why did most parents delegate the education of their children to the public schools? Why did they give up some of their educational prerogatives to the government? (We say some because despite the ever-increasing institutionalization of children for educational purposes, families no doubt continued to teach their children propositions and skills as well as dispositions.) First, parents sent their children to school, usually of their own volition, because they believed that schooling offered status and opportunity for economic advancement. In other words, there was a "pay-off" for relinquishing some parental authority.[13] Second, with several notable exceptions, for example, Roman Catholics, most nineteenth-century parents supported the public schools' goals of Christian character building and literacy training as well as the means of attaining them.[14] Third, despite the often-decried centralizing innovations, for example, the establishment of state and county superintendencies, nineteenth-century public education was intensely localistic. In 1890, for example, better than seventy-five percent of American children attended school in rural areas. Even as late as 1913, around fifty percent of American school children were enrolled in 212,000 one-room schools.[15] Many of these schools included children from only four or five families. Thus, parents looked upon the school as an extension of family and community educational and religious preferences rather than an instrument of alien state authority. Finally, it is likely that some parents were simply pleased to have the public school relieve them of part of the responsibility of raising their children, a task made more arduous by the separation of the father and the workplace from the household.

Not all nineteenth-century parents shared in the often tension-filled consensus regarding common schooling. Parents expressed dissent regarding curriculum, structure, and the belief system embodied in the common school. Among others, Roman Catholics, Lutherans, and Reformed Protestants established alternative schools in order to maintain tightly knit communities in which the family, church, and school propagated the same doctrines of the faith.[16] For class, religious, medical, pedagogical, and geographical reasons, some children were educated to a greater or lesser extent at home rather than in school. Indeed, Edward and Elaine Gordon have pointed out that during the better part of the nineteenth century, literature on "domestic" or "fireside" education was widely available to those interested in the "family school" movement.[17] Just how many parents, relatives, and tutors taught children at home is unknown. Several children who received at least part of their education at home, however, are well known. In addition to the often-cited eighteenth-century luminaries like theologian Jonathan Edwards, George Washington, James Madison, Benjamin Franklin, and Abigail Adams, nineteenth-century public figures who were taught by their parents include Thomas A. Edison, who was instructed at home after school officials labeled him "addled"; Jane Addams, who received most of her precollegiate formal education at home due to poor health; Andrew Taylor Still, a colleague of abolitionist John Brown and founder of osteopathic medicine, who was largely educated by his father, and Alexander Campbell, founder of the Disciples of Christ, who received part of his education from his father.[18] Lesser lights, such as Daniel Dawson Carothers, Chief Engineer of the Baltimore and Ohio Railroad from 1904 to 1909, who received his primary schooling from his mother before attending an academy, are occasionally discovered in obituaries, memorials, diaries, and family records.[19]

Homeschooling in the Twentieth Century

From the turn of the twentieth century until the 1960s, homeschooling virtually disappeared from the educational landscape of the United States. The cultural, social, and political tumult of the 1960s and 1970s, however, proved fertile soil for criticism of institutional schooling and the creation of alternatives to public education, including a revival of parent-directed education. Countercultural activists and parents who embraced the ethos of the "free" and "alternative" school movements of the 1960s and 1970s led the renaissance of homeschooling in the 1970s. Disillusioned with established social institutions and critical of what they believed was the "oppressive" nature of schooling, these dissenters opted for home education as a means of "freeing" their children from "authoritarian schooling."[20] Many agreed with the words of John Holt, one of the most influential advocates of homeschooling in the late 1970s and early 1980s, and founder of the widely circulated magazine, *Growing Without Schooling*: "My concern is not to improve 'education,' but to do away with it, to end the ugly and anti-human business of people-shaping and let people shape themselves."[21] Influenced by critics of contemporary efforts to reform the public schools and schooling in general, such as Holt, Ivan Illich, Paul Goodman, Allen Graubard, and Herbert Kohl, these "educational conscientious objectors" viewed the home as the natural environment in which children could explore their own interests and develop as healthy, autonomous individuals.[22] By the mid-1970s, the number of children taught at home in these progressive, child-centered environments probably numbered only between 10,000 and 20,000. A few short years later, however, the number of homeschooled children would burgeon as a different population dissented, for somewhat different reasons, from the dominant paradigm of institutional schooling. This, in turn, led to clashes between homeschoolers and legislators, social workers, and public school officials regarding the legitimacy of home-based education.[23]

While forces that undergirded the liberal, alternative education movement influenced the homeschoolers of the 1970s, some of the same forces that drove the Christian day school movement affected the vast majority of parents who chose to homeschool in the 1980s and 1990s. Though sharing with their more secular predecessors a commitment to the individual needs of children and the sanctity of the family, concerns about the inflexibility of institutional schooling, and a distrust of education professionals, conservative Christian parents chose to homeschool their children primarily for religious rather than pedagogical reasons. Like the founders and patrons of Christian day schools, they objected to what they believed to be the religion of secular humanism in the public schools and desired to inculcate a Christian worldview in their children. The Darwinian orientation of the science curriculum, explicit sex education, and lack of attention to Christian perspectives in the social sciences and literature were particularly troubling to them.[24] According to Brian Ray, a leader in the Christian homeschool community and widely respected researcher on home-based education, though parents usually give several reasons for homeschooling—including individualized instruction, family enhancement, parent-determined socialization, and safety—the "most frequently cited reason is concern for the development of their children's values and way of life. They desire to teach and transmit their philosophical, religious, or cultural values, traditions, and beliefs, and a particular world view, in a preferred moral environment."[25]

As a small, but growing number of conservative Protestants became more disillusioned with institutional schooling in general and public schooling in particular and desirous of reclaiming education as a family function, the number of homeschooled children in the United States increased rapidly in the 1980s and 1990s. By 1985, the number had reached around 200,000; by 1990 over

400,000; by 1995 over one million; and by 2002 around 1.6 million. Though exact numbers are difficult to determine, the growth rate is impressive. Indeed, one expert estimates an annual growth rate between the early 1990s and the early 2000s of seven to fifteen percent per year. As homeschooling became more prominent on the educational landscape in the 1980s and 1990s, its legal status often was contested in state legislatures and courts.[26]

Between the early 1980s and mid-1990s, clashes between homeschooling advocates and government officials about the appropriate balance between parental liberty and the state's interest in education were commonplace throughout the United States. Homeschooling parents and state education officials often battled each other in state courts and legislatures over curriculum, testing, certification, and "approval" of home-based education. These confrontations resulted in significant advances in the legal status of home education. In 1980, only three states, Utah, Nevada, and Ohio, had laws specifically recognizing the right to homeschool. By the early 2000s, however, it was legal in every state, though regulations varied considerably from state to state.[27] South Carolina, where state authorities and a rapidly growing number of homeschoolers were involved in numerous legislative and legal confrontations between the mid-1980s and early 1990s, provides an instructive example of how parents dissenting from the public school paradigm achieved a significant and unique recognition of parental liberty in education. Here one can readily see the significant role of mothers in the homeschool school movement—not only as the primary teachers in the home but also as political organizers and educational entrepreneurs.[28]

Securing Parental Liberty in South Carolina

The modern history of homeschooling in South Carolina can be divided into four distinct time periods: pre-1984, 1984–1988, 1988–1992, and 1992 until the present. The first three periods marked periods of escalating tension and hostility between homeschool families and school officials. Since 1992, however, homeschoolers' relationship with government officials in South Carolina has been relatively peaceful.

In the years prior to 1988, a "substantial equivalence law" governed homeschool programs. Section 59–65–40, Code of Laws of South Carolina, 1976 and State Board of Education Regulation 43–246 provided the legal basis for what was then termed "instruction at a place other than school." According to Section 59–65–40: "Instruction during the school term at a place other than school may be substituted for school attendance, provided such instruction is approved by the State Board of Education as substantially equivalent to instruction given to children of like ages in the public or private schools where such children reside."

In 1976, the South Carolina State Board of Education adopted Regulation 43–246, delegating the approval (or disapproval) of homeschooling programs to the school board of the district in which the homeschooling family resided. This regulation also established the State Board of Education as the first avenue of appeal in the event the local school board disapproved of a particular home instruction program.

In 1981, the South Carolina State Department of Education (hereafter the SDE) adopted guidelines to aid local school boards and administrations in determining the ambiguous standard of substantial equivalence. In a letter dated June 19, 1981, Associate Superintendent Ernest B. Carnes stated that these guidelines were implemented after conducting "extensive research into the issues concerning instruction at a place other than school."[29] The guidelines contained two separate documents: one offering suggestions to local school districts researching instruction at a place other than school, and the other providing indicators of quality of instruction at a place other than school. These indicators included the following four areas: teacher qualification, instructional program, student evaluation, and place of instruction.

Under the area of teacher qualification, the guidelines reminded local school personnel that requiring teacher certification might not be appropriate since the law allowed for substantial equivalence to be demonstrated in accord with private schools that were not required to employ certified teachers, as was the case with public schools. Therefore, in demonstrating substantial equivalence to a private school that does not require teacher certification, a parent would not have to be a certified teacher to homeschool. This caveat notwithstanding, many public school districts in the state mandated certification of homeschooling parents.

The guidelines for instructional programs recommended requesting information as detailed as the number of minutes parents planned to devote to each subject per day, week, and year. They suggested that parents provide a daily schedule including beginning time, recess, lunch, and ending time. In a section requesting information on additional materials available at the place of instruction, even the number of books in the home was solicited. Under "Place of Instruction," the guidelines urged an "on-site evaluation of the facility . . . , prior to approval of the program."[30]

The Years Prior to 1984

Prior to 1984, the homeschooling "movement" in South Carolina was small, unorganized, and largely unnoticed. Although many date the beginning of the modern homeschooling movement as early as 1970, the development of the homeschooling community in South Carolina lagged almost a decade behind the rest of the country—probably in part because of the state's hostile legal environment and cultural conservatism. Though the exact number of families homeschooling prior to 1984 is not known, one activist has estimated that no more than two dozen, and, of those families, less than a handful homeschooled prior to 1980.[31]

Some of these families taught at home "underground"; others worked out very simple arrangements with their school districts; some were denied permission to homeschool by local school boards; and at least one family was taken to court. According to Phoebe Winter with the Office of Research for the South Carolina SDE:

> Each local school district could establish its own criteria for determining whether a home-schooling instruction program provided 'substantially equivalent' instruction. The district criteria established ranged from requiring the home instructor to hold a high school diploma to requiring the parent or guardian to be a certified teacher. At least one district disapproved all requests for home instruction. Parents wishing to teach their children at home could be eligible to do so in one district but be barred from providing home instruction in a neighboring district.[32]

At least one family went to court prior to 1984. Scott and Susan Page began homeschooling two children in 1982. The Calhoun County School Board initially denied their request to teach their offspring at home. The State Board of Education then upheld this decision. The matter ended in family court when Judge Alvin Biggs rendered his decision on June 28, 1983. He opined:

> I find that the Calhoun County Board's rejection of the Pages' request to teach their children in their homeschool was based upon the unfettered discretion of the Calhoun County School Board. I find the Board did not provide the Pages with any definite standards to guide them after they sent their original letter in August 1982 requesting permission to teach at the home school, nor did they provide them with any guidelines for future compliance. I find the Calhoun County Board was guided only by their own personal ideas and concepts. . . . I find the law has laid an unequal hand on anyone who wants to provide his child with a home school. . . . I find that the Pages' home school qualifies under S.C. Code 59–65–10 (1976) as a "school," and that the Board's decision shall be modified accordingly. I find that the Pages or any other person in

South Carolina, if they qualify under set definite ascertainable standards, should be allowed to teach in a home school. I find this is a basic constitutional "liberty" guaranteed by the U. S. Constitution and the 14th Amendment of the U. S. Constitution.[33]

Judge Biggs' decision was the last positive ruling the homeschooling community in South Carolina would see for years to come.

1984–1988

Between 1984 and 1988, the number of homeschooling families in South Carolina grew dramatically. By 1987, an estimated five hundred to six hundred children were being taught at home, although these numbers were considerably lower than those in neighboring states.[34] The increased interest in home-based education caught the attention of public school officials, who determined they must do something to control the growing numbers of homeschooling parents as well as the process itself.

Zan and Joe Tyler are among the pioneer homeschooling parents in South Carolina. Their experience illustrates the trials and tribulations these dissenters faced in the state and elsewhere when they clashed with government officials over the extent to which the state could regulate their liberty to direct the education and upbringing of their children. Between 1984 and 1988, many educators in South Carolina, fearful of the growing number of parents choosing to opt out of institutional schooling, decided that home-based education needed to be regulated and, if possible, limited. When Zan Tyler, a twenty-eight-year-old mother, applied to her local school board for permission to homeschool in June of 1984, she did not know that she was inadvertently stepping into a hornet's nest and about to become the symbolic whipping boy for homeschooling in South Carolina. Employees at the SDE later informed Tyler that her case in particular, in conjunction with growing statewide interest in home-based schooling, prompted the SDE and local school district personnel to promulgate stringent regulations for homeschooling parents.[35]

In March 1984, Tyler enrolled her oldest son in kindergarten at a local public school in Columbia, South Carolina. Although he would turn six in May, at the behest of the clinical psychologist who tested him, she decided to hold him back a year. The assistant principal who completed his enrollment assured Tyler this was no problem. In May, however, the principal of the school informed the young mother that due to South Carolina's Education Improvement Act of 1984, she could not hold her son back a year—he would have to be put in first grade. This grade placement was simply unacceptable to the family. By that time, all the suitable private kindergartens were filled for the 1984–1985 school year. Tyler then called the assistant superintendent of the district, who had been her high school principal. After explaining the situation with her son, she pleaded with him to help secure a place for him in a K–5 class rather than a first-grade class. When he refused, Tyler stated, "Well, I have no choice then, but to home school my son next year." She was bluffing in order to secure an accommodation and really did not want to homeschool. Much to her surprise, he replied, "Well, the school board has become lenient with that kind of thing." Later she discovered the district had approved one family to homeschool, and the teaching parent was a certified instructor.[36]

Tyler was then baptized with fire into the homeschooling movement. First, the school district and the State Board of Education refused to provide her with information on how to comply with the law as a teaching parent. At that time, little help was available for a novice. Local support and accountability groups, now numbering over 120 in South Carolina, were nonexistent. No statewide organization had been formed. Home School Legal Defense Association (HSLDA), an organization led by attorneys committed to protecting the right of parents to teach their children at home and in 2006 claiming about 80,000 member families, was in its second year of operation. Indeed, according to Tyler, she neither knew nor could find another family in the state that was teaching their children at home. Her only source of support and encouragement was *Home Grown Kids*, by Raymond and Dorothy Moore, child development specialists, critics of academic education at a young age, and early champions of home-based education.[37]

Tyler immediately hired an attorney simply to decipher the laws governing homeschooling in the state of South Carolina. In June, she delivered a forty-plus page application to the local school district. In July, the school board denied her request to teach her son, although she had very carefully complied with all items outlined in the "guidelines for instruction at a place other than school." She again hired an attorney to help her navigate the appeals process. She was discovering firsthand the veracity of Judge Biggs' 1983 prophetic words: "The law has laid an unequal hand on anyone who wants to provide his child with a home school."[38]

During the appeals process, Tyler paid an unannounced visit to Charlie Williams, State Superintendent of Education. As a friend of the family, she thought that he would understand the problem and help resolve it. Believing that her decision to homeschool was due to a district error, she expected a sympathetic response to her story. She was shocked, however, when Williams responded: "You know, Mrs. Tyler, you can be put in jail for truancy." (The State Board of Education decided to delay her appeal until after the commencement of school in August.) Everyone seemed to know that the State Board of Education would not reverse the local school board's denial of her home-schooling program, reinforcing another portion of Judge Biggs' 1983 decision: "The State Board delegated its decision making authority to the Local Board and in effect 'rubber stamped' any decision by them."[39]

After the State Superintendent of Education threatened her with impris-onment, Tyler informed her father, a well-connected attorney, of her plight. Up to that point in time, she had told no one of her plan to homeschool. According to Tyler, in 1984 upstanding citizens simply did not homeschool in South Carolina. It was not, in historian David Tyack's words, part of the recognized "grammar" of schooling.[40] Her father immediately contacted United States Senator Strom Thurmond's office and explained his daughter's situation. (She had worked for the Senator during her senior year in high school.) As Tyler's hearing with the State Board was less than a week away, Senator Thurmond immediately flew from Washington, DC, to Columbia to meet with Superintendent Williams. The senator's staff had already examined the case to make sure it met the letter of the law in every regard. After the Thurmond-Williams meeting, things changed dramatically for Tyler. A week later, to no one's surprise, the State Board of Education overturned the school district's deci-sion—authorizing the mother of two young boys to homeschool for the 1984–1985 school year.[41]

Tyler's homeschooling program was approved in a relatively painless man-ner for the 1985–1986 school year. Her plans to teach her son at home for only one year dissipated as she became enamored of the concept of homeschooling. During 1984 and 1985, she began collecting names of people across the state who advocated (the overwhelming majority were not actually homeschooling) home-based instruction. Her sources for these names were private education foundations and attorneys across the nation. As interest in homeschooling in the state began to build somewhat, persons began contacting her for informa-tion on how to get started, as well as how to comply with the law. As home-schooling families moved to South Carolina from out-of-state, her name was given to them as a contact person. In her own words, she "felt compelled to help as many families as I could weather the hostility of the SDE and local school boards."[42]

By the fall of 1985, Tyler had a mailing list of approximately four hundred names of persons interested or engaged in home based education, but was

uncertain about how it might be used. She had learned from "sources," however, that public educators were not happy that her program had been approved,
and they were particularly unhappy that the State Board of Education had overturned the local school board's ruling in her case. The animosity and hostility
she experienced as a teaching parent baffled her. One educator, however, clar-
ified the situation for Tyler. Off the record, she remarked, "Zan, it is okay for
pockets of homeschoolers to exist as long as school districts feel they are still
in control. Even underground homeschoolers are okay—that means they're
scared. But you have become a threat because they stacked the deck against you
and you still won. To them you have opened Pandora's box."[43] Mere parents had
challenged educators' professional expertise.

On October 22, 1985, the SDE served public notice in the *State Register*
regarding the promulgation of homeschooling regulations in South Carolina.
A task force, consisting of five public school officials and three private school
administrators, was appointed to draft new, stringent regulations. At least two
of the five public school officials had aggressively denied parents the right to
teach at home in their districts. None of the task force members had a working knowledge of home-based education and none was a homeschooling advocate, though one member was slightly sympathetic to parent-directed
education.[44]

Tyler fortuitously learned of the task force and requested that homeschooling parents have an opportunity to testify before the committee. At the January
1986 meeting, five parents addressed the committee. Tyler pointed out that
other states in the region had made more progress in balancing parental rights
and state interests and were doing so in a less adversarial manner. After the task
force heard the testimony of the participating parents, it took a short break.
Upon reconvening, Steve Quick, Elementary Supervisor in the Accreditation
Section at the SDE, handed out the drafted regulations that the SDE would be
recommending to the General Assembly. The task force had allowed homeschooling parents to speak but not intended to utilize their input. The regulations apparently had been drafted before the hearing. Among the most
draconian of the proposed regulations were: 1) a requirement that the teaching parent hold a college degree from an accredited, four-year institution; 2) a
requirement that parents only be allowed to use state-approved texts in their
homeschooling programs; and 3) a requirement that all homeschooled students
participate in the statewide testing program.[45]

Tyler again retained an attorney to learn how to derail these regulations.
He advised her that the state agency would be required to hold a public hear-

ing on the proposed regulations if it received twenty-five letters of request. A public hearing, Tyler surmised, would at least postpone submission of the regulations to the Senate Education Committee and the House Education and Public Works Committee for approval from the 1986 legislative session to the 1987 session, buying time to organize effective opposition.

Not knowing how many homeschooling parents were on her mailing list or how many might respond, Tyler sent out letters regarding the public hearing. Within two weeks of the mailing, she received over one hundred letters requesting a hearing on the proposed regulations. She delivered the letters to the SDE, and in March was notified that the public hearing would be held on May 13,1986. She then spent two months working intensely with homeschooling parents, attorneys, and Raymond Moore, who flew in for the hearing. A few weeks before the hearing, the SDE notified Tyler that homeschooling advocates would be allotted only twenty minutes for their comments. After some behind-the-scenes political pressure, the State Department set aside the limit, thus ensuring the growing number of activists adequate time to present their case.[46]

Over 350 parents, many with children in tow, and homeschooling advocates descended upon the Rutledge Building, home of the SDE, in Columbia on May 13. Parents provided almost four hours of well-organized testimony against the regulations. Even the SDE's internal publication, *Newsline*, reported "a well-organized group of parents and supporters presented their cases for teaching their children at home."[47] Nevertheless, the SDE sent the regulations to the General Assembly for approval with the objectionable portions still intact.

The public hearing did buy homeschooling proponents valuable time. During the summer, Tyler paid a visit to her state senator, Warren K. Giese. A retired University of South Carolina head football coach with an earned doctorate in education, Giese was outraged by the treatment parents had received from government officials. He agreed to ask the Senate Education Committee, of which he was a member, to hold a hearing on the proposed regulations during the 1987 legislative session.[48]

On February 4, 1987, the Senate Education Committee held a hearing on the proposed regulations and invited the House Education and Public Works Committee to attend. Almost seven hundred parents, many with their children, and homeschooling advocates attended, once again testifying to the growing ability of the homeschooling community to participate effectively in the political process. In response to the hearing and the great outcry against the regulations, both committees refused to approve the regulations.[49]

Defeating the regulations had been both a time-consuming and expensive adventure. Many of the dissenters thought the issue had been settled. The day after the hearing, however, a young legislator called Tyler at home and advised her that while homeschoolers had momentum on their side, they should take the initiative to submit proactive legislation. When she hesitated, he said he had seen the legislation the SDE was planning to introduce and assured her that she would not like it.

A few days later, Representative David Beasley filed H. 4224 in the House, and Senator Warren Giese filed S. 457 in the Senate. Ed Garrison, Chairman of the Senate Education Committee, appointed an ad hoc committee made up of three homeschooling advocates, representatives from the SDE, and senators. Its task was to draft legislation that respected both the rights of parents and the state's compelling interest in education. Homeschooling members of the committee were not willing to compromise on two requirements that were part of the defeated SDE regulations, i.e., the minimum level of parental education for the teaching parent and the freedom of choice in textbook selection. They maintained that the minimum educational requirement for teaching parents should be a high school diploma or a G.E.D. certificate and that parents must not be limited in their choice of textbooks to only those on the state-approved list. SDE's requirements would sharply curtail the number of parents eligible to homeschool and, in effect, would allow the state to dictate a particular worldview via the curriculum. In return, the Senate responded that homeschooling parents had to document that education was occurring in the home. The committee's deliberations resulted in compromise legislation that stipulated the following conditions for homeschooling:

1. The teaching parent must hold a high school diploma or a G.E.D.;
2. The instructional day must consist of a minimum of four-and-a-half hours and the instructional year must consist of a minimum of 180 days;
3. The curriculum shall include, but not be limited to, the basic instructional areas of reading, writing, mathematics, science and social studies;
4. As evidence that a student is receiving regular instruction, the instructor shall maintain the following records: (a) a plan book, diary, or other written record indicating subjects taught and activities in which the student and instructor engage; (b) a portfolio of samples of the student's academic work; (c) a record of evaluations of the student's academic progress; and (d) a semiannual progress report including attendance records and individualized assessments of the student's aca-

demic progress in each of the basic instructional areas specified in item 3;

5. Students must have access to library facilities; and
6. Students must participate in the annual statewide testing program and the Basic Skills Assessment Program approved by the State Board of Education for their appropriate grade level.[50]

Since the SDE and homeschooling advocates had participated equally in the compromise process, most observers assumed that the bill would be enacted with minimal debate. The SDE, however, immediately withdrew its support of the bill. Nevertheless, the bill passed the Senate Education Committee and the full Senate with few problems. The bill also was reported favorably out of the House Education and Public Works Committee for consideration by the full House. Passing the House of Representatives presented a new challenge. The bill was placed on the contested calendar and remained there as the House adjourned in June.[51]

The bill languished in the Rules Committee until March of the 1988 legislative session, when homeschoolers' intense lobbying brought it to the House floor. When the bill came to a vote in late May, it was substantially changed. Although representatives attached a few benign amendments, one so altered the substance of the bill that the homeschooling community withdrew its support of the bill in the amended form. The unpalatable amendment required teaching parents without a four-year college degree to make a passing score on the Education Entrance Examination (EEE) before they would be allowed to teach their children at home. (South Carolina developed the EEE to screen prospective professional teachers.) Since its inception in 1985, the task force had discussed the concept of "front-end credentialing" for teaching parents, but the homeschooling community had vehemently opposed it. Nevertheless, the bill passed in its amended form.[52]

One of the goals of passing legislation was to standardize the application process that heretofore had been left to the total discretion of local school boards. By instituting reasonable standards, homeschool advocates had hoped to put an end to the avalanche of litigation. Instead, the inception of the EEE ushered in a new era of legal activity regarding the right to homeschool unencumbered by restrictive regulations. At one point HSLDA had more lawsuits filed in South Carolina than in the other forty-nine states combined.[53]

Members of the homeschooling community had hoped by the end of 1988 to lay to rest the hostility and legal turmoil surrounding home-based education in South Carolina. Instead, the problems escalated. In a letter to members in July 1988, HSLDA President Michael Farris asserted: "Homeschoolers in South Carolina need to be banded together for future actions on all fronts. You are saddled with one of the most cumbersome laws in the country. Of all states, you all need to stick together."[54]

1988–1992

From July 1988 to July 1989, a deceptive calm ensued throughout the state. Although the homeschooling law took effect in July 1988, the EEE requirement was not imposed for another year, allowing the SDE to complete the study required by law validating the EEE for use with the homeschool population. While local school boards denied approval to fewer parents for that one year, many school districts required more information on their homeschool applications after the law passed than they did before. The forms became so far removed from the intent of the law, that HSLDA sent a letter to South Carolina members encouraging them not to give their school districts more information than the law required.

When the EEE requirement took effect, local boards denied approval to unprecedented numbers of parents. Those without college degrees who had been homeschooling successfully for years were suddenly disqualified, unless they took and passed the EEE. Some veteran homeschooling families who moved to South Carolina from other states were not allowed to continue to teach their children at home. One of the major problems with the EEE was logistical. While homeschooling parents as a group had a high pass rate for the EEE they experienced problems because it was only administered three times annually.[55]

At this point HSLDA intervened and filed a class action suit on behalf of its 369 member families in South Carolina. The major contention of the lawsuit was that the validity study for using the EEE with the homeschooling population had been done poorly and failed to meet professional and governmental standards. In February 1989, HSLDA lost the lower court case in a disappointing one-sentence ruling from Judge Drew Ellis.

During 1989, the South Carolina Home Educators Association (SCHEA), a statewide support group for which Tyler was the Legislative Liaison, developed a two-fold strategy for the 1990 legislative session. The first goal was to reduce the sting of the EEE by making it a requirement in the absence of a high school diploma rather than a college diploma. SCHEA's second goal was to provide for private sector supervision of homeschooling programs. Tyler met with key legislators in both the House and the Senate before the beginning of the 1990 legislative session, and they concurred that the chances to amend the homeschooling law looked positive. Only a month into the session, however, the same key legislators reversed course and asserted that the legislative option was not possible.[56]

In February of 1990, Tyler began researching the feasibility of creating an accrediting organization for homeschools in the private sector, "a mediating structure" between the state and parents, thereby negating the need for them to gain approval from their local school districts. On July 20, 1990, the South Carolina Association of Independent Home Schools (SCAIHS) was incorporated.[57] The association was founded on the premise that the South Carolina compulsory attendance law provided the legal basis for its existence. According to 59-65-10 of the South Carolina Code of Laws: "All parents or guardians shall cause their children or wards to regularly attend a public or private school or kindergarten of this State which has been approved by the State Board of Education or a member school of the South Carolina Independent Schools' Association (SCISA) or some similar organization. . . ."[58] The "some similar organization" clause served as the key element in the establishment of SCAIHS. Patterned after SCISA, SCAIHS fulfilled that part of the compulsory attendance law allowing a private school to be a member of SCISA or some similar organization. In addition, key to the legal basis for SCAIHS was the establishment of member homeschools as private schools. Because of the tenuous legal position of the association, the anticipated membership the first year was thirty-five to fifty families. Within the first two months of existence, however, 120 homeschooling families had joined.[59]

SCAIHS had not been in existence for three months before legal problems commenced. On October 5, 1990, Lexington-Richland School District Five charged eleven families with truancy. The County Solicitor agreed to delay prosecution of these families until an Attorney General's opinion could be rendered regarding the legal status of SCAIHS and its members. Many other school districts contemplating prosecution of SCAIHS families also agreed to wait for the impending opinion. In January 1991, the state's chief legal officer ruled that SCAIHS did not fulfill the intent of the compulsory attendance law, thus setting the stage for litigation. Early in 1991, HSLDA's Michael Farris and Dewitt Black filed a declaratory judgment suit in Lexington County on behalf of the affected SCAIHS families. Richland County School District One filing a declaratory judgment to establish the school district's rights under the homeschooling law followed this action. SCAIHS lost both cases at the trial level and appealed both decisions to the South Carolina Supreme Court.[60]

During the fall of 1991, when the future of SCAIHS looked very bleak, several events occurred that would begin to change the landscape of homeschooling in South Carolina. A state attorney mentioned to Tyler the need for new legislation to resolve the mounting legal tension surrounding SCAIHS. Newly elected State Superintendent of Education Barbara Nielsen (R) also made it clear that she did not view homeschoolers as "the enemy" and was open to a legislative remedy to the "SCAIHS problem."[61]

On December 9, 1991, the South Carolina Supreme Court rendered its ruling on the EEE case. It reversed the lower court's decision and opined that the state had not properly validated the EEE for use with homeschooling parents. This was a landmark decision for teaching parents in South Carolina, carrying with it national implications as well. In *The Home School Court Report*, HSLDA founder Michael Farris, one of the most visible of the national homeschool leaders, claimed: "We viewed this law with utmost seriousness as a grave danger which had the potential of spreading across the nation. Accordingly, we went after this South Carolina test with everything we had. We have learned a lot about the world of test validity. We are ready if any other state decides to try this again."[62]

The ruling had significant ramifications for SCAIHS because one of the biggest complaints leveled against the association had been its lack of minimum educational requirements for teaching parents (i.e., SCAIHS did not require a teaching parent to possess a baccalaureate degree or a passing score on the EEE). When the Court ruled against the EEE requirement, it laid to rest one of the major objections against SCAIHS.

In December of 1991, the SCAIHS Board of Directors appointed a legislative committee to pursue the possibility of introducing SCAIHS legislation during the 1992 legislative session. This committee met with legislative and education officials, as well as representatives from the governor's office. By January of 1992, several members of both the House and the Senate agreed to sponsor the following legislation: "In lieu of the requirements of 59–65–40 [the home-schooling law requiring school district approval], parents and guardians may teach their children at home if the instruction is conducted under the auspices of the South Carolina Association of Independent Home Schools. Bona fide membership and continuing compliance with the academic standards of SCAIHS exempt the home school from the further requirements of Section 59–65–40."[63]

Considering the rocky road the prior homeschooling legislation had encountered, the bill proceeded through the House of Representatives with relative ease and speed. This was due in large part to the expert guidance of Rep. David Wright, bill sponsor and Chairman of the K–12 Subcommittee, and Rep. Olin Philips, Chairman of the House Education and Public Works Committee. At the bill's final reading in the House, a threatening amendment was offered but averted, and the House unanimously approved the legislation with the following benign amendment: "By January thirtieth of each year the South Carolina Association of Independent Home Schools shall report the number and grade level of children home schooled through the association to the children's respective school districts." The bill was then sent to the Senate and assigned to a subcommittee of the Senate Education Committee. On March 4, the subcommittee passed the bill unanimously. Several persons warned SCAIHS representatives, however, that a potentially crippling amendment would be considered at the full Senate Education Committee meeting on March 18.[64]

Following a massive phone campaign and lobbying effort initiated by SCAIHS, the Senate passed the House version of the bill and the objectionable provisions of the threatening amendment were defeated. The Senate version did contain the following amendments, which were viewed as harmless since SCAIHS had already implemented the requirements into the association's membership guidelines: A parent must hold at least a high school diploma or G.E.D certificate; the instructional year must be at least 180 days; and the curriculum must include, but not be limited to the basic instructional areas of reading, writing, mathematics, science, and social studies, and in grades seven through twelve, composition and literature. Parents retained the right to select their own curriculum.[65]

On March 25, the bill went to the full Senate, which approved it unanimously. Six days later the House concurred with the Senate version of the bill. On April 8, 1992, the late Governor Carroll A. Campbell, Jr., signed the bill, and the SCAIHS legislation became law, thus ending a decade of intense legal and political hostility toward homeschooling parents. Furthermore, South Carolina became the only state to vest a specific voluntary association with authority equal to that of local school boards to approve homeschooling programs. Regarding the SCAIHS legislative victory, Michael Farris, President of HSLDA, remarked, "South Carolina was the most active state in the nation in taking homeschoolers to court. The South Carolina legislature responded to this bad situation by allowing responsible self-government for homeschoolers.

This is an advancement of an important legal principle."[66] Confrontation had given way to accommodation.

1992 Through the Present

Since its inception in 1990, SCAIHS has grown from two employees and 120 member families to eighteen employees, all of whom are women and most of whom have homeschooling experience, and over 1,200 families, representing more than 2,000 children. With the cessation of political and legal problems, SCAIHS has been able to focus its energy on developing support services for homeschooling families. The association has instituted the High School Program, which has grown from five students to over five hundred students. Every college and university in South Carolina accepts the SCAIHS transcript and diploma, and most graduates have been accepted to the college of their first choice—with many attending on scholarships. The association has implemented a Special Needs Program to provide specialized counsel to those parents of children with learning disabilities. SCAIHS publishes a regular newsletter, provides thousands of hours of curriculum counseling each year, sponsors teacher training workshops and seminars, represents the homeschooling viewpoint to the community at large, maintains an active presence in the legislature, and provides services to homeschooling families overseas. Foundational to the association's mission is, of course, the provision of accountability and encouragement by and for parents who teach their children at home.[67]

Conclusion

As was the case in South Carolina, homeschooling families in most states established their right to teach their children at home via either legislation or litigation between the mid-1980s and mid-1990s. During that time, these dissenters from conventional schooling broke the "grammar barrier." Once thought odd, heretical, and even harmful to children, homeschooling is now well established on the increasingly pluralistic educational landscape and a part of the grammar of American education. Aside from some critics in the academy, who believe homeschooling detracts from the "public good"; professional educational associations, such as the National Education Association, which assert that parents are not qualified to offer quality instruction; and an occasional social worker, who believes that homeschooling is a form of "educational neglect," homeschooling families in the United States now enjoy a high level of public support and admiration as well as a generally positive press.[68] Furthermore, homeschooled children as a whole are academically successful by any measure, and preliminary research suggests that they are regularly involved in community life. Part of their propensity for social and political engagement may be the result of their exposure to the political arena in which their parents fought to secure their right to teach them at home sans intrusive state regulation.[69]

Though conservative white Protestants still dominate homeschooling in the United States, the new millennium has witnessed an increasing diversification of the backgrounds and motivations of parents teaching their children. Growing numbers of Roman Catholics, Secularists, Mormons, New Agers, Muslims, Libertarians, Communitarians, and African-Americans are joining the ranks of those rejecting institutional schooling and the separation of education from the household, thus making homeschoolers more representative of the population at large and enhancing their acceptance in the society. Furthermore, parents committed to teaching their children tend to have more offspring than most parents. They are "natalists" or people whose personal identity, according to David Brooks, "is defined by parenthood" and who "are more spiritually, emotionally, and physically invested in their homes than in other spheres of life, having concluded that parenthood is the most enriching and elevating thing they can do." In the words of Peter Augustine Lawler, "they understand themselves more as parents than as individuals." Indeed, homeschooling families have on average just over three children compared to the national average of two children, and one-third of homeschooling parents have four or more children.[70] If these trends continue, the number of homeschooled children in the United States may reach three million by 2010, accounting for about half of the students educated outside the government system.[71] These diverse dissenters from the dominant educational paradigm, united by their belief that the home is the best place to educate the young, are clearly here to stay and their tribe increases by both conversion and conception.

Notes

1. Brian D. Ray, *Worldwide Guide to Homeschooling*, Nashville, TN: Broadman & Holman, 2005, 7–8, 29. See also US Department of Education, National Center for Education Statistics, *The Condition of Education 2005*, Washington, DC: US Government Printing Office, 2005, 32.

2. Anabaptists made the most radical attempt during the Protestant Reformation to renew the church. They rejected the role of government in the reformation of the church. In addi-

tion to their embrace of pacifism and the principle of love, they insisted on a complete separation of church and state and asserted that the church was distinct from society. To varying degrees, homeschooling parents believe that the education of the young is the responsibility of the family, not the state, and that education is not synonymous with schooling. See John H. Y. Briggs, Robert D. Linder, and David F. Wright, eds., *Eerdmans Handbook to the History of Christianity*, Grand Rapids, MI: William B. Eerdmans, 1977, 399–403.

3. Mark A. Noll, *A History of Christianity in the United States and Canada*, Grand Rapids, MI: William B. Eerdmans, 1992, 7–8, 205.

4. Cotton Mather, *A Family Well-Ordered* [Microfilm], Boston: Green & Allen, 1699, 66.

5. Steven Mintz and Susan Kellogg, *Domestic Revolutions: A Social History of Family Life in America*, New York: Free Press, 1988, xiv.

6. Lawrence A. Cremin, *American Education: The Colonial Experience, 1607–1783*, New York: Harper & Row, 1970, 124.

7. Jan Lewis, "Mothers as Teachers: Reconceptualizing the Role of the Family as Educator," in *Education and the American Family*, ed. William J. Weston, New York: New York University Press, 1989, 126.

8. James C. Carper, "Home Schooling, History, and Historians," *The High School Journal* 75 (April-May 1992): 253–54. See also Carl F. Kaestle, *The Evolution of an Urban School System: New York City, 1750–1850*, Cambridge: Harvard University Press, 1973, 1–27; and Maris A. Vinovskis, "Family and Schooling in Colonial and Nineteenth Century America," *Journal of Family History* 12 (1987): 19–37.

9. Mintz and Kellogg, *Domestic Revolutions*, 23.

10. James C. Carper, "The Changing Landscape of U. S. Education," *Kappa Delta Pi Record* 37 (Spring 2001): 107–8.

11. Carl F. Kaestle, *Pillars of the Republic: Common Schools and American Society, 1780–1860*, New York: Hill and Wang, 1983, 62–103.

12. Allan Carlson, "Will Family-Centered Education Strengthen Families?" *The Family in America* 12 (September 1998): 1–7. See also Charles L. Glenn, *The Myth of the Common School*, Amherst, MA: University of Massachusetts Press, 1987; and E. Vance Randall, *Private Schools and Public Power*, New York: Teachers College Press, 1994.

13. Kaestle, *Pillars of the Republic*, 160–61.

14. Robert T. Handy, *A Christian America: Protestant Hopes and Historical Realities*, New York: Oxford University Press, 1971, 102.

15. Larry Cuban, *How Teachers Taught: Constancy and Change in American Classroom, 1890–1980*, New York: Longman, 1984, 18; and Andrew Gulliford, *America's Country Schools*, Washington, DC: Preservation Press, 1984, 35–45.

16. See James C. Carper and Thomas C. Hunt, eds., *Religious Schooling in America*, Birmingham, AL: Religious Education Press, 1984.

17. Edward E. Gordon and Elaine A. Gordon, *Centuries of Tutoring: A History of Alternative Education in America and Western Europe*, Lanham, MD: University Press of America, 1990, 280–88.

18. For information on home-based education of public figures, see Allen Johnson, et al., eds., *The Dictionary of American Biography*, vols. 1–20, New York: Scribner's, 1928–1936. See also Raymond Moore and Dorothy Moore, *Home Style Teaching*, Waco, TX: Word Books, 1984;

David W. McCullough, *American Childhoods: An Anthology*, Boston: Little, Brown, 1987; and Christopher Klicka, *Home Schooling: The Right Choice*, Nashville: TN: Broadman & Holman, 2002, 159–74.

19. I. G. Rawn et al., *Daniel Dawson Carothers: A Memoir*. N. P.: American Railway Engineering and Maintenance of Way Association, 1909.

20. Mitchell L. Stevens, *Kingdom of Children: Culture and Controversy in the Homeschooling Movement*, Princeton, NJ: Princeton University Press, 2001, 6, 34–38; and Carper, "The Changing Landscape of U.S. Education," 109–10.

21. John Holt, *Instead of Education*, New York: Dutton, 1976, 4.

22. Scott Walter, "Free School Movement," in *Historical Dictionary of American Education*, ed. Richard J. Altenbaugh, Westport, CT: Greenwood Press, 1999, 145. See also Graeme Hunter, "Untenured Radical: Ivan Illich's *Deschooling Society*," *Touchstone* 18 (December 2005): 11.

23. Ray, *Worldwide Guide to Homeschooling*, 28–36; and Klicka, *Home Schooling*, 251–401.

24. James C. Carper and William J. Weston, "Conservative Protestants in the New School Wars," *History of Education Quarterly* 30 (Spring 1990): 79–87; and Richard A. Baer, Jr. and James C. Carper, "'To the Advantage of Infidelity,' or How Not to Deal with Religion in America's Public Schools," *Educational Policy* 14 (November 2000): 600–21. For a discussion of the centrality of Darwinism in widely used textbooks produced by the Biological Science Curriculum Study (BSCS), see Pamela R. Winnick, *A Jealous God: Science's Crusade Against Religion*, Nashville, TN: Nelson Current, 2005, 115–33. One of the best current critiques of Darwinism is Phillip E. Johnson's *Darwin on Trial*, 2nd ed, Downers Grove, IL: InterVarsity Press, 1993.

25. Ray, *Worldwide Guide to Homeschooling*, 42.

26. Ibid., 7–8, 28–29.

27. Klicka, *Home Schooling*, 379–81.

28. For a discussion of homeschooling mothers as organizers, activists, and entrepreneurs, see Stevens, *Kingdom of Children*.

29. Ernest B. Carnes, *Guidelines Concerning Instruction at a Place Other Than School*, Columbia, SC: South Carolina State Department of Education, 1981.

30. Ibid.

31. Zan P. Tyler and James C. Carper, "From Confrontation to Accommodation: Home Schooling in South Carolina," *Peabody Journal of Education* 75 (2000): 34.

32. Phoebe C. Winter, "Regulation of Home Schooling Parents in South Carolina: The State's Perspective." Paper presented at the annual meeting of the American Educational Research Association, San Francisco, March 1989.

33. *Calhoun County Department of Education v. Scott Page and Susan Page*, Calhoun County Family Court, June 1983.

34. *Charleston* [SC] *News and Courier*, February 13, 1987, 5b.

35. Tyler and Carper, "From Confrontation to Accommodation," 35–36.

36. Ibid.

37. Raymond S. Moore and Dorothy Moore, *Home Grown Kids*, Washougal, WA: Hewitt Research Foundation, 1981.

38. *Calhoun County Department of Education v. Scott Page and Susan Page*.

39. Ibid.

40. David Tyack and Larry Cuban, *Tinkering Toward Utopia: A Century of Public School Reform.* Cambridge, MA: Harvard University Press, 1995, 85–88.

41. Tyler and Carper, "From Confrontation to Accommodation," 37.

42. Ibid.

43. Ibid., 38.

44. Ibid.

45. Ibid.

46. Ibid., 39–40.

47. *Newsline*, South Carolina State Department of Education, May 16, 1986.

48. Tyler and Carper, "From Confrontation to Accommodation," 40.

49. For discussions of the political savvy of homeschoolers and their occasional disagreements about strategy, see Klicka, *Home Schooling*, 389–422; and Stevens, *Kingdom of Children*, 107–77.

50. Tyler and Carper, "From Confrontation to Accommodation," 41.

51. Ibid., 42.

52. Ibid.

53. Zan P. Tyler, "South Carolina Home Schoolers Celebrate Legislative Victory," *Home School Court Report*, May-June 1992, 3–5.

54. Tyler and Carper, "From Confrontation to Accommodation," 43.

55. Ibid.

56. Ibid.

57. Charles L. Glenn describes mediating structures as value-oriented agencies that "mediate between individuals and the state." They are associated with community, church, family, and voluntary associations. He asserts that American public policy is ripe for an approach that puts "services and decisions about services closer to those being served . . . even in their own hands." In the case of SCAIHS, educational accountability resides in a voluntary association created by and for homeschooling families rather than in a state agency. Teaching parents report their children's progress to the association. SCAIHS, in turn, assures the state that its interest in an educated public is being met. See Charles L. Glenn, *The Ambiguous Embrace: Government and Faith-Based Schools and Social Agencies*, Princeton, NJ: Princeton University Press, 2000, 3–5. See also Peter L. Berger and Richard John Neuhaus, *To Empower People: The Role of Mediating Structures in Public Policy*, Washington, DC: American Enterprise Institute, 1977.

58. *Code of Laws of South Carolina*, 59–65–10.

59. Tyler and Carper, "From Confrontation to Accommodation," 44.

60. Ibid.

61. Ibid.

62. "Home Schoolers Win EEE Case," *Home School Court Report*, January-February 1992, 4.

63. Tyler and Carper, "From Confrontation to Accommodation," 45.

64. Ibid.

65. By the 1992 legislative session, SCAIHS had developed a sophisticated communication system capable of generating hundreds of phone calls to legislators on short notice. Members of the Board of Directors were professionals and several held advanced degrees. Articulate and well-informed, they provided convincing testimony before various legislative committees and earned the trust of many legislators skeptical of homeschooling and the prospect

of granting authority to SCAIHS to supervise home-based education programs in the state.

66. Tyler, "South Carolina Home Schoolers Celebrate Legislative Victory," 3.

67. Tyler and Carper, "From Confrontation to Accommodation," 46–47. In 1996, the South Carolina General Assembly passed a third homeschooling law (59–65–47) that allows for the establishment of other accountability organizations in South Carolina. More than twenty "third option" organizations operated in South Carolina in 2006.

68. For criticisms of homeschooling and responses, see articles by Chris Lubienski, Michael Farris and Scott A. Woodruff, Michael W. Apple, and Brian D. Ray in *Peabody Journal of Education* 75 (2000): 207–93. See also Bruce S. Cooper, ed., *Home Schooling in Full View: A Reader*, Greenwich, CT: Information Age Publishing, 2005. Randall Balmer's *Thy Kingdom Come: How the Religious Right Distorts the Faith and Threatens America: An Evangelical's Lament*, New York: Basic Books, 2006, is one of several recent volumes that contend that the so-called "religious right," including its supposed manifestations, such as homeschooling, Christian schools, and vouchers, threatens democracy, reason, pluralism, and the Christian faith. For a sharply critical review of *Thy Kingdom Come* and three similar volumes, see Ross Douthat, "Theocracy, Theocracy, Theocracy," *First Things* 165 (August/September 2006): 23–30.

69. Ray, *Worldwide Guide to Homeschooling*, 48–85.

70. One scholar argues that homeschooling is associated with reinvigorated, "child rich" families. Allan Carlson, "Reinventing the Schoolroom: Education as Homecoming," *The Family in America* 19 (January 2005): 6. See also Peter A. Lawler, "Homeless on 'Paradise Drive': Two Views of Americanization," *The Intercollegiate Review* 40 (Fall/Winter 2005): 24–25.

71. Ray, *Worldwide Guide to Homeschooling*, 28.

· 10 ·

FINAL THOUGHTS

State establishment of religion inevitably breeds dissent, which in turn, often leads to persecution of nonconformists. One needs to look no further than the history of sixteenth- and seventeenth-century Europe where Catholics and Protestants alike sought religious uniformity in their respective dominions. Dissenters from the prevailing orthodoxy often suffered unspeakable persecution. Indeed, as James Hutson has pointed out, "In the name of Jesus Christ, Catholics killed Protestants and Protestants killed Catholics; both groups harassed and killed dissenting coreligionists." The fate of many Anabaptists in Germany is a case in point.[1] Though certainly less violent, harassment of dissenters continued in the New World, where colonies established churches, taxed for their support, and imposed legal and financial liabilities (or worse) on religious minorities, particularly those living in seventeenth-century Virginia, where Anglicanism was established, and New England, where Congregationalism reigned. In the eighteenth century, however, the English Bill of Rights, various acts of toleration, and increasing religious pluralism in the provinces contributed to growing religious freedom. As Sidney Ahlstrom has asserted, "By 1775 toleration verging on freedom had become a fundamental part of the long-term American revolution being enacted in the colonies."[2]

Accompanying this growing toleration of diverse expressions of Protestant

Christianity (and to a much lesser extent Roman Catholicism) was a movement toward disestablishment of churches. Despite arguments from supporters of tax-supported, state churches that the government should "nurse" religion on the grounds that "civil government depended upon religion and upon the morality it inculcated," by 1800 all but three states, Massachusetts, Connecticut, and New Hampshire, had disestablished their churches, and in these cases dissenters bore relatively minor burdens. In Connecticut, for example, the legislature granted dissenters, primarily Baptists, permission to worship in churches of their choice in 1770, and fourteen years later the state removed all restrictions, except the requirement, which Baptists loathed, that nonconformists certify their minority status in order to avoid paying an assessment for the support of Congregationalism in their community.[3]

One group of dissenters in Connecticut, the Danbury Baptist Association, wrote to Thomas Jefferson in late 1801 hoping to solicit his support for their effort to disestablish completely the Congregational church. The President's response in early 1802 contained the well-known and still much debated "wall of separation" metaphor that the United States Supreme Court embraced in the *Everson* decision in 1947.[4] While Jefferson hoped his carefully worded reply would influence public opinion, "sowing useful truths and principles" in his words, he informed the Baptists that they would have to address their plight at the state level as the First Amendment prohibition of an establishment of religion applied only to actions of the national government. In 1818, Baptists and their allies in Connecticut accomplished that goal as a new constitution provided that no law could favor any Christian group or mode of worship. New Hampshire followed suit in 1819. In 1833, Massachusetts, home of Horace Mann, often called the "father of American public education," and other strong advocates of a common-school system, abandoned what was left of its Congregationalist establishment. Four years later, Mann assumed the position of Secretary to the Massachusetts Board of Education. From that post, he crusaded tirelessly for the cause of public education, which has functioned in many respects as America's established church.[5]

As was the case with the established churches of Europe and early America, public education has sparked significant dissent. Since its inception in the middle decades of the nineteenth century, dissenters have claimed that tax-supported, state-regulated, compulsory public schooling violates rights of conscience and religious liberty. Specifically, they have objected to the prevailing orthodoxy, purveyed by the state through its public schools in a given era, to paying twice for mandated education (taxes and tuition) in order to exercise their right to educate their children according to their beliefs, and to intrusive state regulation of alternative educational arrangements that embody worldviews that differ from what Stephen Arons has termed "public orthodoxy." Some dissenters have argued that only disestablishment of public education will result in an educational pluralism that matches our confessional pluralism. This, in turn, would enhance individual and family freedom, remove the state from the business of sanctioning a particular worldview, and, finally, likely reduce the enervating conflict regarding, among other things, textbook coverage, religious practices, and moral education—"the public school liturgy"—that often plagues our established church.[6]

Lessons from Dissenters

In the preceding chapters, we have recounted the work and experience of several dissenters and associated dissenting movements in the nineteenth and twentieth centuries. Several lessons emerge from these episodes. First, Roman Catholic dissenters in the nineteenth century and their evangelical Protestant counterparts in the late twentieth century both testify to the fact that education is not, indeed cannot be, value-free. The former asserted correctly that the public school was not neutral or nonsectarian on matters religious. It was, in fact, a quasi-Protestant institution. Reading the Bible without comment, especially the King James Version, was hardly a religiously neutral practice; rather, it reflected the Protestant concept of individual interpretation of Scripture. In Wisconsin, parents succeeded in their efforts to remove Bible-reading from the public school. Ironically, this hastened not only the de-Protestantization of the public schools, but also the establishment of a "godless" institution troubling to devout Catholics and Protestants alike. The latter, on the other hand, have argued recently that removing state-sanctioned prayer and devotional Bible-reading from the government schools in the early 1960s, denuding the curriculum of references to Christianity, promoting moral education without reference to religious authority, and, perhaps unwittingly, sanctioning a naturalistic view of humankind and the cosmos, have established a de facto secularist orthodoxy in the public schools. Though from the state's or a secularist's perspective this may constitute neutrality, it does not seem so to conservative Christian parents.[7] As a result, they are likely either to engage in a rancorous and probably futile war against the prevailing orthodoxy, e.g., recent efforts to encourage criticism of dogmatic Darwinism, or to send their children to a private school or to teach them at home, paying for the exercise of conscience in tuition and fees as well as taxes.

Second, though conflicts regarding the orthodoxy of public education can sometimes be resolved, deeply held beliefs about "first order" matters, e.g., the nature of the cosmos, the basis for morality, or, in the words of the Westminster Shorter Catechism, "the chief end of man," usually are not subject to compromise.[8] Some dissenters point out, then, that a truly "common" public school is a myth. Indeed, public schooling, no matter how well developed, has never met the needs of all families and their children nor will it ever be able to do so. Public education will always transmit a politically determined set of propositions of knowledge, skills, and dispositions of value, appreciation, and belief in a particular institutional environment. No one, therefore, should be surprised that at any given time a minority of Americans of good will and intellect express deeply grounded differences of opinion regarding what constitutes a proper kind of education for their children. Some will become and remain dissenters, choosing nongovernmental schooling until either the prevailing orthodoxy changes by dint of litigation as in the Edgerton case, or they muster sufficient political power to effect desired alteration of the status quo, or their zeal for their beliefs dissipates due to, among other reasons, exhaustion, loss of "vision," lack of resources, strife, or state-sanctioned harassment. Others will remain dissenters regardless of changes in the established church.

Third, the state has not always been accepting of alternative educational institutions and the dissenting subcultures they embody. For better than 150 years, public school advocates have made messianic claims regarding the common school, some of which resemble those made by defenders of traditional established religion. They have asserted that public schooling is the bulwark of American democracy that promotes national unity, creates future citizens, guarantees equality of opportunity, and shapes the national character. In other words, public education is inextricably intertwined with the common good. Nonpublic schools, on the other hand, often have been characterized as undemocratic, divisive, inimical to the public good, and even un-American. Suspicion of dissenting educational arrangements and the beliefs they embody has led recently to the promulgation of intrusive regulation of both Christian schools and homeschooling. In many respects, these efforts mimic the actions of Wisconsin and Illinois in the late nineteenth century and of several states, for example, Oregon, Nebraska, and Hawaii, in the early twentieth century to control or eliminate private schools. Such efforts have highlighted a conflict between parents' desire to speak to the future through their children's education and the interests of the majoritarian state and/or public school leaders, whose professional expertise is implicitly questioned by the mere existence of alternatives to the government-operated school system.[9] Fortunately, most state courts have followed the path blazed by the Ohio Supreme Court in *Whisner*, and Christian schools and homeschools enjoy a significant degree of freedom from comprehensive regulation. That said, however, the ongoing Calvary case in California poses a potential threat to the freedom of private schools to transmit a particular worldview at odds with the dominant culture of a powerful institution. This case involves the University of California System's indirect attempt to control Christian school curriculum by refusing to accept high school courses taught from a Christian viewpoint. While the University System maintains that it has the right to determine admission requirements, Calvary Chapel Christian School claims a violation of First Amendment rights of free speech and free exercise of religion. Should the federal courts rule in favor of the University, Christian schools would have either to significantly alter their curriculum and philosophy or forego a significant public benefit, namely student access to the state's premier institutions of higher education.[10]

Fourth, though dissenting educational institutions and families have achieved a significant degree of freedom to teach their "orthodoxy," the price of liberty of conscience remains high. Like religious nonconformists in late eighteenth-century Connecticut, contemporary dissenters are generally free to educate their children as they see fit, but they must pay taxes to support public education as well as the costs of private education or homeschooling. The present volume does not focus on the varied, and often highly controversial, remedies to what most dissenters view as an injustice similar to that inflicted on dissenters from the established churches of the colonial period. Suffice it to say, some dissenters and advocates of educational justice, present and past, have argued that each child should receive "the same kind and degree of public support" and that "equitable public funding should be offered without regard to the religious, philosophical, or pedagogical differences among the variety of certified schools parents choose."[11] They believe the primary role of government is to insure the education of the public and educational justice rather than to maintain a massive government school system that enjoys almost exclusive claim on tax dollars for education and compromises the liberty of parents, particularly poor parents, to exercise their primary right to direct the education and upbringing of their children. Though embracing the principles of educational justice and parental liberty, some dissenters voice concerns about the potential of this approach, which some would call a universal voucher, to undermine the autonomy of nongovernmental schools via accreditation and certification requirements regardless of their apparent benign intent. They prefer tax credits for educational expenses incurred and for donations to private scholarship-granting organizations. Such an approach, they assert, avoids potential entanglement with "public money" and state regulation. Arizona, Pennsylvania, Illinois, Iowa, and Minnesota are among the states that recently have embraced this approach. Neither equitable distribution of public funds for education nor tax credits is a new idea. Many Catholic leaders, such as John Hughes, and a few Protestants, such as Charles Hodge, proposed similar remedies to burdens on conscience imposed by taxation for public schools.

A few dissenters have gone so far as to suggest a complete separation of school and state. Groups such as the Alliance for the Separation of School & State, founded in 1994, echo Robert L. Dabney's contention that education is strictly a family responsibility and that government should not be involved in "K–12 school attendance, content, teacher and school approval, and financing." The government, the Alliance asserts, has no more business being involved in "Monday-school" than in "Sunday-school." Alliance members oppose charter schools and tax-funded vouchers on the view that these reforms, primarily designed to enhance competition rather than insure justice and protect parental liberty, in fact encourage family dependency on the government. These libertarians of various religious, business, educational, and policy backgrounds, argue that the separation of school and state will free the approximately 500 billion dollars currently spent each year on pre-K–12 public education for a massive tax cut that will enable most Americans to purchase the education they desire. Charitable giving, they predict, will assist the minority of parents who need help to cover tuition costs.[12]

Finally, one wonders if the current educational landscape might be different if nineteenth-century evangelical Protestants and Roman Catholics could have set aside their theological differences and animosities born of the Reformation and its immediate aftermath and rekindled by growing Catholic immigration in the 1830s and 1840s as well as the excesses of Protestant revivalism and Catholic rhetoric at that time. Many Catholic leaders, including John Hughes, asserted that as a matter of justice Catholic schools were due a share of tax dollars for education. Though most Protestants rejected that claim and lent their support to the supposedly nonsectarian common school, a few recognized the legitimacy of the Catholic position. Charles Hodge, the redoubtable Princeton theologian, was highly critical of the theology and polity of the Roman Catholic Church and believed the public schools should teach Protestant beliefs held by the majority of Americans. Nevertheless, he stated on several occasions over his lifetime that Catholics either should receive a share of the school fund or an exemption from school taxes out of respect for freedom of conscience. Though Robert Dabney opined that the state should not be involved with the provision of schooling, he did recognize the validity of Roman Catholics complaints about the content of public education and the injustice of paying taxes for its support. In sum, a basis for a more pluralistic educational arrangement did exist in mid-nineteenth-century America, but the hand of history was too heavy. That said, however, the Roman Catholic Church as well as some Lutheran, Reformed, and other Protestant bodies did create, often in the face of opposition, and fund alternative educational institutions to cultivate and protect their religious and/or cultural identities.[13]

The Future of Dissent in American Education

What of the future of dissent? Some scholars suggest that the American educational landscape is changing rapidly. They point out, for example, that a growing number of children are attending schools of choice. One source recently estimated that about twenty-six percent of low-income children are currently attending schools other than the public school to which they are assigned. Furthermore, with the various tuition tax credit and tax-funded voucher programs operating in twelve states and the District of Columbia, the line between public and private schools is not as sharp as it was fifty years ago. Indeed, in some respects the current educational landscape with its increasing diversity of options is starting to resemble the landscape of pre-common-school America. Whether this trend will encourage, co-opt, or dampen dissent remains to be seen.[14]

Though dissenters from the public school paradigm remain a small minority, the two most visible nonconformist movements of the late twentieth and early twenty-first centuries are still growing. Christian day school enrollments are still increasing, albeit at a slow pace. Homeschool enrollments, on the other hand, continue to climb at a rate estimated at between seven and fifteen percent a year. At that pace, their number may approach three million by 2010. Whether that level of growth will continue is an open question. Clearly, the homeschooling population is becoming more diverse each year.[15] With new populations exploring homeschooling, e.g., Roman Catholics, the potential for growth increases. Moreover, several outspoken dissenters introduced resolutions at the annual meeting of the Southern Baptist Convention in 2004 and 2006 urging members to remove their children from the public schools and secure a Christian education via either private or homeschooling. Neither resolution reached the convention floor. Instead, delegates in 2006 recommended that Southern Baptists exert "godly influence" on the public schools and support released-time religious instruction. Nevertheless, a movement clearly is afoot in the largest Protestant denomination, particularly among neo-Calvinists, to forsake attempts to reform public education by, for example, checking the "homosexual agenda" or countering Darwinism in science classes, and to opt for an exit from the government school system. Whether this dissent will eventually translate into significant increases in Christian school and home-school enrollments remains to be seen. That said, however, it is clear that a small but growing number of Southern Baptists who were once staunch support-ers of public education now view it as indifferent at best and hostile at worst to their Christian worldview. As one commentator remarked, why should Christian parents send their children to Nineveh for an education?[16]

Though dissenters have remained a distinct minority since the advent of public schooling, the current political climate, which seems increasingly favor-able to parental choice; demography (homeschooling parents and conservative religionists from whose ranks dissenters are often drawn have more children than average); and a general lack of confidence in public education certainly suggest that their number will grow. That said, however, a majority of citizens and the politically and culturally powerful still revere public education and often oppose mechanisms to enhance parental liberty that might "hurt" pub-lic schooling.[17] But even if dissenters remain a distinct minority for the foresee-able future, they may now have a unique opportunity to prompt Americans to give careful consideration to whether public education in its current form vio-lates the conscience of those who desire a different kind of education for their children than that offered by the state, forcing them not only to pay taxes for the support of that orthodoxy but to pay again for the right to educate their chil-dren as they see fit. Such an arrangement differs little from that faced by Connecticut Baptists prior to 1784; free to worship according to the dictates of conscience but burdened by taxes for the established church. Perhaps the time is indeed ripe for Americans to consider, in the words of Rockne McCarthy, James Skillen, and William Harper, "Distablishment a Second Time."[18]

Notes

1. James H. Hutson, *Religion and the Founding of the American Republic*, Washington, DC: Library of Congress, 1998, 2–5.
2. Sidney E. Ahlstrom, *A Religious History of the American People*, New Haven, CT: Yale University Press, 1972, 379–80.
3. Ibid., 380. For a discussion of the arguments offered by proponents of established religion, see Hutson, *Religion and the Founding of the American Republic*, 60–65.
4. Philip Hamburger, *Separation of Church and State*, Cambridge, MA: Harvard University Press, 2002, 155–62. For a detailed account of the relationship between church and state in the seventeenth and eighteenth centuries, see Anson Phelps Stokes and Leo Pfeffer, *Church and State in the United States*, New York: Harper & Row, 1964, 3–103.
5. Daniel L. Dreisbach, *Thomas Jefferson and the Wall of Separation Between Church and State*, New York: New York University Press, 2002, 25–54; and Ahlstrom, *A Religious History of the American People*, 380. See also Richard A. Baer, Jr. and James C. Carper, "'To the Advantage of Infidelity,' or How Not to Deal with Religion in America's Public Schools," *Educational Policy* 14 (November 2000): 600–21; Charles L. Glenn, Jr., *The Myth of the Common School*, Amherst, MA: University of Massachusetts Press, 1988; Ivan Illich, *Deschooling Society*, New York: Harper & Row, 1970; and Sidney E. Mead, *The Lively Experiment: The Shaping of Christianity in America*, New York: Harper & Row, 1963.
6. Stephen Arons, *Compelling Belief: The Culture of American Schooling*, New York: McGraw-Hill, 1983, vii–xi, 189–220.
7. For a discussion of the importance of perspective in the matter of "neutrality," see Richard John Neuhaus, "The Couture of the Public Square," *First Things* 38 (December 1993): 66–68.
8. For examples of resolution of conflict over religious issues, see Charles C. Haynes and Oliver Thomas, *Finding Common Ground: A Guide to Religious Liberty in Public Schools*, Nashville, TN: First Amendment Center, 2001; and Benjamin Justice, *The War That Wasn't: Religious Conflict and Compromise in the Common Schools of New York State, 1865–1900*, Albany, NY: State University of New York Press, 2005.
9. See William J. Reese, "Changing Conceptions of Public and Private in American Educational History," in *Public or Private Education?: Lessons from History*, ed. Richard Aldrich, London: Woburn Press, 2004, 150, 156; E. Vance Randall, *Private Schools and Public Power: A Case for Pluralism*, New York: Teachers College Press, 1994; and William G. Ross, *Forging New Freedoms: Nativism, Education, and the Constitution, 1917–1927*, Lincoln: University of Nebraska Press, 1994.
10. As of October 2006, Federal District Judge S. James Otero had set aside the University of California's motion to dismiss the lawsuit brought by the Association of Christian Schools International (ACSI), Calvary Chapel, and several students, thus allowing the religious discrimination suit to proceed. Judge Otero implied that University might have violated First Amendment free speech rights. Lynn Vincent, "Systemic Flaw," *World*, August 19, 2006, 22. See also Naomi Schaefer Riley, "Keeping Out the Christians," *Education Next* 6 (Summer 2006): 50–56.
11. Center for Public Justice, *Education*, Washington, DC: Center for Public Justice, n.d.

12. Separation of School & State Alliance, *Who Should Control a Child's Education? Parents or Government?*, Fresno, CA: Separation of School & State Alliance, n.d. . See also Samuel L. Blumenfeld, *Is Public Education Necessary?*, Old Greenwich, CT: The Devin-Adair Company, 1981; and Sheldon Richman, *Separating School and State*, Fairfax, VA: Future of Freedom Foundation, 1994.

13. Thomas C. Hunt and James C. Carper, eds. *Religious Schools in the United States, K–12: A Source Book*, New York: Garland Publishing, 1993.

14. James C. Carper, "The Changing Landscape of U.S. Education," *Kappa Delta Pi Record* 37 (Spring 2001): 106–10; and Reese, "Changing Conceptions of Public and Private in American Educational History," 160–63.

15. Brian D. Ray, *Worldwide Guide to Homeschooling*, Nashville, TN: Broadman & Holman Publishers, 2005, 7–8, 33.

16. Jessica L. Tonn, "Southern Baptists Urge School Board Activism, Off-Campus Bible Study," *Education Week*, June 21, 2006, 7. For a stinging, but somewhat overwrought and needlessly sarcastic, indictment of public education by a well-known Southern Baptist layman, see Bruce N. Shortt, *The Harsh Truth About Public Schools*, Vallecito, CA: Chalcedon Foundation, 2004. In a similar vein, the Director of the Exodus Mandate Project urges Christian parents to immediately abandon, not reform or takeover, public education, which he believes pulls children away from their parents' faith. See E. Ray Moore, Jr., *Let My Children Go*, Columbia, SC: Gilead Media, 2002.

17. See Randall Balmer, *Thy Kingdom Come: How the Religious Right Distorts the Faith and Threatens America: An Evangelical's Lament*. New York: Basic Books, 2006, 71–108.

18. Rockne M. McCarthy, James W. Skillen, and William A Harper, *Disestablishment a Second Time: Genuine Pluralism for American Schools*, Grand Rapids, MI: Christian University Press, 1982. Critics of an educational arrangement that mirrors our pluralist society often claim that the multiplication of schools rooted in particular worldviews would result in the transmission of bizarre beliefs and questionable propositions, and that the dissolution of the public school system might lead to a breakdown in American community. We believe that part of living in a free society is accepting the fact that parents and schools teach things that others find distasteful and/or wrongheaded. The state must be neutral on such matters unless, of course, clear and compelling evidence exists that a particular kind of education is significantly harmful to children and/or others. Regarding the threat of diverse schooling to the community, Michael McConnell, a former professor of law at the University of Chicago and now a federal appellate judge pointed out: "I remind you that this was the same question that was asked at the beginning of our nation's history. Previously in history, religion itself had been the glue that held most nations together; the experience of having citizens attend whatever church they wanted was a rather scary proposition. It has worked rather well, and I am inclined to think it would work well for education, too, in that it depoliticizes the culture war. If we privatized education, then the most serious sources of divisiveness, anger, and contention that have occurred when we have had to fight it out in the public arena would be eliminated." Michael W. McConnell, "Commentary," in *Curriculum, Religion, and Public Education: Conversations for an Enlarging Public Square*, eds., James T. Sears and James C. Carper, New York: Teachers College Press, Columbia University, 1998, 33–35.

INDEX